Windows® 7 For Seniors
FOR
DUMMIES®

by Mark Justice Hinton

WILEY

Wiley Publishing, Inc.

Windows® 7 For Seniors For Dummies®

Published by
Wiley Publishing, Inc.
111 River Street
Hoboken, NJ 07030-5774

www.wiley.com

Copyright © 2009 by Wiley Publishing, Inc., Indianapolis, Indiana

Published by Wiley Publishing, Inc., Indianapolis, Indiana

Published simultaneously in Canada

For general information on our other products and services, please contact our Customer Care Department within the U.S. at 877-762-2974, outside the U.S. at 317-572-3993, or fax 317-572-4002.

For technical support, please visit www.wiley.com/techsupport.

Wiley also publishes its books in a variety of electronic formats. Some content that appears in print may not be available in electronic books.

Library of Congress Control Number: 2009932714

ISBN: 978-0-470-50946-3

Manufactured in the United States of America

10 9 8 7 6 5 4 3 2

WILEY

About the Author

A computerist for more than 30 years, **Mark Justice Hinton** has written two books on digital photography, one on Microsoft Windows Vista, and this new book on Windows 7: www.mjhinton.com/author/. He has taught computer classes since 1988 for the University of New Mexico Division of Continuing Education. Mark lives — in the best sense of the word — in front of a computer. He writes a blog on computer topics: www.mjhinton.com/help. He posts favorite photos, as well: www.flickr.com/photos/mjhinton/.

Dedication

To Lucky Dog, our handsome, gentle, old friend — a true gift from the Universe.

Author's Acknowledgments

It takes a lot of people to put this book into your hands. The author gets the fame, the fans, and the fat check, but he couldn't do it without so many other people, too many of whom go unnamed here. Thanks to everyone at Wiley for their part in producing this book. Special thanks to editorial manager Jodi Jensen, my acquisitions editor Amy Fandrei, project editors Leah Cameron and Jean Nelson, copy editor Virginia Sanders, technical editor Russ Mullen, and senior editorial assistant Cherie Case. My deepest thanks, again, to Merri Rudd, long-time senior advocate, photographer, writer, and editor, as well as *mi corazón*.

Peace,
mjh

Publisher's Acknowledgments

We're proud of this book; please send us your comments at http://dummies.custhelp.com. For other comments, please contact our Customer Care Department within the U.S. at 877-762-2974, outside the U.S. at 317-572-3993, or fax 317-572-4002.

Some of the people who helped bring this book to market include the following:

Acquisitions, Editorial

Editors: Leah Cameron, Jean Nelson, Virginia Sanders

Acquisitions Editor: Amy Fandrei

Technical Editor: Russ Mullen

Editorial Manager: Jodi Jensen

Sr. Editorial Assistant: Cherie Case

Cartoons: Rich Tennant (www.the5thwave.com)

Composition Services

Project Coordinator: Patrick Redmond

Layout and Graphics: Ana Carrillo, Christin Swinford

Proofreaders: Caitie Copple, Betty Kish

Indexer: BIM Indexing & Proofreading Services

Special Help: Kathy Simpson

Publishing and Editorial for Technology Dummies

Richard Swadley, Vice President and Executive Group Publisher

Andy Cummings, Vice President and Publisher

Mary Bednarek, Executive Acquisitions Director

Mary C. Corder, Editorial Director

Publishing for Consumer Dummies

Diane Graves Steele, Vice President and Publisher

Composition Services

Gerry Fahey, Vice President of Production Services

Debbie Stailey, Director of Composition Services

Contents at a Glance

Table of Contents

Introduction

*W*indows 7 is the latest generation of Microsoft's operating system, the master program that makes a computer useful and provides support to other programs, including word processors, photo viewers, and Internet browsers. Much as an education equips you to read a novel or play a game, Windows 7 equips your computer to perform a wide range of activities. You can use Windows 7 and other software (programs) to read or write a novel, play games or music, and stay in touch with friends and family around the world.

As Windows has evolved over the last 30 years, so have computers — the *hardware*. Today, you can buy a computer as small as a paperback book, and even such a little computer is unimaginably more powerful than computers were just 10 years ago, and at a fraction of the price. The hardware provides the mechanisms — the display, the keyboard, the mouse, and more — you use to work with Windows 7.

It doesn't take much time with a computer to conclude there has to be an easier way to do things. At times, computers seem overly complex and inscrutable. Have you used a cellphone lately? Or a TV remote control? Why are the controls on every microwave oven different? Why does every new tool offer countless options you don't want that hide the ones you do? Well, I don't have the answers to those questions, but I do have step-by-step instructions for many tasks you want to perform using Windows 7, which isn't as dry as that sounds, but which is quite practical.

After 30 years working with computers, I find computers reward patience, curiosity, and a little methodical exploration. In this book, you find the instructions for doing practical activities, such as creating a letter or sending e-mail. In addition to the steps that are necessary, you see what's possible and what's consistent (and inconsistent) between different programs.

Seniors, in particular, know that learning never really stops and that new things keep one young, at least figuratively. The computer is a unique tool. Tomorrow, your TV won't do something new, but with your computer, you'll do things you don't yet imagine.

By the end of this book, you may be a multitasking computerist performing virtual gymnastics with Windows 7. On the other hand, if the computer does only one thing for you — whether it's e-mail, browsing the Web, enjoying photos, music, or DVDs — that one useful thing may be all you need.

About This Book

Age is just a number. This book is intended for anyone getting started with Windows 7 who wants step-by-step instructions without a lot of discussion. The *Get ready to . . .* bullets at the beginning of each chapter lead you to the practical tasks that you want to find out about. Numerous figures with notes show you the computer screen as you progress through the steps. Reading this book is like having an experienced friend stand behind you as you use Windows 7 . . . someone who never takes the keyboard away from you.

Foolish Assumptions

I assume that you have a computer and want clear, brief, step-by-step instruction on getting things done with Windows 7. I also assume you want to know just what you need to know, just when you need to know it. This isn't Computers 101. This is Practical Windows 7. As an old friend of mine says, "I don't want to make a watch; I just want to know what time it is."

Why You Need This Book

Technology always comes with its own terms and concepts, but you don't need to learn another language to use a computer. You don't need any prior experience with computers or Windows. Step-by-step instructions guide you through specific tasks, such as starting a program and saving your documents. These steps provide just the information you need for the task at hand.

You can work through this book from beginning to end or simply look at the table of contents and find the content you need to solve a problem or help you learn a new skill whenever you need it. The steps in each task get you where you want to go quickly without a lot of technical explanation. In no time, you'll start picking up the skills you need to become a confident Windows 7 user.

Conventions Used in This Book

This book uses certain conventions to highlight important information and help you find your way around, including these:

➠ **Tip icons:** Point out helpful suggestions related to tasks in the steps lists.

➠ **Bold:** I use bold on the important, find-it-now stuff:

- When you have to type something onscreen using the keyboard

- Figure references

    Many illustrations and figures have notes or other markings to draw your attention to a specific part of the figure. The text tells you what to look for; the figure notes help you find it.

➠ **Web site addresses:** They look like this: www.website.com. See Chapter 9 for information on browsing the Web.

➡ **Menu choices:** Look for this arrow symbol: ➪. This shows a sequence of steps in a computer menu. For example, Start➪All Programs➪Accessories means to click the Start button, click All Programs, and then click Accessories.

➡ **Options and buttons:** Although Windows 7 often uses lowercase in options and on buttons, I capitalize the text for emphasis. That way you can find a button labeled Save Now, even though onscreen it appears as *Save now*.

 On the computer, you single-click the left mouse button to select an option or object. A single click of the right mouse button always produces a special *context, or shortcut, menu* with commands tailored to the situation. When appropriate, I tell you to click the right mouse button as *right-click*. All other times when I tell you to *click* the mouse, you can assume that I mean the left button. See Chapter 1 for more on using the mouse.

When you're to use the keyboard, I tell you to *press* a particular key, such as *press the Enter key*. Later in the book, after you get comfortable with the steps, you may see shorthand for keyboard shortcuts. For example, ⊞+E means press and hold the Windows logo key (with the flag icon on it, between Ctrl and Alt on most keyboards), press the E key, and then release both. Knowing a few keyboard shortcuts can be very handy.

How This Book Is Organized

This book is divided into six parts to help you find what you need. You can read from cover to cover or just jump to the page that interests you first.

➡ **Part I: Getting to Know Windows 7.** In Chapter 1, turn the computer on and get comfortable with essential parts of Windows 7, such as the desktop and Start menu. In Chapter 2, explore the parts of a *window* (an area of the screen). In Chapter 3, use WordPad to create a note or letter. In Chapter 4, discover the organization Windows 7 creates for you and make it your own.

➡ **Part II: Getting Things Done in Windows 7.** In Chapter 5, use programs for displaying the time and weather, performing calculations, and taking notes. In Chapter 6, install additional programs or remove programs you don't need. In Chapter 7, set up a printer or other device, such as an external hard drive.

➡ **Part III: Discovering the Internet.** In Chapter 8, connect to the Internet at home or on the road. (You may want to do this sooner, rather than later.) In Chapter 9, browse the World Wide Web, which can be your international library and marketplace. In Chapter 10, create an e-mail account and then send and receive e-mail.

➡ **Part IV: Having Fun with Windows 7.** If you haven't been having any fun until now, I've failed you. In Chapter 11, play the games Windows 7 includes, such as Solitaire. In Chapter 12, enjoy photos on Windows 7 and put your own photos on the computer if you have a digital camera. In Chapter 13, listen to music or watch a DVD movie.

➡ **Part V: Having It Your Way with Windows 7.** Hint: If something about Windows 7 bothers you or is hard to use — for example, things on the screen are too small — turn to this section now. In Chapter 14, make changes to the look of Windows 7. In Chapter 15, adjust the taskbar and Start menu to work better for you. In Chapter 16, change the size of objects on the screen and turn on features intended to make Windows 7 easier to use.

➡ **Part VI: Staying Safe and Keeping Windows 7 Healthy.** In Chapter 17, keep Windows 7 up-to-date. In Chapter 18, protect your computer against bad software (called *malware*), such as viruses. (Another thing you should do sooner, rather than later.) In Chapter 19, back up the documents and photos you'd hate to lose.

Time to Get Started!

Scan the table of contents or the index for a topic that interests you most. Or, just turn the page and start at the beginning. It's your book.

Comments and suggestions are welcome. Write me at mark@ mjhinton.com. Visit the book's Web site for supplemental material: www.mjhinton.com/w7fs.

Part I

Getting to Know Windows 7

The 5th Wave   By Rich Tennant

Before installing Windows 7, Dwayne prepares to partition the hard drive.

Getting Comfortable with the Windows 7 Desktop

Chapter 1

Microsoft Windows 7 is a special type of program or software — tools for getting things done with a computer — called an *operating system*, which is the master control of a computer. Windows 7 gives a computer essential functions that enable you to run other programs and work with documents, photos, and music.

Whether you already have a computer or you intend to buy a new computer with Windows 7 installed, this chapter takes you into Windows 7 for the first time, from turning the computer on, looking around, to turning it off again.

Get familiar with common terms and concepts, such as the *desktop*, which you see soon after you start. Use the *Start menu* to start programs. Take advantage of the *taskbar* to see what's going on. You work with these parts of Windows 7 every time you use your computer.

In the process of exploring the major features of Windows 7 for the first time, come to grips with the mouse, your pet for prodding Windows 7 into action. The mouse and its buttons enable you to point and click your way to happiness. From time to time, I emphasize when the keyboard provides a good alternative to the using the mouse.

Get a New Computer with Windows 7

Although this is not the book to tell you everything there is to know about buying a new computer, I do have a few suggestions for you as you shop. The first consideration is what style or size of computer do you want? Choose from these types of computers (see **Figure 1-1**):

Desktop   Laptop   Netbook

Figure 1-1

➡ A **desktop computer** is usually shoebox sized or larger. Often, a desktop computer is a vertical tower that sits under a desk or table. This desktop box usually accepts numerous hardware upgrades internally, but not everyone wants to open the box and insert new hardware. A desktop has a separate *screen* (also called a *display* or *monitor*) that displays what the computer is doing, a keyboard for typing, plus a mouse for doing things onscreen. (More on these components shortly.)

➡ A **laptop computer** is not only smaller than most desktop computers, it is portable. Even if you never intend to leave the house with your computer, you may enjoy taking the computer from one room to another. A desktop computer requires you to connect a few different parts during setup. A laptop computer is ready to go when you get it.

➡ A **netbook** is a small laptop computer that may be less powerful than a more expensive laptop. A netbook is a great *beginner's computer* because netbooks are much cheaper than other machines ($250 to $400). The small size of a netbook may suit you perfectly, but look closely at the size of any laptop or netbook. Is the computer too big to carry comfortably? Will your hands fit the keyboard?

In the rest of the book, when I use the words computer or machine, I mean any style of computer. I use the words desktop or laptop (including netbook) to emphasize differences between those machines, as needed.

For more information on buying a computer, see *Computers For Seniors For Dummies*, by Nancy C. Muir.

When you buy a new computer, check the ad or the box or talk with a salesperson to find out whether that computer comes with Microsoft Windows 7 installed. Ask which *edition* you're buying. The various editions of Windows 7 have different features and capabilities. You are most likely to see one of these editions:

➡ **Starter Edition:** Many of the Windows 7 visual effects are missing from the Starter Edition, and so are some of the useful accessories discussed in Chapter 5. This edition may be too stripped down to give you the real benefits of using Windows 7.

➡ **Home Premium Edition:** This is a good choice for most computer users and is likely to be the version already installed if you are buying a new PC. It has media options, such as music and video. Home Premium supports all the slick visual effects of Windows 7. Some people dismiss these visual effects as eye-candy, but these effects, such as semi-transparent objects onscreen and rich colors, are part of the fun of using Windows 7.

➠ **Ultimate Edition:** This version has everything Windows 7 can provide. (The name says as much.) Ultimate may include some advanced features — including options for backing up your files — that you won't immediately need. This is the Edition that *may* impress your teen-aged kids or grandkids, if anything does.

 Through a program called Windows Anytime Upgrade, you can upgrade from Starter to Home Premium or Ultimate. See Chapter 17 for more information.

 You can buy a DVD with Windows 7 and use that to install Windows 7 on an older computer that currently uses Windows XP or Vista. Sometimes, upgrades work flawlessly; but the older the computer, the greater the odds that some hardware or software won't work with the brand new Windows 7. It is often more reliable to get a new version of Windows on a new computer. (At least, that's what the marketing department says.)

Turn On Your Computer

1. If your computer is a laptop, find the latch on the front edge of the computer that releases the screen from the keyboard. You may need to push the latch in or slide it to the right to open the laptop. Raise the lid so you can see the screen and the keyboard.

2. Locate the power switch. On most laptops, the switch is located near one of the hinges of the lid. On a desktop computer, the power switch is usually on the front of the computer box or tower (see **Figure 1-2**). Push in or slide the power switch from left to right; then release the switch to turn on the computer. You should hear some noise from the fan or see lights on the keyboard or screen soon after you turn it on.

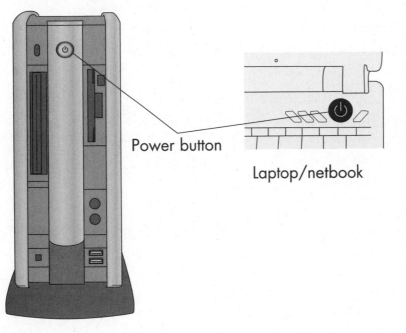

Power button

Laptop/netbook

Desktop

Figure 1-2

3. The very first time you turn on a computer running Windows 7, you may have to create a user account with the following information:

- **User name and computer name:** Your user name appears throughout the system, from the log-in screen to the Start menu to the folder containing all your documents. Use a simple, clear name. Your first name is just fine. Your computer needs a name, as well. Windows 7 suggests your user name plus **-PC**, but you can change that, if you wish. (See **Figure 1-3.**) Click Next.

Enter a user name and computer name...

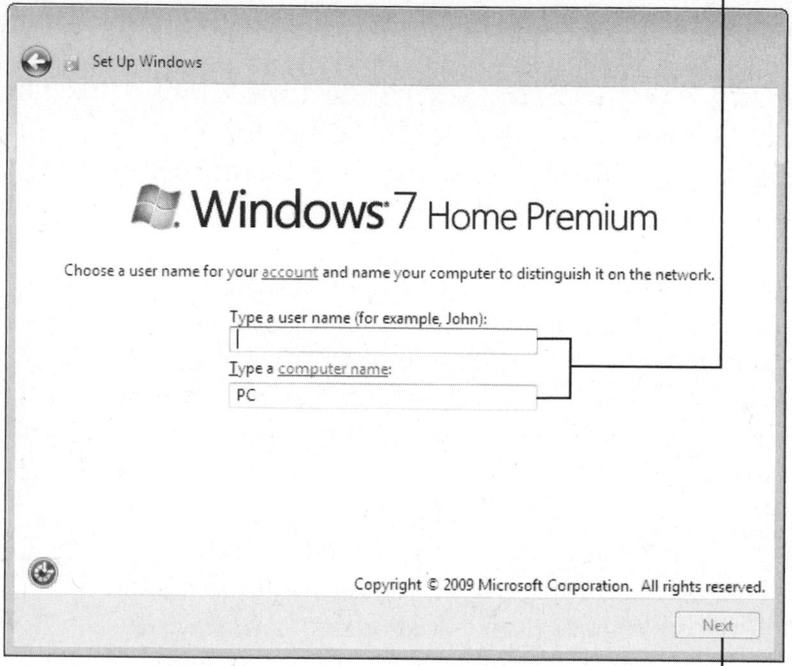

Windows 7 Home Premium

Set Up Windows

Choose a user name for your account and name your computer to distinguish it on the network.

Type a user name (for example, John):

Type a computer name:

PC

Copyright © 2009 Microsoft Corporation. All rights reserved.

Next

...And then click Next.

Figure 1-3

- **Password:** A password is an optional security measure. If you enter a password when you create your user account, that password is required each time you start the computer. If someone other than you tries to start your computer, he or she will have to know (or guess) the password to get into your files. (Don't put your password on a note stuck to the computer or nearby.) Click Next.

 For home computers, passwords may be unnecessary unless you need to keep someone else in the house out of your business. Laptop users should always create a password, however, because it is easy to lose a laptop. Don't make it easy for a thief to use your computer.

- **Use Recommended Settings:** After the password screen, you select settings for updating and securing Windows 7. Click Use Recommended Settings.

- **Date and Time Settings:** Select your time zone. Check or uncheck Automatically Adjust for Daylight Saving Time, as appropriate. Confirm the current time. Click Next.

- **Select Your Computer's Current Location:** Your computer may detect an Internet connection automatically. If you are at home, click Home Network. Otherwise, click Public Network. See Chapter 8 for more information about network connections.

 After the initial setup, every time you turn on the computer, you may be asked to log in under the user account you created in Step 3, including a password if you created one. If you are the only user of the computer and did not create a password, Windows 7 logs you in automatically.

Check Out the Windows 7 Desktop

1. After you turn on the computer and log in with your user name and (if necessary) password, you see a screen indicating that Windows is starting. Then you see the Windows desktop. **Figure 1-4** shows a common desktop setup, although yours may be different.

 Often, an interesting picture or photo is displayed on the desktop. You see how to change this picture in Chapter 14.

Icon

Icons

Desktop

Figure 1-4

2. Examine your desktop for *icons* — small pictures that represent programs, which perform functions, or documents such as letters and photos. Icons provide a way to run a program or open a document. The Windows 7 desktop displays an icon for the Recycle Bin, where deleted documents go. The Recycle Bin may be the only icon on your desktop, or you may see others.

3. Finally, the desktop displays *gadgets*, which are usually larger than icons. Gadgets display information, such as the time (in a clock) or the current weather report. See Chapter 5 for more about using gadgets.

Try Out the Mouse

1. If your computer came with a mouse pad, which is a thin, flexible rectangle with a very smooth surface, place the mouse pad under the mouse.

2. Move the mouse, which is typically about the size of a bar of soap and has two buttons at one end. Your mouse may have a wheel between the buttons. Use the wheel in long documents or on Web pages (see Chapter 9) to scroll to areas below or above the area displayed on your screen.

 Hold the mouse gently so that you can click either button easily without having to reposition your hand.

Instead of a mouse, a laptop usually has a *touchpad* — a small rectangle below the keys on the keyboard with buttons below it that do the same things as the mouse buttons. Drag your index finger over the touchpad to move the mouse pointer (see Step 3) over the screen.

 You can use more than one mouse or other pointing device with any computer. If your current mouse is too small or big or hard to use, buy a wireless mouse. In addition to mice, other pointing devices include trackballs, which you roll to move the mouse pointer, and pens that you use on a separate tablet or directly on the screen.

3. As you move the mouse, an arrow called the *mouse pointer* moves on your computer screen (see **Figure 1-5**). Try moving that pointer over the screen. With experience, you'll become very comfortable using the mouse. For practice, pat your head while rubbing your stomach.

Icon

Recycle Bin

Mouse pointer
Figure 1-5

4. Try out the mouse or touchpad buttons in the following ways:

- Move the mouse pointer on top of an icon or gadget on the desktop, such as the Recycle Bin. Let the mouse pointer sit there for a moment — this is *hovering* — you may see a pop-up message (called a *tooltip*) with information about the icon you hover over. Press and release (*click*) the left mouse button. This action highlights, or *selects*, that icon or gadget. As you work with *menus*, which are lists of items (see Chapter 3), you put the mouse pointer on the menu item you intend to use and then click the left mouse button to select the item.

 In this book, when you see the words *point* or *hover*, they mean move the mouse pointer to the specified location but don't click. The word *click* means a single, quick press and release of the left mouse button. A *double-click* is two rapid clicks of the left mouse button. A *right-click* is a single press and release of the right mouse button.

- Place the mouse pointer on an icon and then double-click the left mouse button to open the object associated with that icon, such as an e-mail program or a document that you want to read, edit, or print.

Sometimes you don't know for sure whether you need to click or double-click. One way to tell is to hover over the icon you want to use. Often, a little bit of help info pops up, telling you what the icon is for (see "Get Help When You Need It," later in this chapter). Then click the left mouse button to see whether anything happens. If nothing does, double-click the icon. In other words, you may not always have to double-click to open a document or run a program, so don't assume that you have to until you get more familiar with when one click is sufficient.

- Place your mouse pointer over any object on the screen and right-click (click the right mouse button one time). You see a menu of *options*, related to the item your mouse pointer is over. This menu is called a *context menu* because it changes with the context or the position of the mouse pointer and is different for different items. Right-clicking a photograph's icon, for example, displays a menu of options for viewing that photo, and right-clicking a music file's icon displays a menu of options for playing the music. A few options, such as Open and Properties, appear in most context menus, but others change depending on the context (what the mouse pointer is pointing at).

The right mouse button is the key to the kingdom because of context menus. Try right-clicking various areas of the screen. You almost never double-click the right mouse button, though.

5. With the mouse pointer over an icon, such as the Recycle Bin, click and hold down the left mouse button; then move the mouse to the right or down the screen. As you move the mouse, the icon moves in the same direction on the screen. This process is called *click and drag*. When you release the left mouse button, the icon stays where you moved it. Click and drag the Recycle Bin or any other icons you see on the desktop to some other places on the desktop. Fun, huh?

6. You can also click and drag with the right mouse button. Hover the mouse pointer over an icon, such as the Recycle Bin or any other icon or gadget on the desktop; click and hold down the right mouse button; and move the mouse. When you release the right mouse button, a small context menu pops up. You use this menu to copy or move documents in Chapter 4.

 If you have a laptop, you can click, double-click, and click and drag by using your finger on a touchpad and the buttons near it. Keep in mind, too, that you can use a mouse with a laptop (though it's not easy if you have the laptop on your lap!).

Go with the Start Button

1. The Start button, located in the bottom-left corner of the screen, provides easy access to all the programs you use. This circular button displays the Windows logo — a four-colored flag. Click the Start button to display the Start menu, which is a list of options (see **Figure 1-6**).

2. Move your mouse pointer slowly over each item on the left side of the menu. As you hover, some menu items display a tooltip. A menu item with a triangle to the right displays a pop-out list called a *jump list*. See Chapter 15 for more information about using jump lists.

3. Click the All Programs item to display a menu of all the available programs on your computer.

4. On the All Programs menu, find a yellow icon for Games or Accessories, and click that icon to display more programs. (Later, to play a game or open an accessory, you click its name.)

Click an item to start that program.

Start typing to find the program you want.

Start button

Figure 1-6

5. Click Back near the bottom of the All Programs menu to return to the first Start menu. You can also press the Esc (Escape) key to back up through the menus.

6. You don't have to dig through menus by clicking as you did in the preceding steps. Instead, you can type part of the name of the program you want to run. When the Start menu opens, the *cursor,* which is a vertical or horizontal line indicating where words you type will appear, is automatically in the box labeled Search Programs and Files. Start typing **solitaire**, and you see several programs listed, including the game Solitaire. Note that the game appears in the list as soon as you type the letter **s**. By the time you type **sol**, Solitaire is at the top of the list. Click the Solitaire item to start the game. See Chapter 11 for information about Solitaire and other games.

 You can perform most actions with the mouse, the keyboard, or a combination of the two. Another way to display the Start menu, for example, is to press the Windows logo key, which is located between the keys labeled Ctrl (Control) and Alt (Alternate) near the spacebar — the largest key on the keyboard. The Windows logo key has the same four-part flag icon as the Start menu (although not in color). From here on, I'll refer to this key as the *Win key*.

7. Tap and release the Win key to display the Start menu; tap the Win key a second time to remove the Start menu from the screen. If you want to run something else, you can type the name of the program you want and press Enter or click the program name. This is the easiest way to start any program you know the name of. You may need to type only a few letters to run a program.

 See Chapter 15 for information on customizing the items that appear on the Start menu.

 Learning keystroke shortcuts is especially valuable if you don't like using the mouse or other pointing device, which is a common complaint laptop users have about the touchpad.

Get Familiar with the Taskbar

1. The area at the bottom of the screen and to the right of the Start button is the *taskbar*, where you see icons for some programs. **Figure 1-7** shows four icons in the taskbar. The first three icons are for programs that aren't running (Microsoft Internet Explorer, Windows Explorer,

Media Player); the fourth icon is for Solitaire, which you started in the preceding task. The mouse hovers over Solitaire to display the thumbnail or the program name.

Taskbar

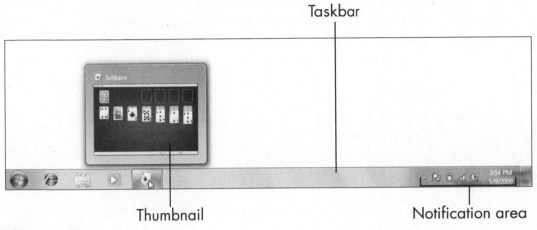

Thumbnail   Notification area

Figure 1-7

Use the taskbar as another way to run programs, in addition to the Start menu. You can use the taskbar to switch between programs by clicking the icon for the program you want to use.

2. Hover the mouse pointer over icons in the taskbar. For programs that are running, you may see a preview or *thumbnail* (small picture) of that program (refer to Figure 1-7).

 Whether your computer has this capability depends, in part, on your edition of Windows 7. The Starter edition, for example, does not show thumbnails in the taskbar. This function also depends on your computer's graphics hardware, so you may not see taskbar thumbnails if you don't have the necessary hardware.

3. The right end of the taskbar is an area called the *Notification area* or *icon tray* (refer to Figure 1-7), which displays the current date and time, as well as icons for

other programs that run automatically when your computer starts. Messages called *notifications* pop up here from time to time. Get information about these icons by hovering the mouse pointer over them. Click any icon in the icon tray to open the associated program, and right-click an icon to see a menu of available options, such as those to change settings or exit the program.

 Before too long, you see a pop-up notification in the icon tray to Activate Windows Now. Windows 7 needs to phone home to Microsoft to check in — that's activation. Ignore this message until you have an Internet connection. See Chapter 8 for information on connecting to the Internet and Chapter 17 for steps to activation.

 To recap: Start a program by using the Start menu, icons on the desktop, or icons in the taskbar. Switch between programs you have started by clicking their icons in the taskbar.

Get Help When You Need It

1. Hover the mouse pointer over anything on the screen to see a pop-up box, or *tooltip*, with a brief explanation of the item.

2. Look for information on the screen. A How to Play box appears briefly when you start Solitaire, for example. The bottom edge of the screen, called the *status bar*, may display help text that changes as you highlight different items on the screen. Some screens display blue links you can click for more information.

3. Many programs, including the one shown in **Figure 1-8**, have a Help menu. Click the Help menu to see a list of help options. You can also press the F1 key near the top of your keyboard to see help information.

Click Help.

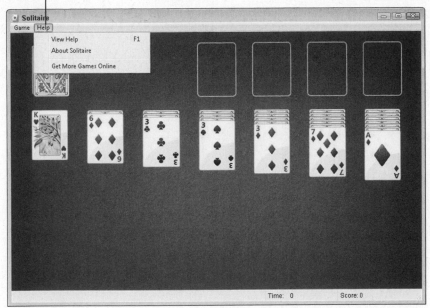

Figure 1-8

 In most programs, choose Help➪About (this program) to find out the name and version number of the program. You may need the version number as you seek help elsewhere.

4. Choose Start➪Help and Support to start the Windows 7 Help program. Click blue links to see more information. Type a term you want help with in the Search Help box at the top of the Help window, and press the Enter key to search for that term. Try this by typing **taskbar** or **start menu**, for example. Search the Help and Support program for **what's new** if you have used Windows Vista or Windows XP (see **Figure 1-9**).

Type a term you want to find more about and press Enter.

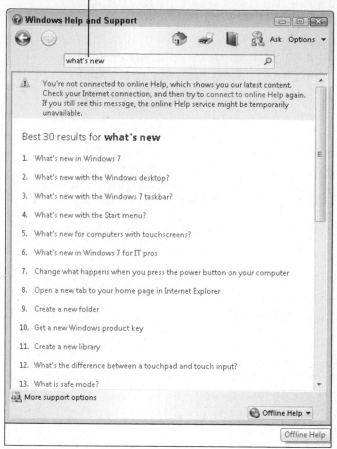

Figure 1-9

Close Windows 7

1. Although you can let Windows 7 run indefinitely, you probably want to turn your computer off if you aren't going to use it for a few hours. To see your options for turning the computer off, click the Start button to open the Start menu (refer to "Go with the Start Button," earlier in this chapter).

2. At the bottom of the Start menu, to the right of the box labeled Search Programs and Files, you see a button with a triangle at its right end. This button usually displays Shut Down, although the button may be programmed to display another option.

3. The Shut Down button has other options, as shown in **Figure 1-10**. Click the triangle to the right of the button for these options. For now, these three options matter most (you may not have all of these):

- **Shut Down:** This option exits Windows 7 and saves power by turning the computer off. In exiting Windows 7, Shut Down closes any programs that are currently running.

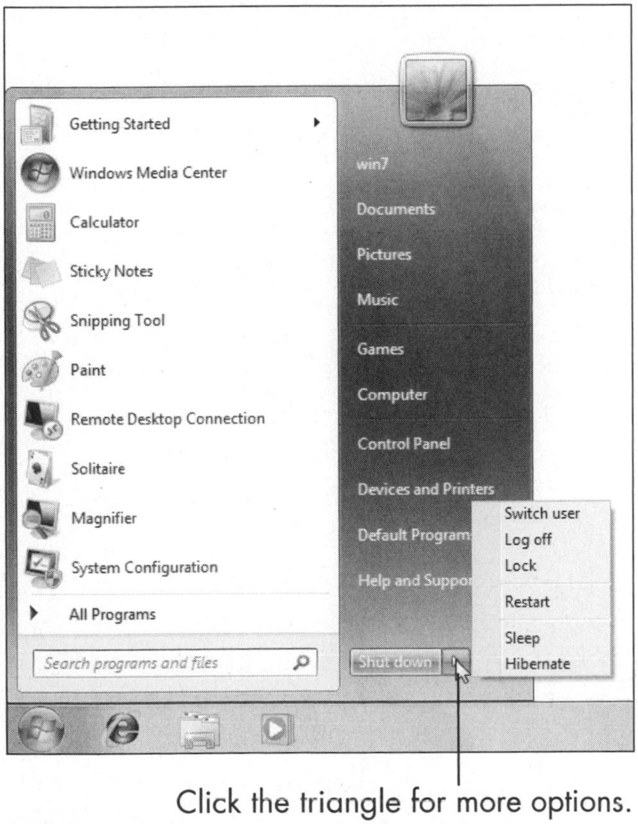

Getting Started

Windows Media Center

Calculator

Sticky Notes

Snipping Tool

Paint

Remote Desktop Connection

Solitaire

Magnifier

System Configuration

All Programs

Search programs and files

win7

Documents

Pictures

Music

Games

Computer

Control Panel

Devices and Printers

Default Programs

Help and Support

Switch user

Log off

Lock

Restart

Sleep

Hibernate

Shut down

Click the triangle for more options.

Figure 1-10

- **Sleep:** This option reduces the computer's power consumption without exiting Windows 7 or closing programs. As a result, when you wake the computer by moving the mouse or touching the keyboard, everything is exactly as you left it: programs and documents are open, if they were before Sleep.

- **Hibernate:** This option combines Sleep and Shut Down. Hibernate records which programs are running but completely shuts down the computer. When you start the computer, Windows 7 opens all programs you were using, just like Sleep.

 Hibernate or Shut Down are equally *green* options — they save the same amount of power. Sleep is a little less green, but saves time in returning to a task you're in the middle of.

4. Choose Shutdown to turn off the computer.

 On most computers, pressing the power switch also shuts down the computer. On a laptop, closing the lid may shut down the laptop or put it into Sleep or Hibernation mode.

 For a desktop computer, consider using a power strip to plug in the computer, the monitor, and the printer. After you shut down or hibernate the computer, turn the power strip off. This saves the most power.

Examining the Anatomy of a Window

At the dawn of the personal computer in the 1980s, computers and their users ran one program at a time. Although you can use Windows to run one program at a time, that's so last-century. Windows is a multitasking system that enables you to run many programs at once. You can listen to music, browse the Web, write e-mail, and play a game — all at the same time.

Windows, with a capital *W*, gets its name from its main feature: windows, with a lowercase *w*. These windows contain activities. Each program you run occupies its own window. One window may contain your word processing program, such as WordPad or Microsoft Word; another may contain your Web browser; and another may contain a game.

A window can occupy part of the computer's screen or fill the entire screen. Individual windows have some common features, which you explore in this chapter. Many windows also have features that are unique to the particular program, such as a slideshow option in a photo program or a play option in a game.

Getting comfortable with capital-W *Windows* means learning to open, close, resize, move, and switch between lowercase-w *windows*, which is the key to juggling multiple activities successfully.

Explore the Parts of a Window

1. To see a window on your screen, click the Start button and type **sol** in the Search Programs and Files box to display the Solitaire game. (See Chapter 1 for information on using the Start button.) **Figure 2-1** shows the window that Solitaire runs in.

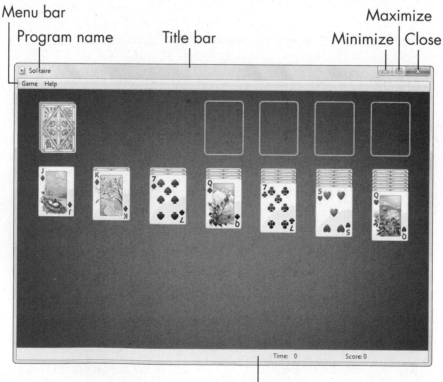

Figure 2-1

2. Explore this example of a window, starting at the top:

- **Title bar:** The *title bar* is the top line of the window, containing the title of the program you're using. When you use a program to create a document, the name of the document also appears in the title bar.

- **View and close buttons:** In the top-right corner of the window are three little buttons with big functions. (One of these buttons changes as you use it.) From left to right, these buttons are:

Minimize: The Minimize button shrinks or hides the window contents. The program that the window contains is still running and open, but the window is out of sight. You'll still see the program's icon in the taskbar. (I cover the taskbar in Chapter 1.) Click the Minimize button when you want to ignore a particular window but aren't actually done with it. To restore the window, click its icon in the taskbar (see Chapter 1).

Maximize/Restore: The Maximize button (the button with a single square) fills the screen with the contents of this window. Click the Maximize button to hide the desktop and other open windows, to concentrate on this one window, and to see as much of the window's contents as you can. Restore (the button with two squares) is the name of the button that appears after you click the Maximize button; it replaces the Maximize button. Click the Restore button to return the window to its previous size, which is in between maximized and minimized.

Close: Close is the red button with the X in the top-right corner of the window. Click the Close button when you are done with the window. Close is also called Quit and Exit.

- **Menu bar:** Below the title bar, starting at the left edge of the window, you see the *menu bar*, which is a horizontal strip containing various menus. Solitaire's menu bar has two menus: Game and Help. Many other programs' menu bars have File, Edit, and View as the first three menus. To use a menu, click its name and a vertical list of related items drops down. Then click the item you want to use.

- **Toolbar:** Below the menu bar, some programs display a *toolbar* of icons that you can click to perform various functions. Solitaire doesn't have a toolbar. You see a toolbar later in this chapter.

- **Program:** The bulk of the window contains the reason you have this particular window open: the program or document you're using.

- **Status bar:** Along the bottom edge of the window, some programs display information about the window or its contents in a *status bar.* Solitaire displays the elapsed time of play and your score in the status bar.

 Scan the edges of windows. Often, important information and functions are pushed to these edges around the main content area.

3. Click the Close button (the red X) to close Solitaire.

Resize a Window

1. To see how to resize a window, open Notepad, a simple program for typing small amounts of text. Click the Start button and type **Notepad**. Notice that Notepad's title bar displays *Untitled* because you're starting a new document.

2. If the Notepad window is maximized (fills the screen), click the Restore button to the left of the Close button to make it smaller.

3. Move the mouse pointer to the right edge of the window. When you have the pointer just over the outside edge of the window, the mouse pointer changes to a double-headed arrow called the *resize pointer*, shown in **Figure** 2-2.

Resize pointer

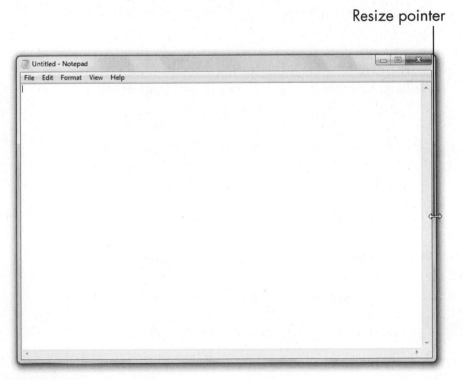

Figure 2-2

4. Click and drag the edge of the window, using the resize pointer. (To drag, click and hold down the mouse button while you move the mouse.) Drag left to shrink the window and right to expand it.

5. Put the mouse pointer over any other edge of the window and then click and drag on the resize pointer to shrink or expand the window.

6. Put the mouse pointer on the bottom-right corner of the window. If your pointer is in the corner over the small triangle of dots, the resize pointer arrows point top-left to bottom-right. Click and drag to resize the window's width and height at the same time (see **Figure 2-3**).

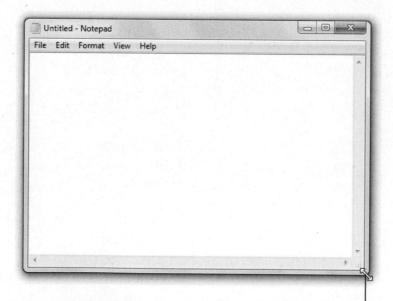

Click and drag to resize both height and width.

Figure 2-3

7. Resize the window by clicking and dragging the resize pointer in any of the other corners (even though you don't see dots in those corners). If you want to see whether you're a mouse master, try resizing the top-right corner without accidentally clicking the Close button.

8. Leave Notepad open as you go on to the next task.

 You may want to resize a window to show just what you want to see, nothing more. Practice resizing from any side or corner.

Arrange Windows

1. Start the WordPad program by clicking the Start button and typing **wordpad**. You may not need to type the whole word before it opens. WordPad is suitable for documents such as letters and journals. (See Chapter 3 for more information about using WordPad.) Notice that WordPad's title bar displays *Document* as the title of this new document. WordPad has a very large tool bar called a *ribbon*.

2. If Notepad isn't still running from the preceding task, start it by clicking the Start button and typing **notepad**. You now see two overlapping windows, as shown in **Figure 2-4**.

 The window in front of others is called the *active* window. All other windows are *inactive*. Notice the title bar of the active window is a different color from the title bar in an inactive window. Clicking anywhere in an inactive window makes it active and moves that window to the front.

Ribbon toolbar   Inactive window

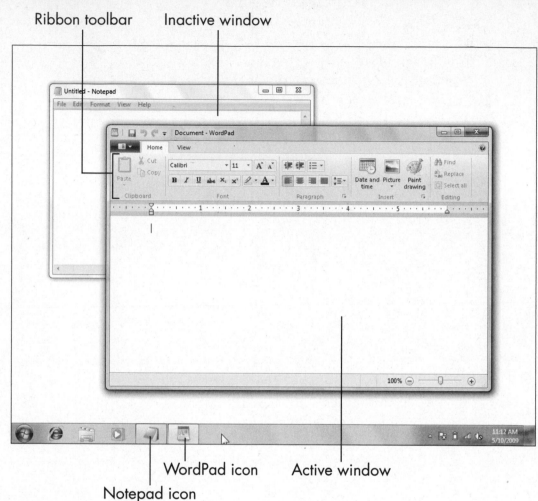

WordPad icon   Active window

Notepad icon

Figure 2-4

3. Click anywhere in the WordPad title bar (avoiding the buttons on the left and right ends), hold down the mouse button, and drag the mouse to move the window a little.

4. Click anywhere in the Notepad title bar (again, avoiding the buttons on both ends), and drag the window.

5. Practice moving both windows a few times. Arranging windows helps you see and do more than one thing at a time.

If you can't see the title bar of the window you want to move, move the other window to uncover the hidden title bar.

6. Leave Notepad and WordPad open for the following task.

Snap Windows

1. Drag the Notepad window to the left edge of your screen. When the mouse pointer touches the left edge of the screen, you'll see a new outline on the screen (see **Figure** 2-5).

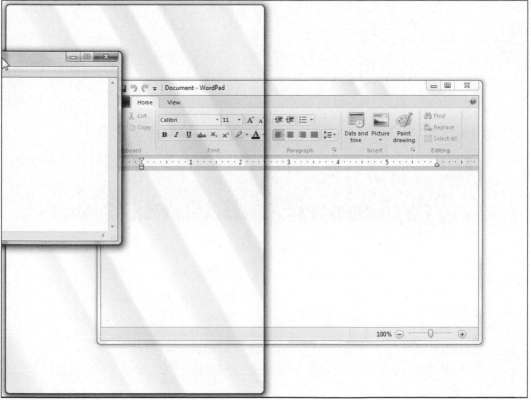

Figure 2-5

2. Release the mouse button. The window should resize automatically to fill the left half of the screen (see **Figure 2-6**). This operation is called *snap*.

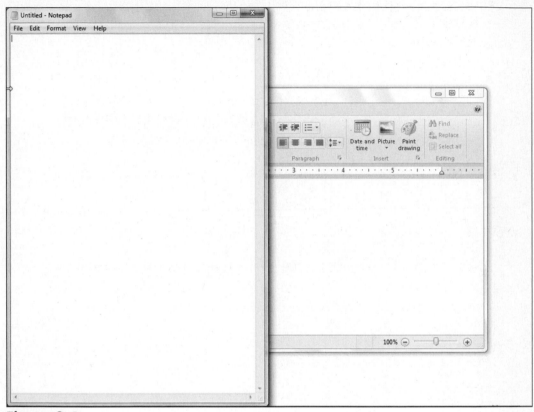

Figure 2-6

3. Drag the WordPad window to the right edge of the screen. When the mouse pointer touches the right edge, you'll see a new outline on the screen.

4. Release the mouse button. The WordPad window resizes automatically to fill the right half of the screen.

 Two or more windows displayed side by side like this are called *tiled*.

5. Drag either window by the title bar away from the edge of the screen. The window returns to its previous size.

6. Drag either window to the top edge of the screen. This action maximizes that window, just as though you clicked the Maximize button (refer to "Explore the Parts of a Window," earlier in this chapter).

7. Drag the title bar of the maximized window away from the top to restore it to its previous size, just as though you clicked the Restore button (refer to "Explore the Parts of a Window," earlier in this chapter).

8. Leave Notepad and WordPad open for the following task.

Stack Windows

1. On your desktop, place the mouse pointer on an empty area of the taskbar and right-click to display the context menu shown in **Figure** 2-7.

More ways to arrange windows

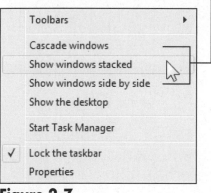

Figure 2-7

2. On that menu, click Show Windows Stacked. All the windows open on your desktop are arranged, one above the other.

3. With the mouse pointer on an empty area of the taskbar, right-click to display the context menu again and choose Undo Show Stacked to put the windows back the way they were.

4. Right-click an empty area of the taskbar and choose Show Windows Side by Side from the context menu (refer to Figure 2-7). The windows are arranged side by side.

 When you snapped the windows in Steps 1–4 of "Snap Windows," earlier in this chapter, you had to drag each window to the edge of the screen. The Show Windows Side by Side option performs this operation in one step.

5. Undo the tiling operation by right-clicking an empty area of the taskbar and choosing Undo Show Side by Side from the context menu.

 Often, you can undo your most recent action by right-clicking to display the context menu and looking for an undo option.

6. Leave Notepad and WordPad open for the next task.

Flip between Windows

1. Notepad and WordPad should be open. Start Solitaire, so that you have all three programs running. Now, you're juggling. To display previews of all open windows using a function called *Flip*, hold down one of the Alt keys (on either side of the spacebar, typically) and tap and release the Tab key. Don't let go of the Alt key yet. You'll see one of two forms of preview of your open windows:

• Windows 7's *Aero Peek* feature provides actual thumbnail previews of the content of each window, as in **Figure** 2-8. The Solitaire thumbnail preview is easiest to recognize in the figure. In addition, the window matching the selected preview appears behind the thumbnail previews.

Switch to the selected window.

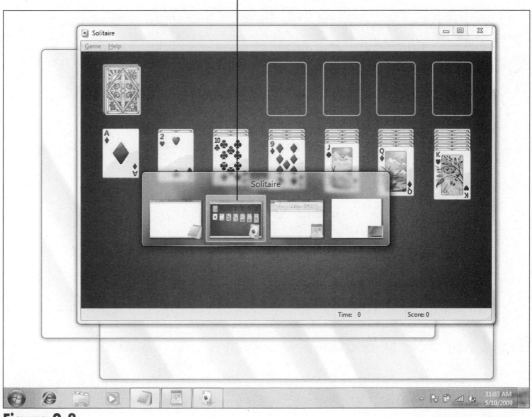

Figure 2-8

- If you have the Starter Edition of Windows 7, Aero Peek is unavailable. In other editions, you may not have thumbnail previews because your graphics card doesn't support it or preview may be turned off using themes discussed in Chapter 14. In this case, you see generic icons in *Flip*. See **Figure** 2-9. In addition, the window matching the selected preview doesn't appear behind the thumbnail previews.

Switch to the selected window.

Figure 2-9

2. Still holding down the Alt key, tap the Tab key as many times as necessary to move the highlight to the window you want to switch to.

3. Release the Alt key. The highlighted window appears in front of the others.

4. For a different — and cooler — preview of all open windows, hold down one of the Win keys that is beside one of the Alt keys, and repeatedly tap the Tab key to bring the window you want to the front. This action produces the effect called *Flip 3D,* shown in **Figure 2-10**.

5. Release the Win key. The selected window appears in front of the others.

Switch to the window in front.

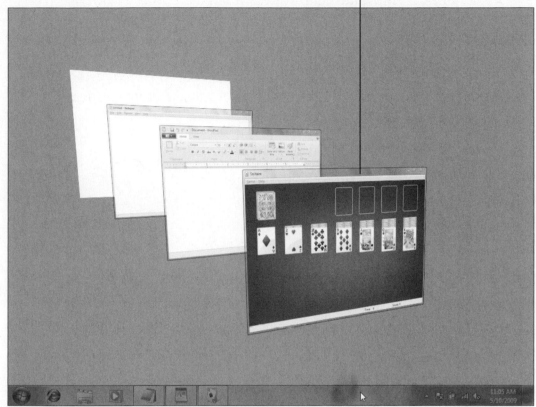

Figure 2-10

 If nothing happens when you hold down the Win key and press Tab, you may have the Starter Edition of Windows 7, which doesn't have this feature; your computer's graphics hardware may not have the necessary capability; or the feature may have been turned off. See Chapter 14 for information about Aero themes, which enable Flip and Flip 3D.

 Flip and Flip 3D have an option to show the desktop, which minimizes all open windows. That option is the last icon on the right of Flip or in back of Flip 3D.

Creating Your First Documents

Chapter
3

You use programs — or *software*, if you prefer that term — to do anything on a computer, including creating documents such as letters, memos, and diaries. That rather dry word *document* includes drawings and other works you create and save on your computer.

You tell a program what you want to do. Often, you have more than one way to command the program to do something. You may see a menu below the title bar of the window. You may find a button in a toolbar below the menu. Or clicking the right mouse button displays a context menu that may contain just the option you are looking for (see Chapter 1 for a refresher on context menus).

Often, you can use keystrokes to perform the most common commands. You don't need (or want, I'll bet) three or four ways to do something, but you have to determine which way is best for you. If the mouse is a problem for you, you may like keystrokes. Buttons in toolbars are often the most obvious choices, but they can be tricky to locate, recognize, or click. In this chapter, I introduce one method for each function and suggest some alternatives to try.

A *dialog box* is a special window that requires input from you. You interact with a dialog box, choosing groups of related options, such as for printing a document. In this chapter, you use dialog boxes and discover more about common features of a dialog box.

For this chapter, you create a letter or similar text using WordPad, one of the programs included with Windows 7. You can create similar documents with Microsoft Word and other programs. Each program you work with has some unique aspects, but try to generalize your experience with WordPad to see how it applies to other programs.

Start WordPad and Type Some Text

1. Start WordPad, and maximize the WordPad window to fill the screen. (See Chapter 2 for information about starting WordPad and working with individual program windows.) **Figure 3-1** shows the WordPad window.

The cursor shows where text will appear when you type.

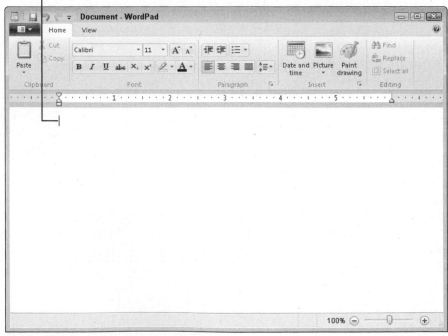

Figure 3-1

2. Start typing any text at all. The *cursor* — the blinking vertical line that shows where the next character you type will appear — moves as you type. Don't worry too much about what you're typing; no one is looking over your shoulder. (You can check to make sure, if you want.) Relax.

 Don't press the Enter key at the end of every line. Just keep typing; your text automatically *wraps* (moves down) to the next line.

3. At the end of a paragraph, press the Enter key. WordPad puts a blank line after each paragraph. A few paragraphs are all you need right now. See **Figure 3-2**.

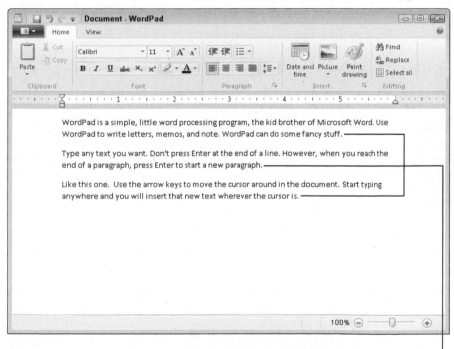

Press Enter at the end of a paragraph.

Figure 3-2

4. If you need to move the cursor before you type more text, click the place in the document where you want to move the cursor, or press the arrow keys that point up, left, down, and right. These keys are between the letters and numbers on a standard keyboard.

 You can't click or move the cursor beyond the last line of the document. To make a document longer, click at the end of the last character and start typing new text, or press Enter to create a new paragraph before typing.

5. Leave your document open for the next task.

Save a Document

1. To save your document, press the Ctrl key and the letter S at the same time, and then release them. This action, or *key combination*, is called Ctrl+S. When you do, the Save As dialog box appears (see **Figure 3-3**). See "Discover How a Dialog Box Works," later in this chapter. The Save As dialog box needs one piece of information from you: What do you want to call this document? Right now, the File Name text box displays the word *Document*, which is highlighted and ready to be replaced as soon as you start typing.

2. In the File Name text box, type a name that you'll recognize as being the name of this particular document, because you'll use it later to open the document again (see "Open a Document," later in this chapter). You could type **My First WordPad Document**, as shown in **Figure 3-4**, or something else.

 The name can be more than 200 characters long, which may be more characters than you have in the document! A few characters or words may suffice for a name. You can use uppercase and lowercase characters, spaces, dashes, and a few other symbols, including underscore (_), parentheses (()), and brackets ([]).

You can't use slashes (/ or \) or a few other symbols that Windows 7 reserves for other functions, including the asterisk (*) and question mark (?).

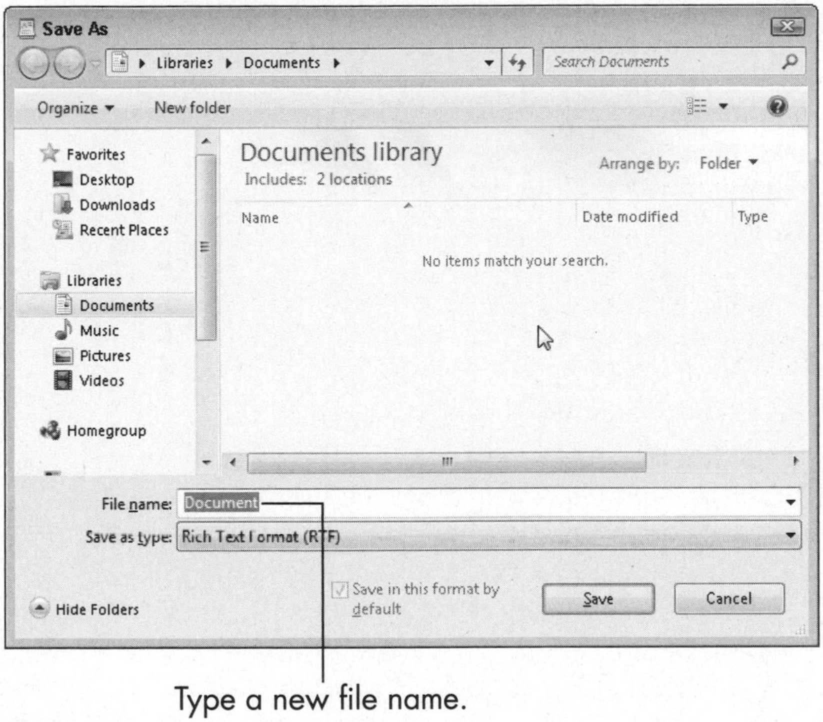

Type a new file name.

Figure 3-3

3. Click the Save button in the dialog box to save your document. When you do, the Save As dialog box closes, and you return to your document. Notice that your document name appears in the title bar to the left of the program name (WordPad).

 Saving a document stores it on your computer's disk as a *file* that you can open later. (See Chapter 4 for information on files and disks.) The saved document remains open so you can continue to work on it.

 Many programs, including WordPad, also have a toolbar button for saving a document. In the WordPad title bar, you see a small icon with a white square on a larger purple square (refer to Figure 3-1). This icon, which represents a disk, is the Save button. You can click this button instead of pressing Ctrl+S, if you prefer; it executes the same Save command and opens the same Save As dialog box. Another way to save your document and open the Save As dialog box is to choose File➪Save As.

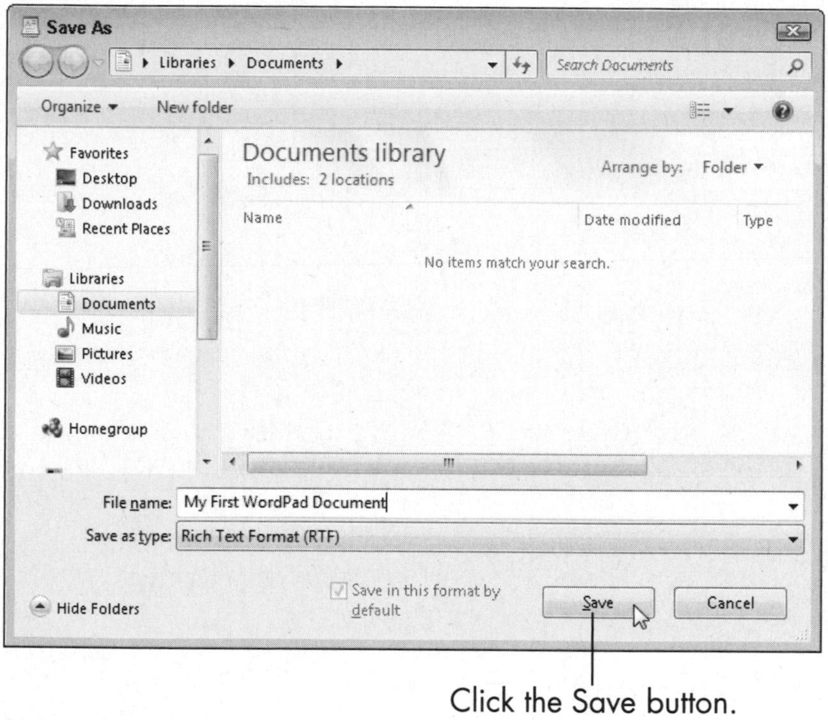

Click the Save button.

Figure 3-4

4. Type some more text in your document.

5. Save your document again, just as you did in the preceding steps. This time, you don't see the Save As dialog box. Why? WordPad knows the name of this file from the first time you saved it, so you don't have to name it again.

 Don't wait until you're done with a document to save it. Every time you make significant changes in a document, save it. Every time you're about to do something in a document that you've never tried before, save it. If you're not sure whether you've already saved a document, save it. Save frequently to reduce the odds of losing everything if the power goes off or you accidentally delete all your text. You can't save too many times, so save early and often. Each time you do, the older version of the file without your latest changes is replaced by the newest version of your file.

 See Chapter 4 for information on where your saved document is and how to find, move, and rename that document.

Add, Delete, Select, and Move Text

1. Add text to the document you created in earlier tasks or any document with text already in it. Click the place in the document where you want to begin typing, or press the arrow keys to move the cursor to that point (refer to "Start WordPad and Type Some Text," earlier in this chapter).

2. Click between two words and type something. The existing text moves to the right and down automatically to make room for the new text.

3. Press the Backspace key. Each time you do so, a character to the left of the cursor is erased. Any text to the right of the cursor moves left.

4. To *undo* what you just did, press Ctrl+Z (press the Ctrl key and the letter Z at the same time, and then let go of both keys at the same time). You can repeat Ctrl+Z to undo previous steps. To *redo* a step — or undo an undo — press Ctrl+Y. Feel free to undo any steps you wish to repeat.

5. With the cursor under some text, press the Delete key. Each time you do so, the character directly above the cursor is erased. Any text to the right of the cursor moves left.

Delete and Backspace both erase text, but Delete erases the text to the right of the cursor and Backspace erases the text to the left of the cursor.

6. Double-click a word to select the entire word and then press Backspace or Delete to erase it.

 When you *select* text, it's highlighted on your screen (see **Figure 3-5**). You select text when you want to do something to it, such as delete it or format it (see "Format Text with Bold, Italics, and More," later in this chapter).

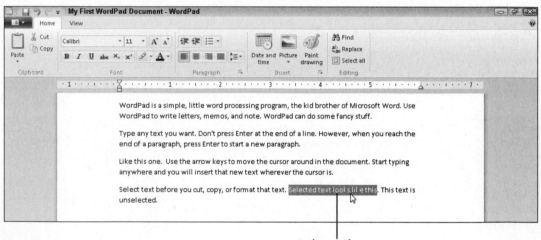

Selected text

Figure 3-5

7. To select more than a single word, click at the beginning of the text that you intend to select; hold down the Shift key; and press the right-arrow key to highlight the text you want to select. Don't let go of the Shift key until you've selected all the text you want. As you hold down Shift, you can also press the down-arrow key to select an entire line of text.

The mouse method for selecting text is clicking and dragging over the text to highlight it (see Chapter 2). Another way to select text with the mouse is to click at the beginning of the text you want to select, hold down the Shift key, and click at the end of the text you want to select. The entire section is highlighted.

8. Select any text and then press Ctrl+X to *cut* it. That text disappears from the screen but is not erased from the document, as it is when you press the Backspace or Delete key (refer to Step 3 and Step 5). Text that you cut is moved to an invisible feature of Windows 7 called the *Clipboard*, which temporarily holds text and graphics that you cut or copy.

 Anything that you cut stays on the Clipboard until you cut or copy something else, which replaces it, or until you turn off your computer.

9. Move the cursor somewhere else in your document, and press Ctrl+V to *paste*. Windows 7 takes the text you just cut from the Clipboard and puts it in the document at the location of your cursor.

10. To copy text instead of cutting it, select that text and press Ctrl+C to *copy*; move the cursor to a new location; and press Ctrl+V to paste. Like cut text, copied text goes to the Clipboard and stays there until you copy something else to replace it or turn off your computer.

 Most programs use the same key combinations for the Copy (Ctrl+C), Cut (Ctrl+X), and Paste (Ctrl+V) commands. Many programs also have an Edit menu that contains these commands. (WordPad doesn't.) If you right-click selected text, these same commands appear in a context menu. Also, many programs have

Cut, Copy, and Paste buttons in the toolbar. Why do programs give you so many options? To let you find out which one works best for you. Try each method to see what you find.

Format Text with Bold, Italics, and More

1. In any document, select some text (refer to "Add, Delete, Select, and Move Text," earlier in this chapter), and press Ctrl+B to make that text **bold** (dark and thick). You see the text become thicker onscreen.

2. With the text still selected, press Ctrl+B again to remove the bold formatting.

3. Select some text, and press Ctrl+I to make the text *italic* (slightly slanted to the right).

4. With the text still selected, press Ctrl+I a second time to remove the italic formatting.

5. Use WordPad's *Ribbon* — the toolbar at the top of the window — to add more text effects (see **Figure 3-6**). In each case, first select the text you want to format; then click one of the following formatting buttons in the Font panel of the Ribbon:

WordPad Ribbon toolbar

The Home tab   The Font panel

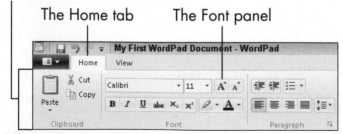

Figure 3-6

- B is **bold**.

- *I* is *italic*.

- U is <u>underline</u>.

- ~~abc~~ is strikethrough.

- X_2 is subscript (like the number in H_2O).

- X^2 is superscript (like the number in $E = mc^2$).

- The highlighter icon to the right of the Superscript button (X^2) highlights the selected text. Click the triangle (down arrow) to the right of the button to select a highlighter color. To use that same color the next time, just click the Highlight button, not the arrow.

- The *A* with a heavy bar under it applies a color to the text itself. Click the triangle (down arrow) to the right of the button to select a text color. To use that same color the next time, just click the Font Color button, not the arrow.

6. Use the buttons in the top row of the Font panel in WordPad's Ribbon (see **Figure** 3-7) to make these changes to selected text:

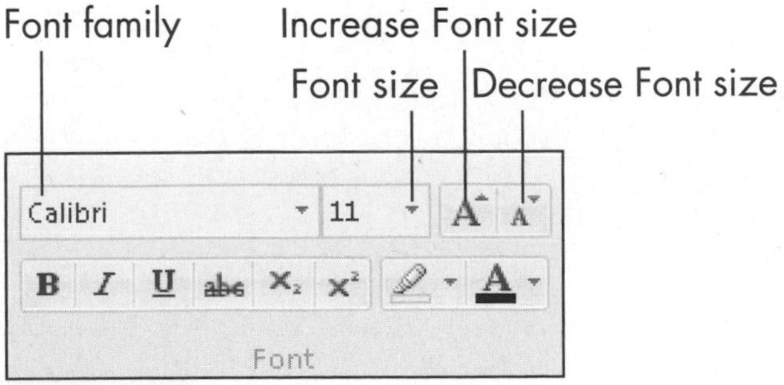

Font family   Increase Font size

Font size |Decrease Font size

Calibri   11   A A

B *I* <u>U</u> ~~abc~~ X_2 X^2 **A**

Font

Figure 3-7

- The Font drop-down list shows options that let you change the *font,* or typeface, in which the text is displayed. Some fonts are easier to read than others; some fonts are prettier than others.

- The Size drop-down list allows you to change the selected text to a specific size measured in *points* — a traditional unit of measure for fonts. Text that is 72 points, for example, is about an inch tall. Most newspapers and books use text between 10 and 12 points. (This text is 12.5 points.)

- The A with a triangle pointing up allows you to increase the font size without using the Size list.

- The A with a triangle pointing down allows you to decrease the font size without using the Size list.

 Programs reward patience and curiosity. Don't be afraid to experiment with formatting in a document that isn't precious to you, so that you can see what works and how. Remember: The Undo command is Ctrl+Z.

Print a Document

1. You can print your document at any time. With the printer connected and the power on, click the WordPad button — the button with the little box and down-pointing triangle on it — to the left of the Home tab in the Ribbon. (You can see this tab in Figure 3-1, earlier in this chapter.) **Figure 3-8** shows the WordPad menu that drops down from this button.

 If you haven't attached your printer to the computer yet, see Chapter 7.

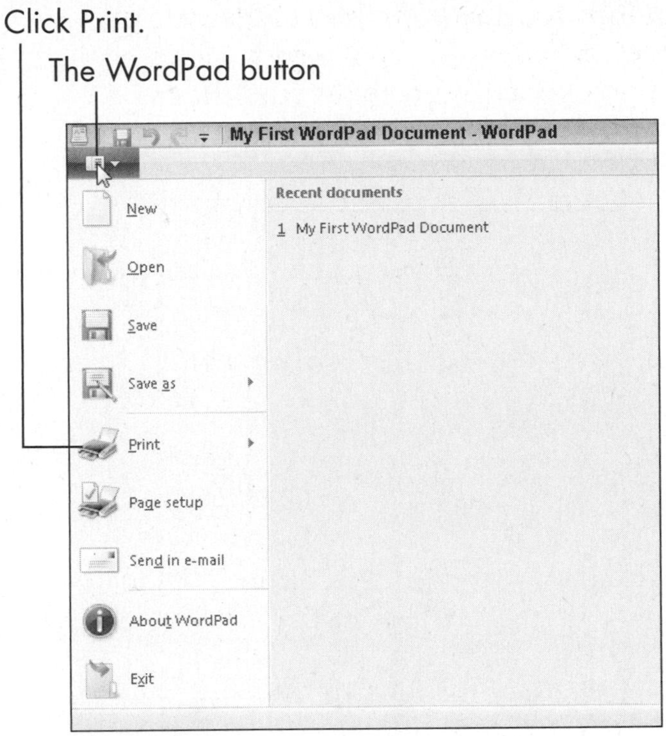

Click Print.

The WordPad button

My First WordPad Document - WordPad

Recent documents

1 My First WordPad Document

New

Open

Save

Save as

Print

Page setup

Send in e-mail

About WordPad

Exit

Figure 3-8

 In most programs, the File menu appears in place of the WordPad button. The File menu displays options similar to those on the WordPad button.

2. Hover over the Print button, halfway down the menu. (Flip to Chapter 1 for a refresher on hovering.) A second menu pops out to the right, listing three printing commands (see **Figure 3-9**).

3. Click the Print Preview item to see what your document will look like on paper (see **Figure 3-10**).

 When you're creating a document, you can't always tell how much of the page the text uses or how many sheets of paper you'll need to print the whole document. Print Preview shows you exactly what will come out of your printer. It may also help you avoid wasting paper if you see a change that you need to make before printing.

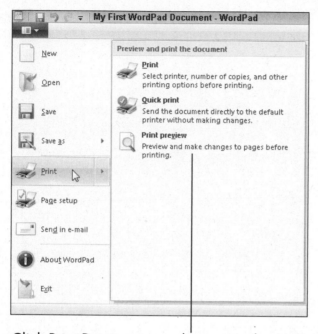

Click Print Preview to see how your document will look when you print it.
Figure 3-9

4. If you're ready to print from Print Preview, click the Print button in the Ribbon (refer to Figure 3-10). If you're not using Print Preview, repeat Steps 1 and 2, then click Print in the pop-out menu. The Print dialog box appears, as shown in **Figure 3-11**.

 Ninety-nine percent of the time, you don't need to set any of the options in the Print dialog box.

Click to print the document.

Click to return to editing the document.

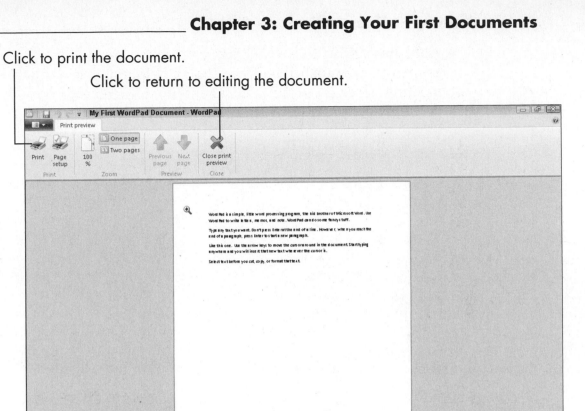

Figure 3-10

5. Click the Print button to print (or, if you don't want to print, click the Cancel button).

 To skip the Print dialog box, choose File⇨Print⇨ Quick Print.

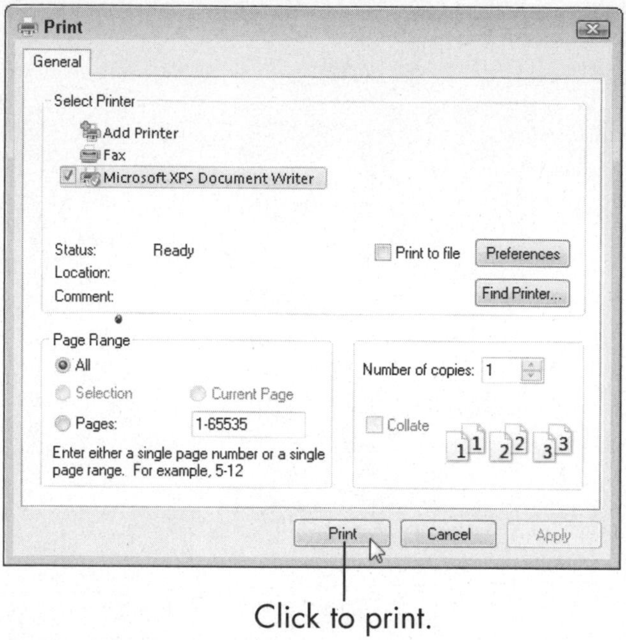

Click to print.

Figure 3-11

Quit WordPad

1. When you're done with WordPad, click the Close box —
the red box with the X on it in the top-right corner of the
program window — to quit the program. *Quit* is also
called *exit* or *close.* (See Chapter 2 for details on closing.)
If you haven't saved your document since making
changes or printing it, WordPad displays the dialog box
shown in **Figure 3-12**.

2. Click one of the three buttons in the dialog box:

- Click the Save button to save your document
before quitting WordPad (your most likely
choice).

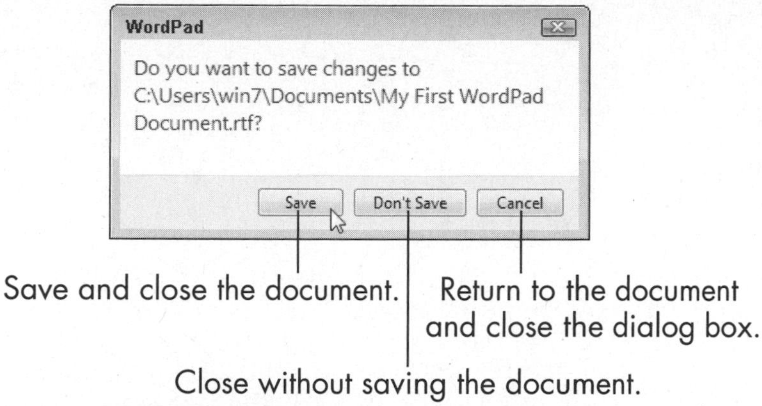

Save and close the document. | Return to the document and close the dialog box.

Close without saving the document.

Figure 3-12

- Click the Don't Save button to throw away your most recent changes. Whatever you did up to the last time you saved the document is still saved, but any changes you made after the save are discarded.

- Click Cancel to dismiss the dialog box and return to WordPad and your document. (Clicking the Close button in the dialog box does the same thing.)

Open a Document

1. To open an existing document to read, change, or print it, click the Start button (see Chapter 1), and start to type the name of the document you intend to open. If you named the document My First WordPad Document, for example (refer to "Save a Document," earlier in this chapter), you could start to type any of the four words in the document name. The Start menu automatically lists matching documents and programs, as you see in **Figure 3-13**.

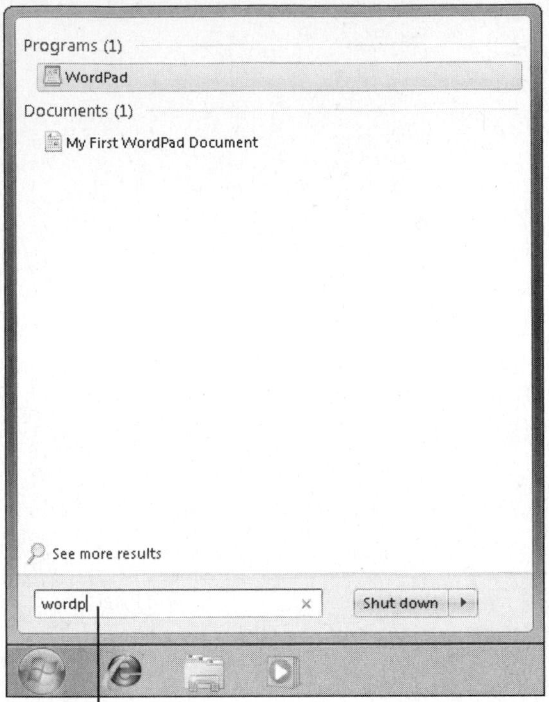

Type text that matches your document's name.
Figure 3-13

2. Click the document name or, if the name is already highlighted, press the Enter key. The document opens in WordPad (or whichever program you used to create the document).

3. Searching for your document from the Start menu, as you just did, is great, but now try this method: Click Start. If you see WordPad in the Start menu, hover over WordPad. A list of recent documents pops out to the right. This list is called a *jump list* (see **Figure 3-14**). Click the document you intend to open. See Chapter 15 for more about using jump lists.

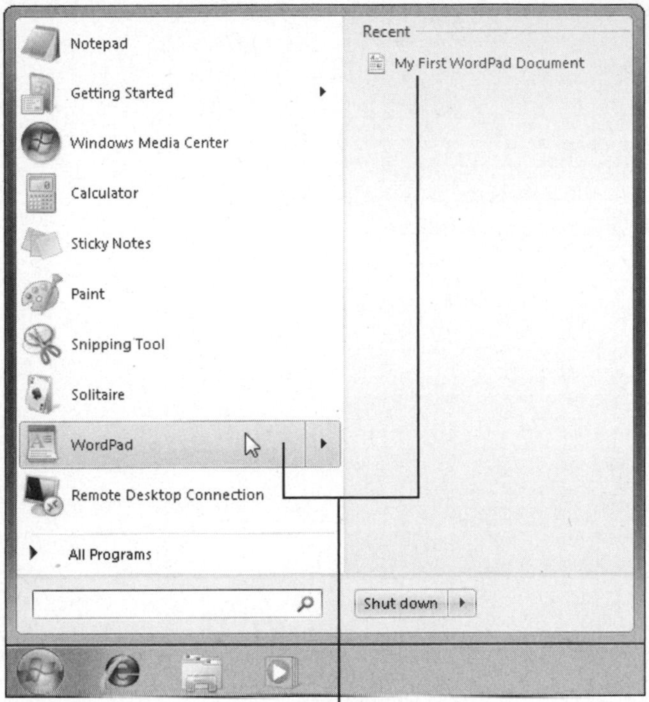

Notepad	Recent
Getting Started ▶	My First WordPad Document
Windows Media Center	
Calculator	
Sticky Notes	
Paint	
Snipping Tool	
Solitaire	
WordPad ▶	
Remote Desktop Connection	
▶ All Programs	
🔍	Shut down ▶

Hover over a program for a jump
list of recent documents.

Figure 3-14

4. Yet another way to open a document: Start WordPad,
and click the WordPad button next to the Home tab in
the Ribbon (refer to Figure 3-9). Your document may be
listed in the menu that drops down. Click the document's
name to open it. If it isn't, choose File⇨Open. Double-
click your document in the dialog box (see **Figure 3-15**).

See Chapter 4 for information on searching for misplaced documents and opening documents from
Windows Explorer.

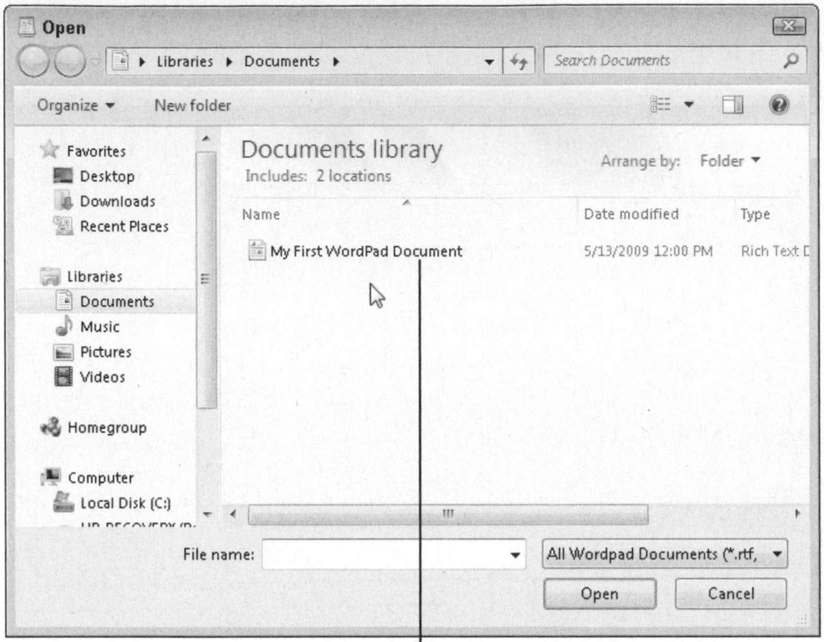

Double-click a document to open it.

Figure 3-15

Discover How a Dialog Box Works

Dialog boxes provide multiple options related to a specific action. In the task "Save a Document," the Save As dialog box provides a *text box* for you to enter the name of the document. You didn't need the options that determine where the document is saved and what kind of file it is. Often, you can accept the default options already set in a dialog box. The following features are common to many dialog boxes, though no dialog box contains every one of these. (For that reason, there isn't an ideal figure to display them all.)

➡ **The OK button:** When you are done with the dialog box — even if you haven't actually changed anything — click OK to accept the options in the dialog box and to continue. In some dialog boxes, the label on this button is for the action to be performed, instead of OK. For example, the button

displays Print in the Print dialog box (**Figure 3-16**).
To see this dialog box on your screen, click the
WordPad button, and then click Print.

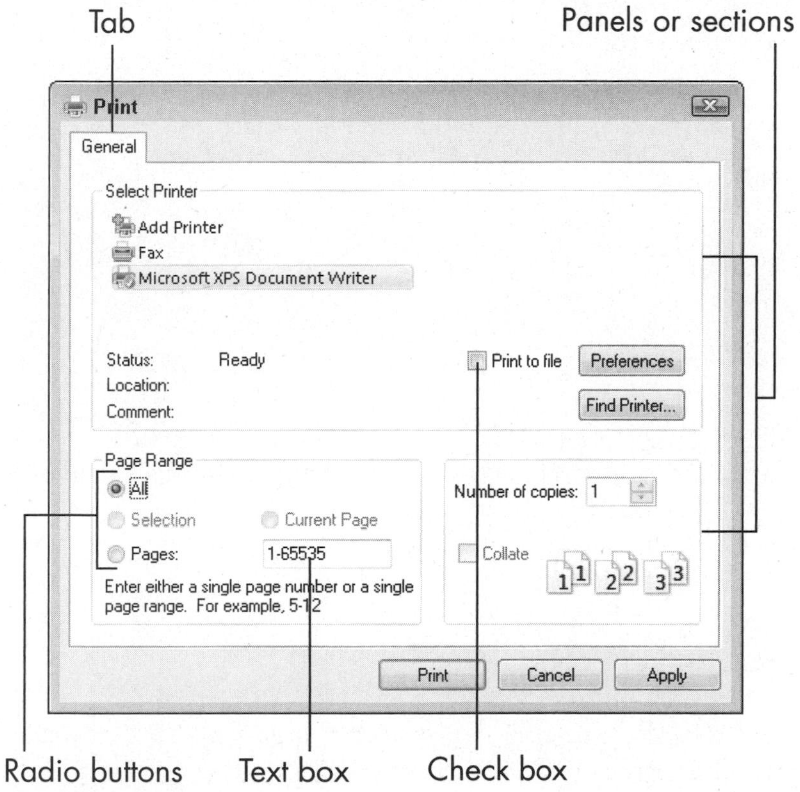

Tab   Panels or sections

Radio buttons Text box Check box

Figure 3-16

> ➠ **The Cancel button**: This button stops any further
> action and undoes selections you made prior to can-
> celing. Use it when you open a dialog box you don't
> want to continue with.

> ➠ **The Apply button**: This button preserves changes
> you make in the dialog box, unlike Cancel. Also
> unlike OK, this leaves the dialog box open for fur-
> ther options. Apply is useful in a dialog box with
> many options, because you can apply the choices
> you've made before you go on to explore others.

➡ **Tabs**: Some dialog boxes have so many options, those options are grouped into tabs arranged across the top of the dialog box. The Print dialog box (see Figure 3-16) only has one tab, labeled General.

➡ **Panels or sections**: Within a dialog box, related options may be grouped into panels or sections. In Figure 3-16, three panels appear. Select Printer and Page Range are labeled. The third panel, containing Number of Copies, is not labeled.

➡ **Text boxes**: You can click in a text box and type. **Figure 3-17** shows four text boxes for the *margins* of the printed page — the area of blank space around the outside of the text. Click in the text box next to Left, backspace to erase the current number, and type a different number. You can change any of the four margins in the same way. To see this dialog box on your screen, cancel the Print dialog box, if it is open. Click the WordPad button, and then click Page Setup.

➡ **Menus or lists**: You pick some options from a list or menu, which often drops down or pops up when you click on the current selection. In Figure 3-17, Size and Source both use drop-down lists.

➡ **Radio buttons**: Radio buttons are small circles. If there is a dot in the center of the circle, the option is selected. Deselected radio buttons are empty or hollow. With radio buttons, you can select only one of the available choices. In Figure 3-17, Portrait is selected, which is standard page orientation, taller than it is wide. If you click on Landscape anywhere from the button through the end of the word, you select Landscape (the page is sideways, wider than it is tall) and Portrait automatically becomes deselected. You can't choose both options.

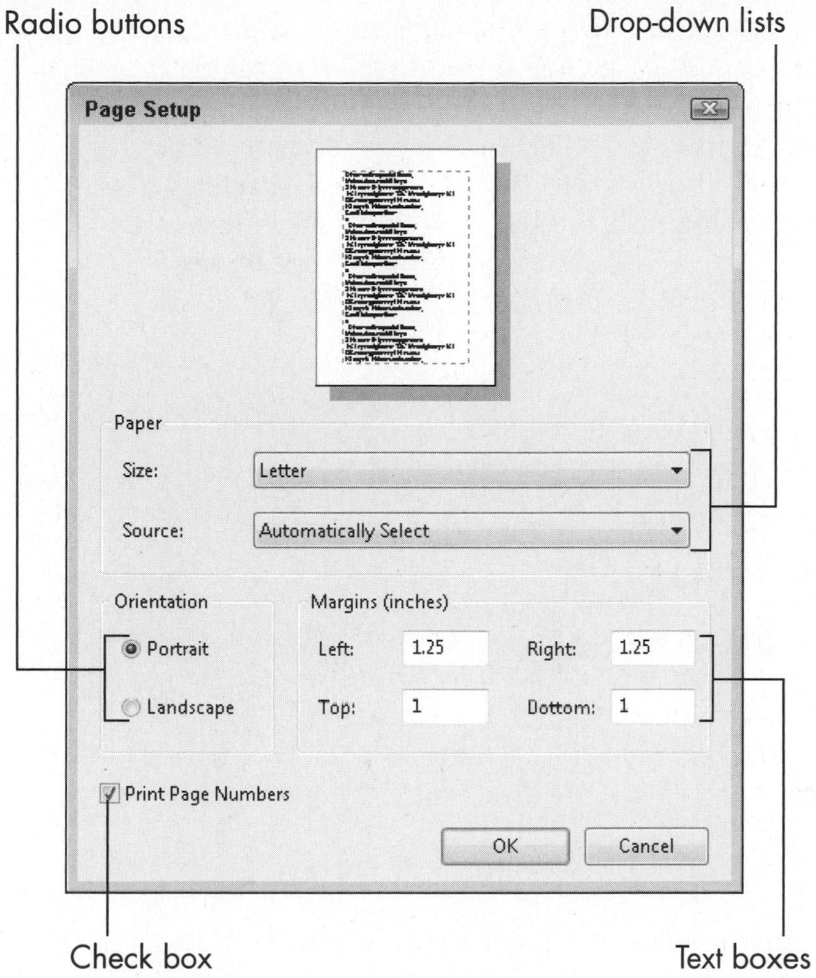

Radio buttons   Drop-down lists

Check box   Text boxes

Figure 3-17

➠ **Check boxes**: Check boxes are small squares. If a check box is selected, it contains a check mark, an X, or it is filled in solid. In Figure 3-17, Print Page Numbers is checked and every page will have a number on it. If you click anywhere from the check box through the end of the word Numbers, you uncheck this option and page numbers will not print. Unlike radio buttons, multiple check boxes can all be checked or unchecked in any combination.

If you want to use the keyboard instead of the mouse in a dialog box, Ctrl+Tab moves from one dialog box tab to the next. The Tab key moves the selection from one panel to another. The down and up arrow keys move radio button selection. The spacebar selects and deselects check boxes. The Enter key chooses the default button — often OK — which appears highlighted differently from Cancel or Apply.

Organizing Your Documents

Chapter 4

*E*verything inside your computer is stored on a disk. Your computer has a primary disk, formally called the internal *hard drive*. (*Drive* and *disk* are interchangeable words.) You may see this disk referred to as the C: drive.

The content of a disk is organized into individual files. When you save a document (see Chapter 3), you create a file on a disk. Many other files on the disk belong to the programs you use, including the thousands of files that make up Windows 7.

Disks also are divided into *folders*, which are containers for files. Windows 7 has a folder for its own files and dozens of other folders inside that one (called *subfolders*). One extra-important folder has the same name as your user name, which you created the first time you turned on the computer (see Chapter 1). Inside or below that user account folder, Windows 7 creates more folders to help you organize your files by type. All your photos go into the Pictures folder, all your documents go into the Documents folder, and so on.

Get ready to . . .

In this chapter, you explore your disk, folders, and documents. You create new folders to organize documents and move files from one folder to another. You also copy files from your hard disk to other disks to take with you or give to other people. It's all much more exciting than it may sound so far.

See All Your Documents As Files on a Disk

1. Click the Start button to open the Start menu.

2. In the folders list on the right side of the Start menu, click your user folder, which is named with your user name. (Mine appears in **Figure 4-1**.) Your user folder opens in *Windows Explorer*, the program you use to . . . well, explore your computer and to work with files and folders outside the programs you use to create files. Windows Explorer is your file manager, as you see in **Figure 4-2**.

Note the following areas in Windows Explorer:

- The **address bar** is at the top of Windows Explorer. If you completed Steps 1 and 2, it currently displays your user name. As you move around in Windows Explorer, the address bar shows where you are in your computer system.

- The **command bar,** which starts with the Organize button, is a toolbar below the address bar. (So many bars!) The buttons in the command bar change depending on where you are in the folders and what you select, if anything.

Click your username.

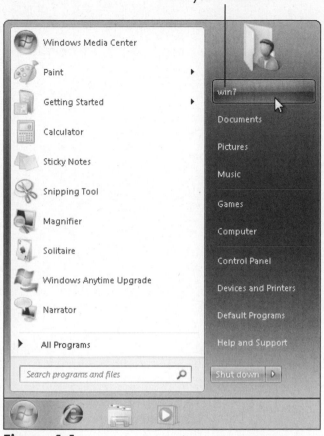

Figure 4-1

- The **navigation pane** runs down the left edge of the screen and has five sections: Favorites, which are folders that you need one-click access to; Libraries, which are groups of folders; Homegroup, which is a network option if you have two or more Windows 7 computers; Computer, which represents your entire computer; and Network, which displays your computer and others on your network, if any, including non-Windows 7 computers, such as those running Windows XP.

Command bar

Navigation pane

Address bar   Your username

Folders for holding your files

View Options

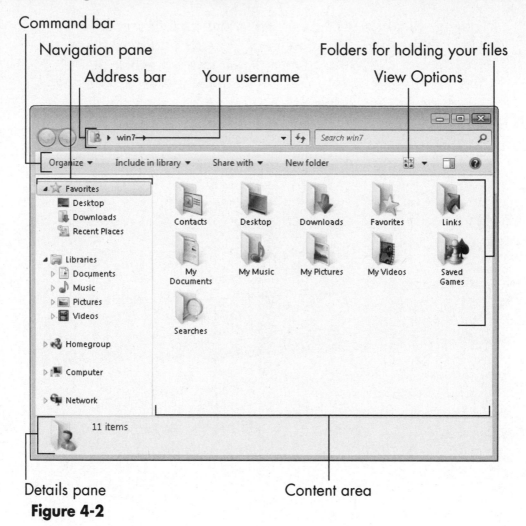

Details pane   Content area

Figure 4-2

- The **content area** displays icons for folders in your user account. Windows 7 creates these folders automatically to help you organize your files by type.

- The **details pane** stretches across the bottom of the window. The information in this pane depends on what you select in the content area, if anything.

3. Change the display of the icons in the content area by clicking the small four-part View Options button at the right end of the command bar. Each time you click the button, the display of the icons changes, as well as the information you see about each icon. Click the triangle to the right of the View Options button to see a list of view options (see **Figure 4-3**). Click the Extra Large Icons option, which is very useful, especially in a folder full of pictures, although you can't see many icons at one time in this view. In each folder you view, use the View Options button to choose the best view for that moment.

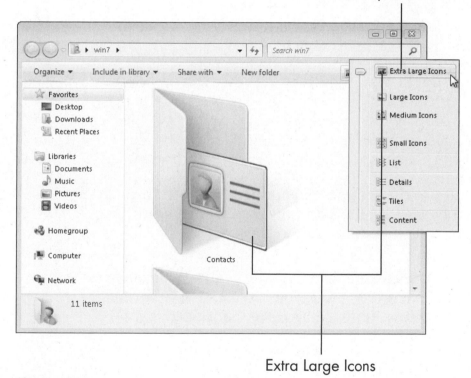

Figure 4-3

4. Double-click the My Documents folder in the content area. You see any files saved in that folder, including (if you're reading this book in chapter order) the one you created in Chapter 3.

 Somewhat confusingly, Windows 7 has a Documents library and a My Documents folder. Just keep in mind that a *library* is a collection of folders and that a *folder* is a collection of files. The Documents library contains lots of files created by Windows 7 and other programs, and some that you create, but the My Documents folder contains *only* files that you create.

5. Click a file name in the My Documents folder, and look in the details pane for some technical information, such as file size in bytes (characters, roughly), date created, and date modified.

6. Click the Preview Pane button at the right end of the command bar. The Preview pane appears on the right side of the window, displaying the contents of the selected file (see **Figure 4-4**), and the Preview Pane button changes to the Hide Preview Pane button.

7. Return to the contents of your user folder (refer to Figure 4-2) by clicking the Back button to the left of the address bar or pressing the Backspace key.

 If you see the folder you want in the address bar or the navigation pane, you can click the folder name anywhere you see it to open that folder.

 You can go directly to the Documents, Pictures, and Music libraries, which are groups of folders, from the top-right side of the Start menu (refer to Figure 4-1).

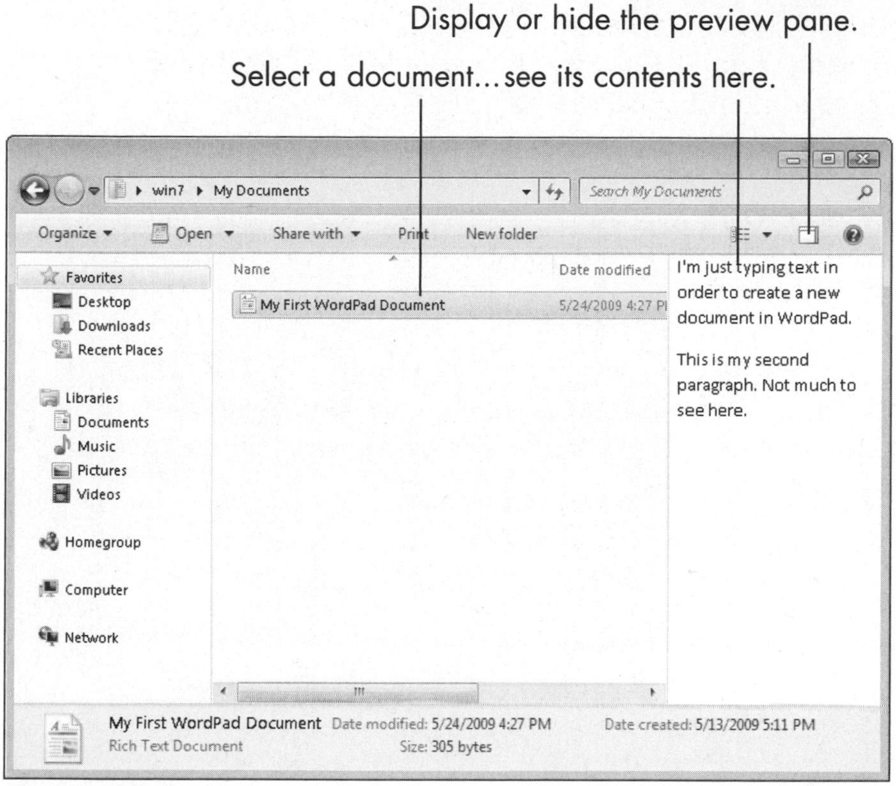

Display or hide the preview pane.

Select a document...see its contents here.

Figure 4-4

Find a Misplaced File

1. To search for a misplaced file, click the Start button and then click your user name to open Windows Explorer with all your folders.

2. In the top-right corner of Windows Explorer, click inside the Search text box (in which the word *Search* is followed by your user name or the folder you are exploring), and type part of the name of the file you're looking for. Windows Explorer displays any matching files, highlighting the text that matches. The search results include extra information that may help you identify the file, including the date it was modified (last changed). **Figure 4-5** shows the results of a search for My First WordPad Document.

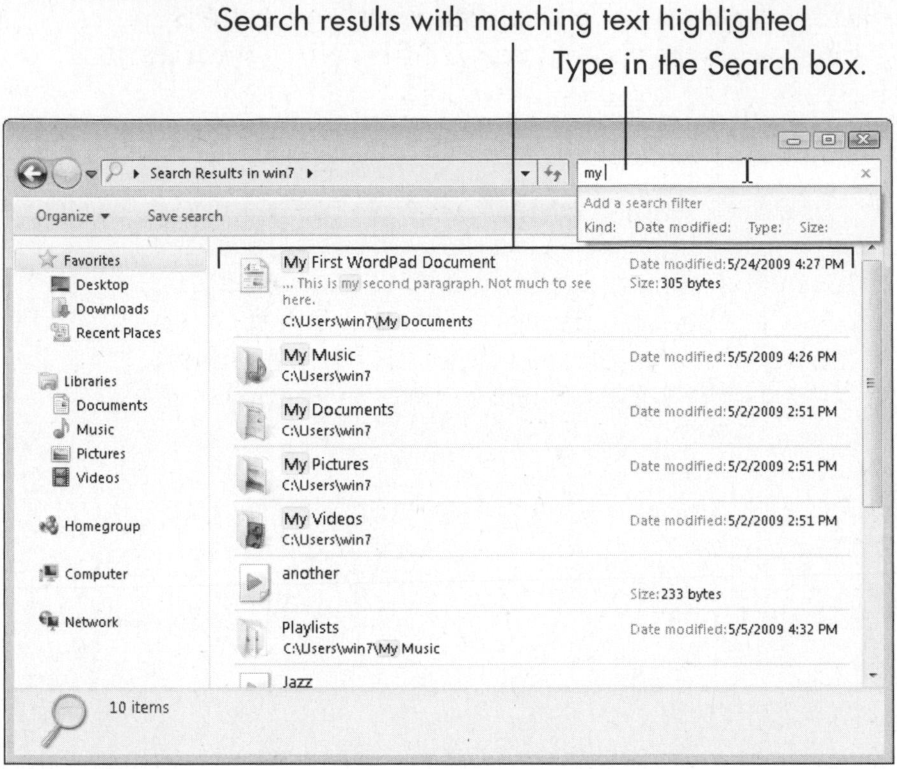

Search results with matching text highlighted

Type in the Search box.

Figure 4-5

3. If the search results include too many files, making it hard to see the one you want, type more of the file name in the Search box. The number of matching files should decrease as you type more text in the box.

 You can find all the documents you changed on a particular date. In the Add a Search Filter pane below the Search box, click Date Modified; then click a date on the calendar that appears. All files modified on that date appear in the search results.

4. If you don't see the file you're looking for, type a different part of the file name in the Search box.

5. If you still don't find your file, click Computer in the navigation pane (refer to Figure 4-2), and repeat Step 2.

This action searches the entire computer, which takes longer and turns up some irrelevant files along with the missing one (you hope!).

Create a Folder to Organize Your Files

1. To create a new folder, start by going to the folder or library that you want your new folder to be part of. For this exercise, you create a new folder in the Documents library, so choose Start⇨Documents to open the Documents library.

2. Click the New Folder button in the command bar. An icon for the new folder appears in the content area, with the name *New folder* next to it, already selected (see **Figure 4-6**).

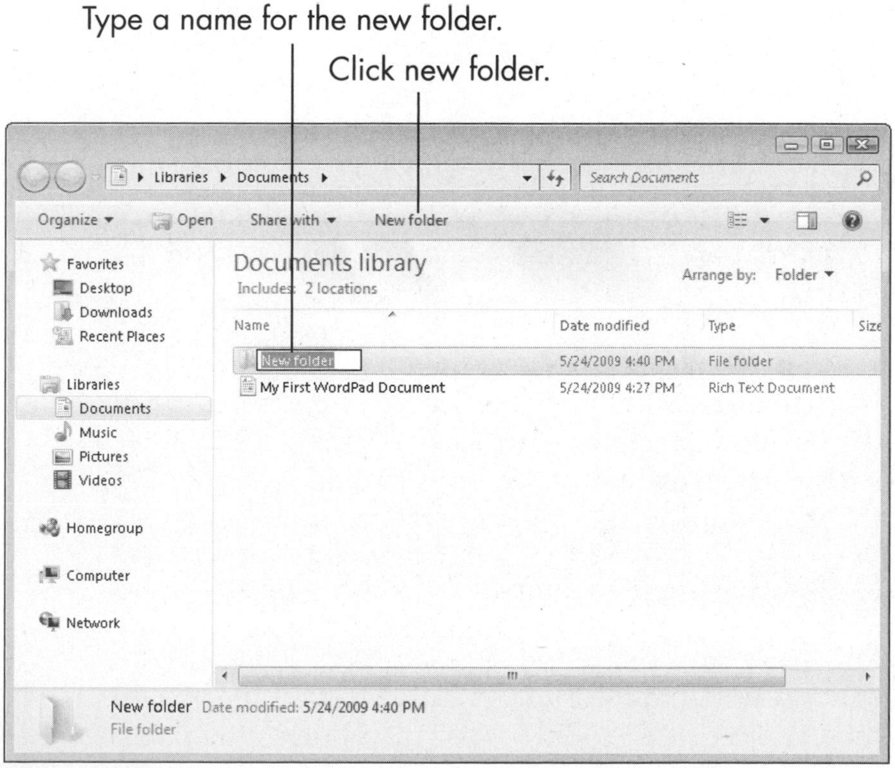

Type a name for the new folder.

Click new folder.

Figure 4-6

3. Type the name you intend to give to the new folder. Don't move the cursor or mouse before you start typing. Your new text will replace the highlighted text automatically.

4. Press the Enter key to make the new name stick.

5. Open your new folder by double-clicking its icon.

6. To return to the Documents folder, click Documents in the address bar, or press the Backspace key.

7. If you want, create more new folders by repeating Steps 2–4.

 Don't worry too much about creating folders as you start out. The folders Windows 7 provides may be all you ever need. As you accumulate more and more files, however, organizing them into folders may help you keep up with them. In the Documents library, for example, you might create a folder called Finances for files related to income, expenses, and investments, and another folder called Family for family-related documents. Which folders to create and how to name them depend entirely on your own sense of order.

Rename a File or a Folder

1. You can change the name of any file or folder you create. With the mouse pointer over the file or folder you intend to rename, click the right mouse button (*right-click* that file or folder). A context menu appears. **Figure 4-7** shows the context menu for a folder.

 For more information on right-clicking and context menus, see Chapter 1.

2. Choose Rename from the context menu. The file's or folder's current name is selected. If you type anything, you erase the current name. If you want to keep most of the current name and edit it, click inside the name or press the left- or right-arrow key to move to the place in the name where you want to type new text.

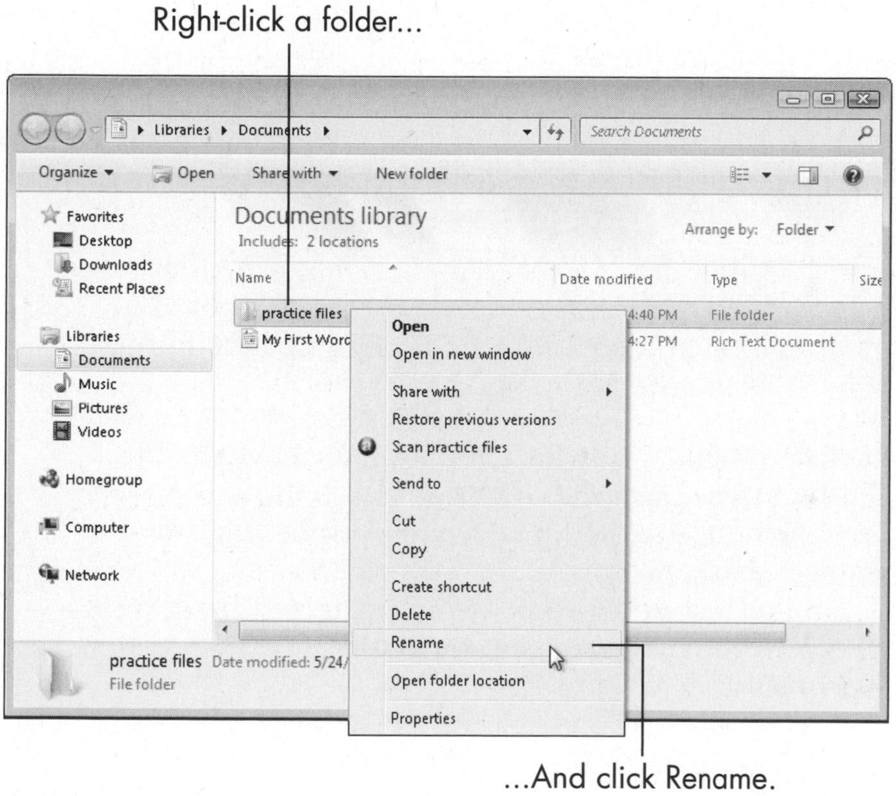

Right-click a folder...

...And click Rename.

Figure 4-7

3. Type the new name, which can be more than 200 characters long (although a dozen characters may be more than enough). You can capitalize letters and use spaces and dashes; you can't use slashes or asterisks, which Windows 7 reserves for other purposes.

4. When you've typed the new name, press the Enter key to finish.

You can undo the renaming and get the old name back, but you have to act now. With the mouse pointer over an empty area of Windows Explorer — not over the renamed folder or file — right-click and then choose Undo Rename from the context menu.

Move a File from One Folder to Another

1. To move a file to a new folder, right-click the file's name or icon in Windows Explorer to open the context menu.

To move more than one file at a time, see "Select Multiple Files and Folders."

2. Choose Cut from the context menu to remove the file from its current location and place it on the Clipboard (see **Figure** 4-8). The file's icon fades, although the file remains in its original location.

3. Right-click the folder to which you want to move the file, and choose Paste from the context menu to move the file (see **Figure** 4-9). The file's icon disappears from its previous location.

For details on cutting, copying, and pasting in a document, see Chapter 3.

4. Open the folder you selected in Step 3 to see your file.

You can move a file in a single step. Click the file's icon and hold down the right mouse button as you drag the file to the folder you want to move it to.

When the mouse pointer is over the folder, release the right mouse button. From the context menu that pops up, choose Move Here.

 Use these same steps to move a subfolder from one folder to another. Don't move the folders Windows 7 creates.

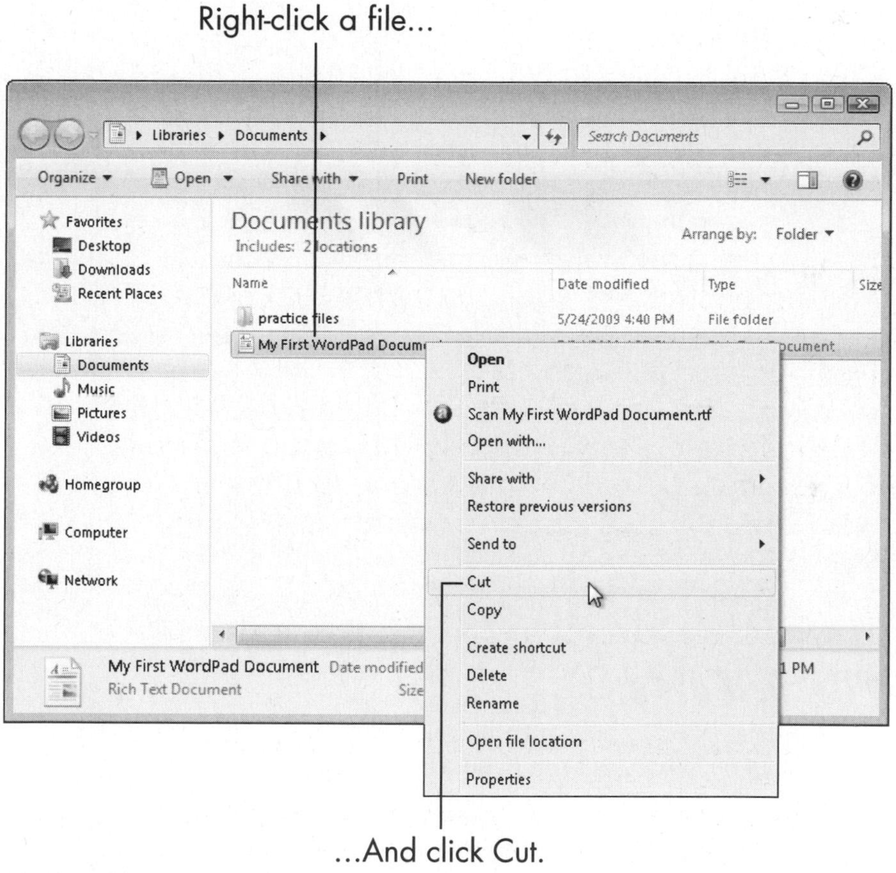

Right-click a file...

Libraries ▸ Documents ▸

Organize ▾   Open ▾   Share with ▾   Print   New folder

Favorites
Desktop
Downloads
Recent Places

Libraries
Documents
Music
Pictures
Videos

Homegroup

Computer

Network

Documents library
Includes: 2 locations

Arrange by: Folder ▾

Name	Date modified	Type	Size
practice files	5/24/2009 4:40 PM	File folder	
My First WordPad Docume...		...cument	

Open
Print
Scan My First WordPad Document.rtf
Open with...

Share with   ▸
Restore previous versions

Send to   ▸

Cut
Copy

Create shortcut
Delete
Rename

Open file location

Properties

My First WordPad Document   Date modified...   1 PM
Rich Text Document   Size...

...And click Cut.

Figure 4-8

Right-click a folder...

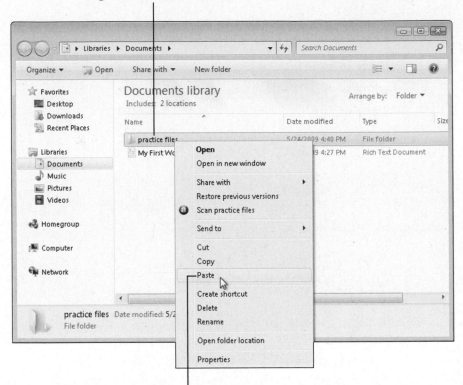

...And click Paste.

Figure 4-9

Delete a File or Folder

1. To delete a file or folder, right-click it and then choose Delete from the context menu. Windows 7 displays a confirmation dialog box as a safety measure (see **Figure 4-10**).

2. Choose Yes unless you've changed your mind about deleting this file or folder; in that case, choose No.

 The context-menu commands that you've used for the tasks in this chapter also appear on the Organize menu in Windows Explorer.

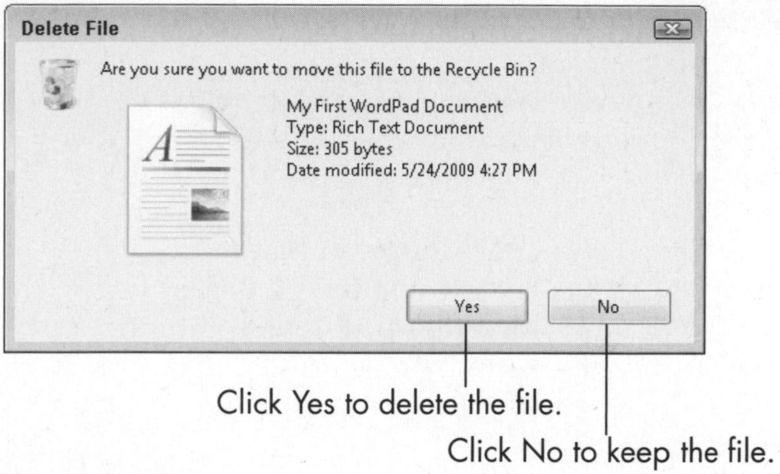

Delete File

Are you sure you want to move this file to the Recycle Bin?

My First WordPad Document
Type: Rich Text Document
Size: 305 bytes
Date modified: 5/24/2009 4:27 PM

Yes   No

Click Yes to delete the file.

Click No to keep the file.

Figure 4-10

Get Back a File or Folder You Deleted

1. If you delete a file or folder and want it back, look for it in the Recycle Bin, which is a special folder to which Windows 7 moves items that you delete (see Chapter 1). To open the Recycle Bin, double-click its icon — which looks like a trash can — on the desktop.

 If you don't see the desktop, you may have to minimize open windows (see Chapter 2) or click the Show Desktop button to the right of the time in the taskbar.

 To open the Recycle Bin from Windows Explorer, click Desktop in the Favorites list in the navigation pane; then double-click Recycle Bin in the list that appears to the right of the navigation pane.

2. If many files or folders are listed in the Recycle Bin window, type the name of the item you want in the Search box in the top-right corner of the window. Files matching what you type, if any, will appear in the content area.

3. To restore a file or folder to its original location, right-click it in the Recycle Bin window and then choose Restore from the context menu (see **Figure** 4-11). The selected file or folder returns to where it was before you deleted it.

4. Files stay in the Recycle Bin indefinitely, so that you can undelete files even months later. If Windows 7 needs room, it will clear out the oldest files first. If you want to get rid of everything in the Recycle Bin, click Empty the Recycle Bin in the command bar.

Double-click the Recycle Bin icon.

Right-click the file and click Restore.

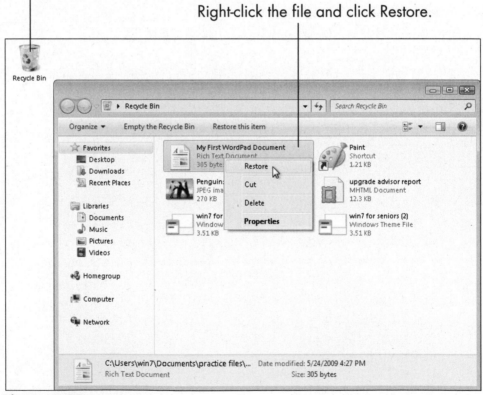

Figure 4-11

After you empty the Recycle Bin, you can't undo your action and undelete any of these files or folder.

 Don't click Restore All Items in the command bar, because it puts every single item in the Recycle Bin back in its original location. Choosing this command would be like dumping the trash can on your living-room floor to find a penny you threw away.

Select Multiple Files and Folders

1. You can work with groups of files or folders at the same time, but first, you have to select them. Try one of these methods for selecting multiple files or folders in Windows Explorer:

- Click the first file or folder you want to select, hold down the Ctrl key, and then click each additional file or folder you want. The selected files are highlighted, and the details pane (refer to Figure 4-2) displays the number of selected items. To unselect one of the selected files, click that file a second time. After selecting all your files, release the Ctrl key.

- Click an empty part of the content area in Windows Explorer, hold down the left mouse button, and drag the mouse pointer towards the files you want to select. A selection box appears on-screen (see **Figure 4-12**). Any file or folder that you touch with that selection box becomes selected. You don't have to surround a file with the box — just touch it.

- To select all files inside a folder, open that folder by double-clicking its icon and then press Ctrl+A or choose Organize⇨Select All.

Click and drag diagonally to select multiple files.

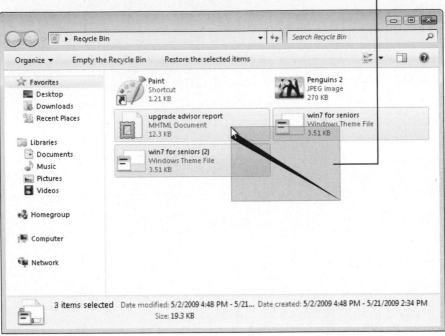

Figure 4-12

2. After selecting multiple files or folders by any method, right-click any of the selected items to display a context menu.

3. Choose a command to apply to all the selected files or folders. For example, Cut to begin a move, or Copy, Delete, or Rename.

Copy Files and Folders to a Flash Drive or Memory Card

1. You can carry your files around with you when you're away from your computer by storing them on portable storage devices. For example, you can store files on a USB *flash drive* (also called a *thumb drive*), which is about the size of a disposable cigarette lighter, and a *memory card*, which is the size of a postage stamp and is most often used in laptop computers and digital cameras.

- To copy files or folders to a flash drive, start by inserting the flash drive into one of your computer's USB ports (see **Figure** 4-13). A *USB port* is a small rectangular slot in the front or back of a desktop or tower computer or on either side of a laptop, marked with a symbol that looks like a trident.

- To copy files or folders to a memory card, start by inserting the card into a slot along the edge of your laptop computer. (Desktop computers rarely have memory-card slots.)

You can buy these portable storage devices at most office-supply and computer stores. They come in various capacities but are large enough to hold many files.

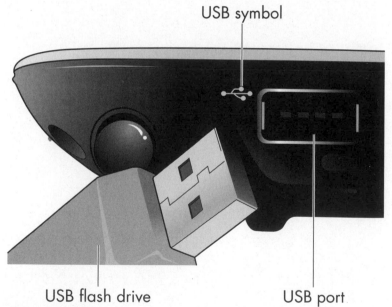

USB symbol

USB flash drive

USB port

Figure 4-13

2. If Windows 7 displays a pop-up message when you insert the flash drive or memory card, close it by clicking the Close box (the red box with the X) in the top-right corner of the message.

3. In Windows Explorer, select the files or folders you intend to copy (refer to "Select Multiple Files and Folders," earlier in this chapter).

4. Right-click one of the selected items, and choose Send To from the context menu. Your flash drive or memory card is probably one of the last items in the submenu of locations that appears (see **Figure 4-14**). The name and letter for your flash drive or memory card will be different from those in Figure 4-14.

5. Choose the flash drive or memory card from this submenu. Your files or folders are copied to the portable storage device.

Right-click a file or folder.

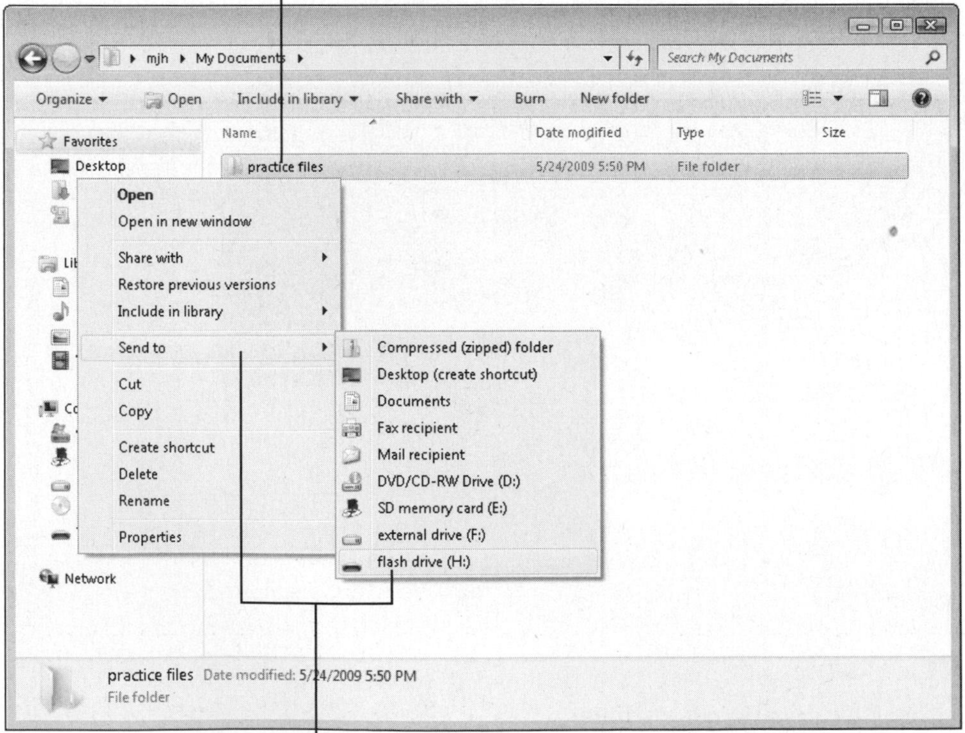

Click Send To and then click your flash drive.

Figure 4-14

6. To see the files or folders on the flash drive or memory card, click Computer in the navigation pane; then double-click the flash drive's or memory card's icon in the content area.

7. To remove a flash drive or memory card, click Computer in the navigation pane. Right-click over the card or drive (**Figure** 4-15). Click Eject. This closes the device. Windows 7 pops up a notification message it is Safe To Remove Hardware (**Figure** 4-16). Gently pull the flash drive out of the USB port. To remove a memory card, press the eject button by the card or push the card in farther and release to cause it to pop up.

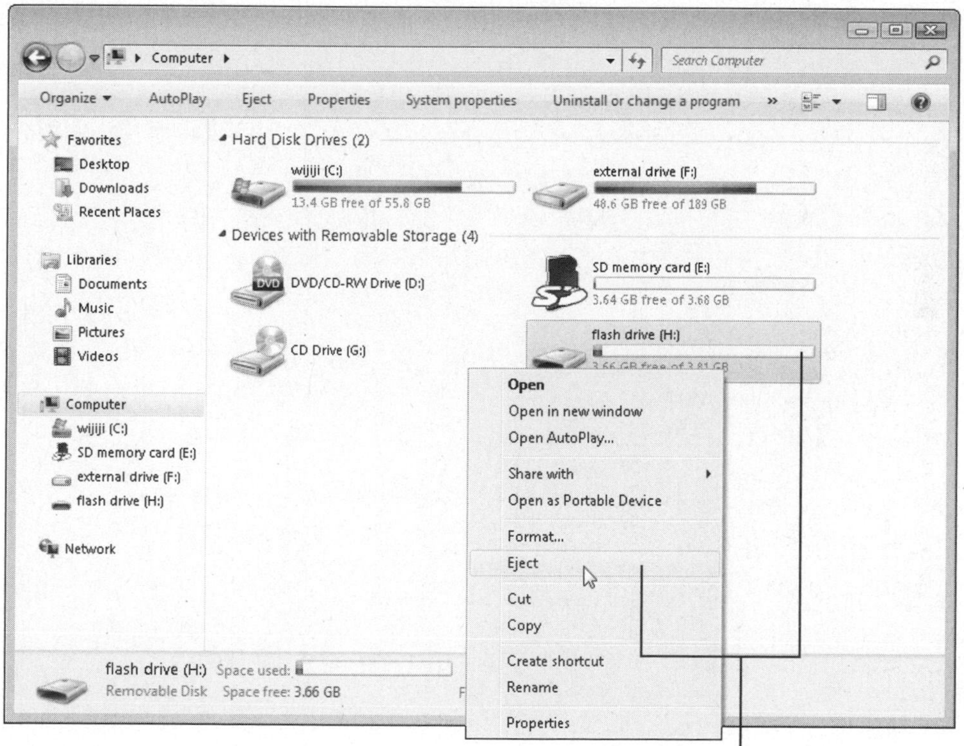

Right-click the flash drive or memory card, and then click Eject.

Figure 4-15

Figure 4-16

 If you have files or folders that you'd be devastated to lose, follow the steps in this task to create backup copies of those items on a portable storage device, and keep that device in a safe place.

Copy Files and Folders from a Flash Drive or Memory Card

1. If you want to copy the files or folders stored on a flash drive or memory card back to your computer's hard drive, insert the flash drive or memory card into the appropriate slot on your computer (refer to "Copy Files and Folders to a Flash Drive or Memory Card," earlier in this chapter). Windows 7 displays the AutoPlay dialog box shown in **Figure** 4-17.

2. Click Open Folder to View Files in the AutoPlay dialog box.

3. Select the files or folders you intend to copy.

4. Right-click one of the selected items, and choose Copy from the context menu.

5. Open the folder on your computer where you want to copy the files.

6. Right-click an empty area of the folder, and choose Paste from the context menu. You should see your copied files.

Click to see the folders
and files on the flash drive.

Figure 4-17

7. To remove a flash drive or memory card, click Computer in the navigation pane. Right-click over the card or drive (refer to Figure 4-15). Click Eject. This closes the device. Windows 7 pops up a notification message it is Safe To Remove Hardware (refer to Figure 4-16). Gently pull the flash drive out of the USB port. To remove a memory card, press the eject button by the card or push the card in farther and release to cause it to pop up.

 See Chapter 12 for information on copying photos to or from a camera or memory card. For information on copying music to or from a CD or MP3 player, see Chapter 13.

Part II

Getting Things Done in Windows 7

The 5th Wave   By Rich Tennant

UBER-USER DWAYNE GRANTZ CHALKS UP BEFORE PUTTING WINDOWS 7 THROUGH ITS PACES.

Taking Advantage of the Windows Accessories

*W*indows 7 includes a few programs called *accessories*. One such accessory is WordPad, which you use in Chapter 3. In this chapter, you add a couple of *gadgets* — small tools for displaying bits of information on your desktop — to display the time and weather. You also work with a simple calculator, a tool that lets you take a snapshot of what's on your computer screen, a drawing program, a sound recorder, and two programs for taking notes.

You may not use the accessories regularly. In some cases, you may replace these programs with others that have even more features. The accessories are, however, a good introduction to what you can use programs for.

You can start any program from the Start menu. If the program already appears on the Start menu, as it will after you run it once, just click the program name. If the program name doesn't appear on the Start menu, simply type enough of the program name to make it appear, then click it. You can also find most of these programs by choosing Start➪All Programs➪ Accessories, where you see all of the accessories. You use a few accessories in this chapter, a few others in later chapters, and there are a few you may never use.

As you use these accessory programs, look for features that you may see again in other programs, such as buttons, tools, and menus.

 Most Windows 7 programs allow you to undo (Ctrl+Z), cut (Ctrl+X), copy (Ctrl+C), and paste (Ctrl+V). See Chapter 3 for details.

Display Gadgets on Your Desktop

1. Gadgets display bits of information on the desktop. Your desktop may already show one or more gadgets from Windows 7 or from the computer manufacturer. To see all of the available gadgets, right-click the desktop and click Gadgets (see **Figure 5-1**). The Desktop Gadget Gallery appears in **Figure 5-2**.

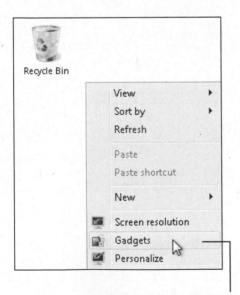

Right-click the desktop
and then click Gadgets.

Figure 5-1

2. Double-click a gadget's icon. You see that gadget on the desktop.

3. Repeat Steps 1 and 2 for any other gadgets you want to add. The two you may use most often — as I do — are the Clock and Weather gadgets, so I discuss them in the following sections.

Double-click a gadget to display it on the desktop.
Figure 5-2

Keep Time with the Clock Gadget

1. If you don't already see the Clock gadget on your desktop, follow Steps 1 and 2 of "Display Gadgets on Your Desktop," earlier in this chapter, to put it there. Hover the mouse over the clock to see the toolbar in **Figure 5-3**.

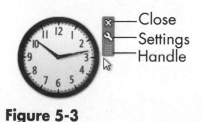

Figure 5-3

2. You can change the way the clock looks and works, if you want. To do so, click the Options tool, which looks like a wrench, or right-click that gadget on your desktop, and choose Options from the context menu. The Options dialog box for the Clock gadget opens (see **Figure 5-4**). (For more information on working with dialog boxes, see Chapter 3.)

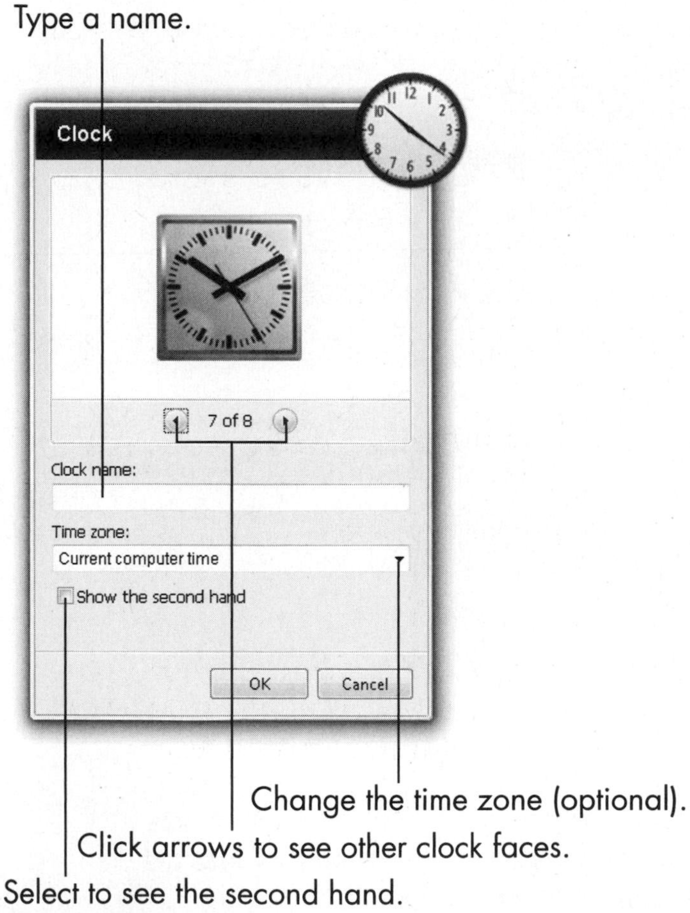
Type a name.
Clock
7 of 8
Clock name:
Time zone:
Current computer time
Show the second hand
OK
Cancel
Change the time zone (optional).
Click arrows to see other clock faces.
Select to see the second hand.

Figure 5-4

3. Experiment with these options:

- View different clock styles by clicking the arrow button to the right of *1 of 8*. Each time you click it, a preview of a new clock face appears above the arrow buttons (see Figure 5-4). Click the left-arrow button to move backward through the clock faces.

- Give the clock a name if you're going to have more than one on the desktop. Just type the name in the Clock Name text box.

  Each time you double-click the Clock gadget in the gallery, you add another clock to the desktop. Why would you want more than one clock? Each clock can display the time in a different time zone. You can create your own wall of clocks, as in a movie newsroom or to track time zones where friends and family live.

- Choose a different time zone from the Time Zone drop-down list. To do this, click the triangle at the right end of the Time Zone box to display the menu; then, on that menu, click the time zone you want to use.

- Check the Show the Second Hand check box, if you want to see one. (Time flies when you have a second hand.) For more information on check boxes, see Chapter 3.

4. Click the OK button to save your changes. You may see that the Clock gadget has changed on the desktop (see **Figure 5-5**).

Clock name (Hawaii)

Figure 5-5

Check the Weather with the Weather Gadget

1. Double-click the Weather gadget in the Desktop Gadget Gallery to display it on the desktop (refer to "Display Gadgets on Your Desktop," earlier in this chapter). If you have an Internet connection, this gadget gets weather information through the Internet. If you don't have an Internet connection, the gadget displays "Cannot connect to service." (See Chapter 8 for information about connecting to the Internet.) Windows 7 guesses your location based on your Internet connection.

2. To change the city in the weather forecast, hover over the gadget and click the wrench icon or right-click and choose Options from the context menu. The Options dialog box for the Weather gadget opens (see **Figure 5-6**).

3. Click inside the Select Current Location text box, type your zip code or city name, and press the Enter key to search for your location. If your location appears, click OK. If your location isn't found, search for a larger city nearby.

 You can add more than one Weather gadget and choose different locations for each gadget — a great idea if you have a bunch of clocks. (Refer to "Keep Time with the Clock Gadget," earlier in this chapter.)

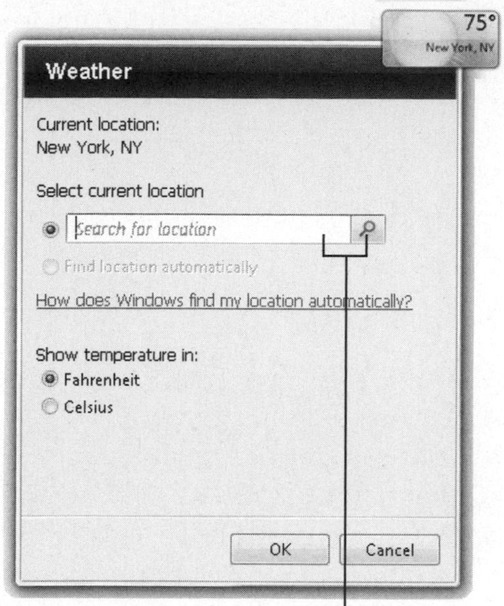

75°
New York, NY
Weather
Current location:
New York, NY
Select current location
Search for location
Find location automatically
How does Windows find my location automatically?
Show temperature in:
Fahrenheit
Celsius
OK
Cancel

Type your zip code or city's name, and click the magnifying glass.

Figure 5-6

4. To expand the gadget to show more information, place your mouse pointer over the gadget on the desktop; a tiny arrow in a box appears to the right of the gadget. Click that arrow. The gadget shows a three-day forecast (see **Figure 5-7**).

Click this button to switch between smaller and larger sizes for the gadget.

72°
Mostly Sunny
84° - 69°
Honolulu
Tuesday
85°
69°
Wednesday
85°
69°
Thursday
86°
70°
© WDT

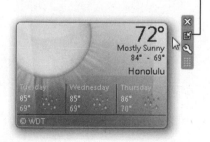

Figure 5-7

5. Click the same arrow-in-a-box button to collapse the gadget into its smaller format.

 You can also expand the Calendar gadget, if you have it on your desktop, to show both the month at a glance and the day. Not all gadgets have the same tools or options.

Use the Calculator

1. To use the Windows 7 Calculator accessory, click the Start button, type **calc**, and click Calculator in the search results. The Calculator appears on your desktop (see **Figure 5-8**), looking much like the standard pocket calculators that you're probably familiar with.

Entry or result appears here.

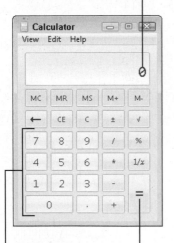

Click the equal-sign button or press Enter to see the result.

Click the buttons or type numbers.

Figure 5-8

2. To perform a simple calculation, use the keyboard to type the first number or click the number buttons with the mouse; type or click the appropriate math-symbol button;

enter the second number; then press the Enter key or click the equal-sign button to see the results.

 Along with the plus (+) and minus (–) buttons, use the asterisk key or button (*) for multiplication and the slash key or button (/) for division. Click the CE button or press the Esc key to clear your most recent entry or click the C button to clear all calculations.

3. After you perform at least one calculation, choose View⇨History. The calculator expands to display your recent calculations, as shown in **Figure** 5-9. Choose View⇨History again to hide the history.

Choose View⇨History to
see recent calculations.

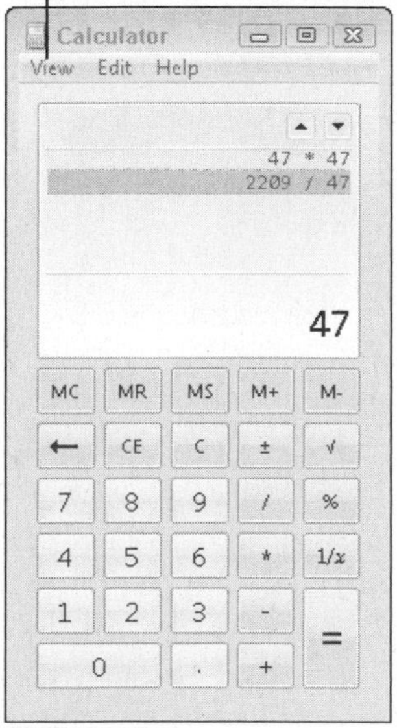

Figure 5-9

4. If you want to, copy or cut results from the Calculator and paste them into another program. Choose Edit⇨ Copy, or Edit⇨History⇨Copy History (only available if History is displayed). (See Chapter 3 for details on copying, cutting, and pasting.)

Capture the Screen with the Snipping Tool

1. The Snipping Tool captures all or part of the computer display screen as a picture. You can save the picture and attach it to an e-mail or paste the picture into a document. (See Chapter 10 for information on e-mail.) Click the Start button, type **snip**, and click the Snipping Tool from the search results. The screen fades slightly and the Snipping Tool toolbar appears (see **Figure 5-10**).

Click and drag over the area
you want to capture.

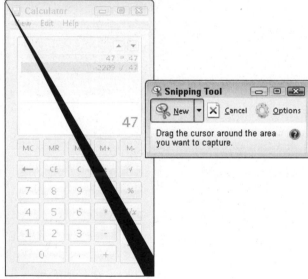

Figure 5-10

 Use the Snipping Tool to capture screens, if you have questions or problems. Send the captures to your own computer expert. Or explain steps to someone using screen captures.

2. Click and drag over the area of the screen you want to capture as a picture. Any area at all will do for this step. **Figure 5-11** shows the area to be captured.

3. After you select an area, release the left mouse button.
Figure 5-12 shows the result of the capture in the
Snipping Tool editor, which appears as soon as you
complete the capture.

The area inside the box you
create by dragging is captured.

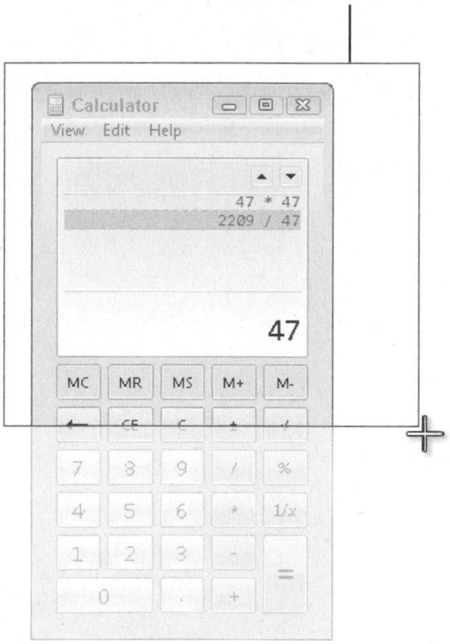

Figure 5-11

4. (Optional) Change the shape of the area you want to
select by clicking the down arrow on the New button
(see Figure 5-12) in the editor or the original capture
toolbar. The options on the menu that appears include
the following:

- **Free-form Snip:** Lets you draw any shape,
  including a rough circle.

- **Rectangular Snip:** Allows you to click and drag a box around the area you want to capture. This is the *default* option if you don't select one of the other options.

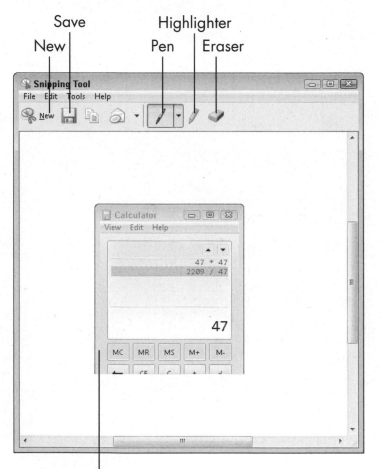

The screen capture

Figure 5-12

- **Window Snip:** Grabs an entire window automatically, which may be less than the entire screen. Move the mouse pointer over the window you intend to capture and click anywhere in that window.

- **Full-screen Snip:** Grabs the entire screen at once.

5. Choose one of these options. A new *snip* begins. Select an area of the screen, unless you chose Full-screen. After you complete the screen capture, the Snipping Tool editor appears with the area of the screen you selected (refer to Figure 5-12).

6. (Optional) You can highlight or annotate your snip with tools in the toolbar (refer to Figure 5-12). Click the Pen tool and draw or write on the picture; click the High-lighter tool and drag a highlight over any area; erase your changes with the Eraser tool.

7. After making all necessary edits, click the Save button or press Ctrl+S to save your snip. Type a filename for your picture when prompted.

 Whether or not you save your snip, you can copy it to the Clipboard to paste into other programs. With your snip still onscreen, press Ctrl+C to copy the snip. Open the other program (such as Paint, described in the next task), and choose Ctrl+V to paste it.

Draw with Paint

1. To use Microsoft Paint — an accessory that provides virtual pens and brushes for use in play, serious art, or art therapy — click the Start button, type **paint**, and click Paint in the search results. The Paint window opens (see **Figure 5-13**). Maximize the window, if it isn't already. (See Chapter 2 for information on working with windows.)

2. The *canvas* is the area you draw on, below the Ribbon (refer to Figure 5-13). To see what Paint is capable of, click and drag your mouse over the white canvas to draw a black squiggle using the default brush and color; then release the mouse button.

If your computer uses a pen or has a touchscreen, you may be able to draw directly on your screen.

3. Move the mouse pointer to a different spot on the canvas, and click and drag to create another black squiggle or line.

Ribbon

Paint button

Home and View tabs   Brushes

Tools panel   Shapes   Color palette

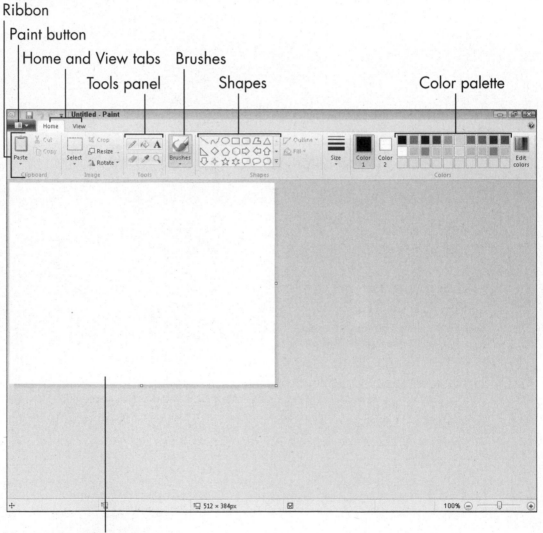

Canvas (drawing area)

Figure 5-13

4. Click the down arrow on the Brushes button in the Ribbon to see a panel of brushes (see **Figure 5-14**). Hover your mouse pointer over each brush to see a tooltip that describes it. (See Chapter 1 for information on hovering and tooltips.)

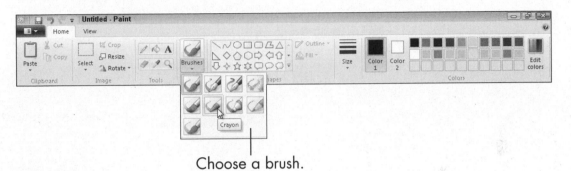

Choose a brush.

Figure 5-14

5. Click one of the brushes in this panel to select it.

6. Click one of the small color boxes at the right end of the Ribbon (refer to Figure 5-13) to select that color.

7. Click and drag your mouse over the canvas again. The new line looks different from the first two lines you drew, because you're using a different brush and a different color.

8. To add text to your drawing, click the A button on the Tools panel (refer to Figure 5-13); then click the canvas and start typing in the text box that appears. When you do, a new Text tab opens above the Ribbon.

9. Select the text you just typed, and choose options in the Text tab to size and format your text. You may need to resize the text box as you change or add text. Your drawing may (or may not) look something like the example in **Figure 5-15**. (For details on text formatting, see Chapter 3.)

10. Save your drawing by pressing Ctrl+S or by clicking the Save button — the tiny disk icon in the Paint title bar (refer to Figure 5-15).

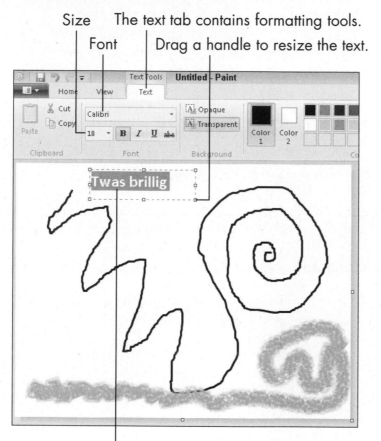

Size The text tab contains formatting tools.

Font Drag a handle to resize the text.

Selected text

Figure 5-15

 Paint is capable of doing more — more than I am. (You can tell that I'm an art-school dropout.) To use premade shapes, for example, click the Shapes button on the Ribbon; click a shape on the panel that drops down; and click and drag in the canvas to draw that shape. Then click the paint-bucket icon on the Tools panel to change the inside (or *fill color*) of the shape.

Copy what's on your screen by using the Snipping Tool, and then paste it into Paint to draw or add text to something displayed on your screen. You can also open a photo in Paint and use Paint's tools to add drawings and text to your photo. Keep in mind that you are changing your original photo unless you make a copy first. See Chapter 12 for information about photos.

Talk to Sound Recorder

1. You can record audio notes or reminders to yourself with the Sound Recorder accessory, if your computer has a microphone.

 If you don't have an obvious external microphone or headset, you may have a built-in microphone, especially with a laptop.

2. To open this accessory, click the Start button, type **sound**, and click Sound Recorder in the search results. Sound Recorder opens (see **Figure 5-16**).

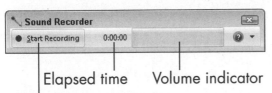

Elapsed time   Volume indicator

Click to start recording.

Figure 5-16

3. To start recording, click the Start Recording button (and people say computers are hard to figure out!); face the computer; and talk for more than a few seconds.

 When you click the Start Recording button, it changes to the Stop Recording button.

4. To stop recording, click the Stop Recording button. Sound Recorder automatically opens the Save As dialog box (see Chapter 3). There are no options to pause and resume.

5. In the File Name text box, type a name you'll recognize later for the recording.

6. Click the Save button. Windows 7 saves your recording as a sound file on your computer's hard drive (see Chapter 4).

7. To listen to your recording, choose Start⇨Documents, find your sound file in Windows Explorer, and double-click the file to open it. The sound file opens in Windows Media Player, which I cover in Chapter 13. (For details on navigating Windows Explorer, see Chapter 4.)

 If you try to play back a recording, but hear nothing, make sure your speakers are on and turned up a little. Check that the speaker icon in the taskbar isn't muted (no red slash across the speaker). Right-click the speaker icon and choose Recording Devices. Is a microphone listed with a green checkmark?

Take Sticky Notes

1. To use Sticky Notes — an accessory that puts those ubiquitous yellow notes directly on your computer's desktop — click the Start button, type **sticky**, and click Sticky Notes in the search results. Sticky Notes opens, as you see in **Figure 5-17**. (Looks just like the real thing, doesn't it?)

2. Start typing. Your text appears where the cursor is on the note.

 To add text to an existing note later, click the end of the text that's already there and type the new text.

Add another note.

Delete

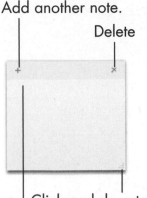

Click and drag to resize note.

Start typing your note.

Figure 5-17

3. To make the note larger, drag the bottom-right corner down and to the right (refer to Figure 5-17).

4. To move the note to another place on your desktop, click the top area of the note between the plus sign and the X, and drag the note to a new location.

5. To add a new note, click the plus sign (+) in the top-left corner of any existing note. A new, blank note appears near the existing note.

6. To delete a note, click the X in the top-right corner. A confirmation dialog box pops up.

7. Click the Yes button to delete the note or No to keep it.

 Sticky Notes doesn't have a Save command, so your notes are saved automatically unless you delete an individual note by clicking the X.

 The next time you start Windows 7, you may not see any of your notes. Start Sticky Notes to display your existing notes.

Installing and Removing Programs

Chapter 6

Your toaster oven isn't getting any smarter. Your computer is different from other machines, in that it can be programmed to do something it's never done before. You expand your computer's capabilities by installing new programs. *Programs*, *software*, and *applications* are all terms for the tools you use to do things.

You don't install new programs because you want your computer to live up to its potential, however. You install new programs so that you can do new things by using those programs — things you can't do with the programs you already have. You can install a program to add new capabilities to your computer, such as creating greeting cards or drafting legal documents. Some programs are free; others cost money. Programs designed for professional work may cost hundreds of dollars. In this chapter, you install programs from DVD and from the Internet.

On the other hand, your computer may already have programs that you haven't begun to explore. The company that sold your computer or the person who set it up for you may have installed extra software.

Your computer may have some programs that you'll never use and wouldn't miss. You don't have to get rid of them, but doing so is easy enough and frees a little space on your computer. In this chapter, you have the option to uninstall a program you are absolutely sure you don't need.

Determine Which Programs Are on Your Computer

1. To take stock and see what's on your computer, click the Start button, and examine the programs listed on the left side of the Start menu, which may look something like **Figure 6-1**. The programs you see include any that you have run recently. Other programs may be recommended by Microsoft or your computer maker.

Click a program to run it.

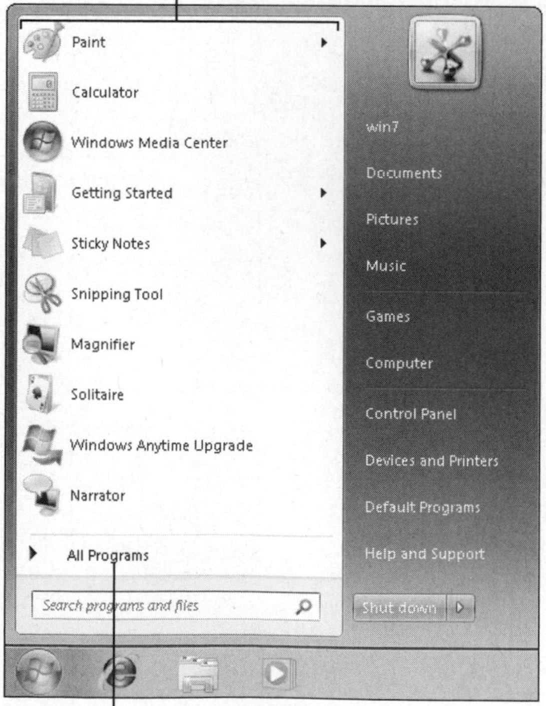

Click to see all the programs on your computer.

Figure 6-1

2. Click All Programs at the bottom of the menu. Windows 7 displays the All Programs menu — an alphabetical list of programs followed by a second list of yellow folder icons representing program groups (see **Figure 6-2**).

All programs

Click folders to see groups of programs.

Figure 6-2

3. Click one of the folder icons, such as Accessories or Games, to see a submenu of all the programs in the group. Some program groups have other program groups inside them.

4. Click the folder icon again to hide the group submenu.

5. To start any program listed in any of these menus, click its name.

Starting a program by clicking through menus seems slower to me than typing part of the program name in the Start search box, especially if you don't know which program group a program is in or if it's several folders deep. However, sometimes you need to see what programs are available by digging a little.

Install a New Program from a CD or DVD

1. To install a program that comes on a CD or DVD, insert the program disc into your computer's disc drive or tray, label side up (or, if your computer has a vertical disc slot instead, insert the disc with the label side facing left). The AutoPlay dialog box appears (see **Figure 6-3**). Click the option to run Install or Setup. User Account Control may ask if you really want to run this program. (Windows 7 tries to keep you from installing software unintentionally by asking for confirmation.)

Click to install the new program.

Figure 6-3

If nothing happens when you insert the disc, choose Start⇨Computer to open the Computer window; double-click the icon for your DVD or CD drive; and then double-click a program named Setup or Install.

2. If the installer offers a language selection, choose yours.

3. Many installers require you to accept an end-user license agreement (EULA). You can read the EULA or not, but you can't install without agreeing to its terms.

4. If the installer offers Express or Custom installation options, choose the Express option to let the installer set up the program without further input from you. The Custom option or Advanced Settings allows you to specify where to install the program and, perhaps, which parts of the program to install. Some installers provide other options, such as the one shown in **Figure 6-4**, to install documentation, other programs, or to register the program.

5. As the installer program continues to run and display dialog boxes, click the Next or Continue button in each dialog box to proceed to the next step.

6. Click the Finish or Close button in the last step of the installer program to complete the process. In a few cases, the setup program may ask you to restart Windows 7. In this case, you don't have to restart immediately, but you won't be able to use the new program until you do restart.

Click to...Install the program.

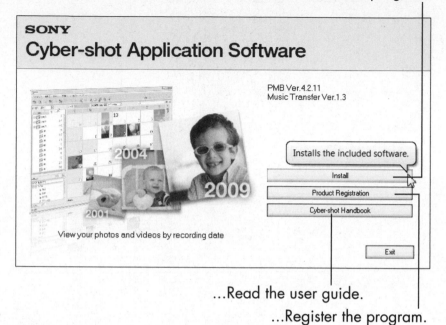

SONY
Cyber-shot Application Software

PMB Ver.4.2.11
Music Transfer Ver.1.3

2004

2009

2001

View your photos and videos by recording date

Installs the included software.

Install

Product Registration

Cyber-shot Handbook

Exit

...Read the user guide.

...Register the program.

Figure 6-4

7. The new program may appear automatically at the bottom of the first screen of the Start menu, as shown in **Figure 6-5**. Look under All Programs, as well. Newly installed programs are highlighted in color. Some installers add a program icon to the desktop.

 Many programs try to connect to the Internet for updates during installation or when you run the installed program. The first time you run a program, you may be asked if you want to register the program or configure some aspect of the program. Go with default (assumed) responses, if you're not sure.

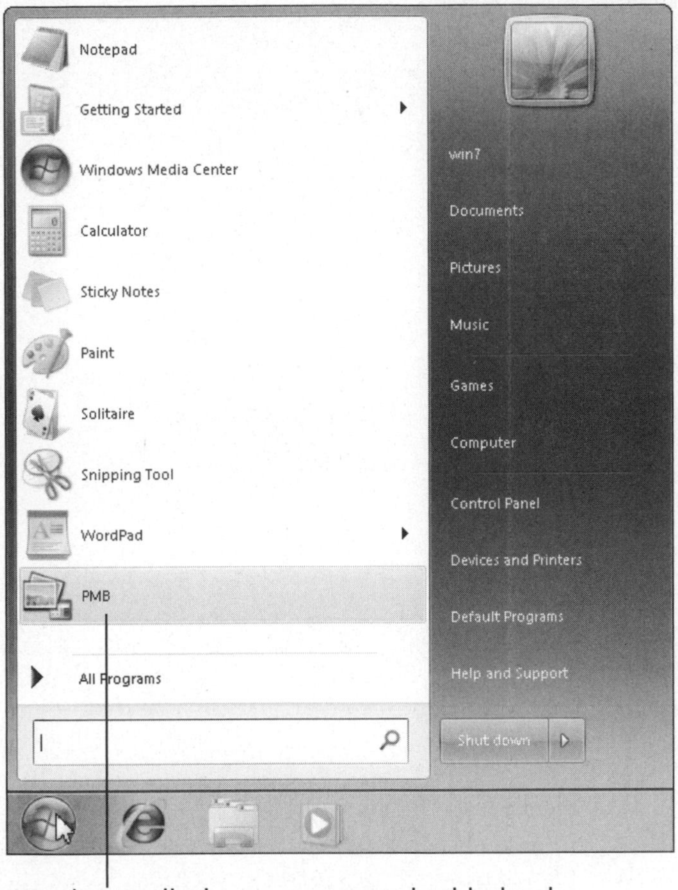

Newly installed programs are highlighted.

Figure 6-5

Install a New Program That You Downloaded from the Internet

You may want to read Chapter 8, about connecting to the Internet, and Chapter 9, about using Internet Explorer, before you try this task. You need to download a program to perform these steps.

1. To install a program that you've downloaded from the
Internet, choose Start⇨Computer to open the Computer
window; then click Downloads on the left side of the
window. The contents of the Downloads folder appear
under your user name. See **Figure 6-6** (your folder surely
has different contents).

Downloads folder   Double-click to install.

Figure 6-6

2. Double-click the downloaded program to start the
installer. User Account Control may ask if you really
want to run this program. (Windows 7 tries to keep you
from installing software unintentionally by asking for
confirmation.)

3. If the installer offers a language selection, choose yours.

4. Many installers require you to accept an end-user license agreement (EULA). You can read the EULA or not, but you can't install without agreeing to its terms.

5. If the installer offers Express or Custom installation options, choose the Express option to let the installer set up the program without further input from you. The Custom or Advanced Settings option allows you to specify where to install the program and, perhaps, which parts of the program to install.

6. As the installer program continues to run and display dialog boxes, click the Next or Continue button in each dialog box to proceed to the next step.

7. Click the Finish or Close button in the last step of the installer program to complete the process. In a few cases, the setup program may ask you to restart Windows 7. In this case, you don't have to restart immediately, but you won't be able to use the new program until you do restart.

8. The new program may appear automatically at the bottom of the first screen of the Start menu (refer to Figure 6-5). Look under All Programs, as well. Newly installed programs are highlight in color. Some installers add a program icon to the desktop.

 Many programs try to connect to the Internet for updates during installation or when you run the installed program. The first time you run a program, you may be asked if you want to register the program or configure some aspect of the program. Go with default (assumed) responses, if you're not sure.

 This tip is a warning, really: Although you can download many good programs from the Internet, you can also download dangerous ones. Never install a program that you get in an e-mail message, for example, no matter who sent it. See Chapter 18 for more information about protecting your computer.

Remove Programs You Don't Use

1. If you don't want a particular program on your computer, you can uninstall it. Begin by clicking the Start button, typing **programs**, and then clicking Programs and Features (not Default Programs). The Programs and Features window opens, listing all the programs that you can uninstall (see **Figure 6-7**).

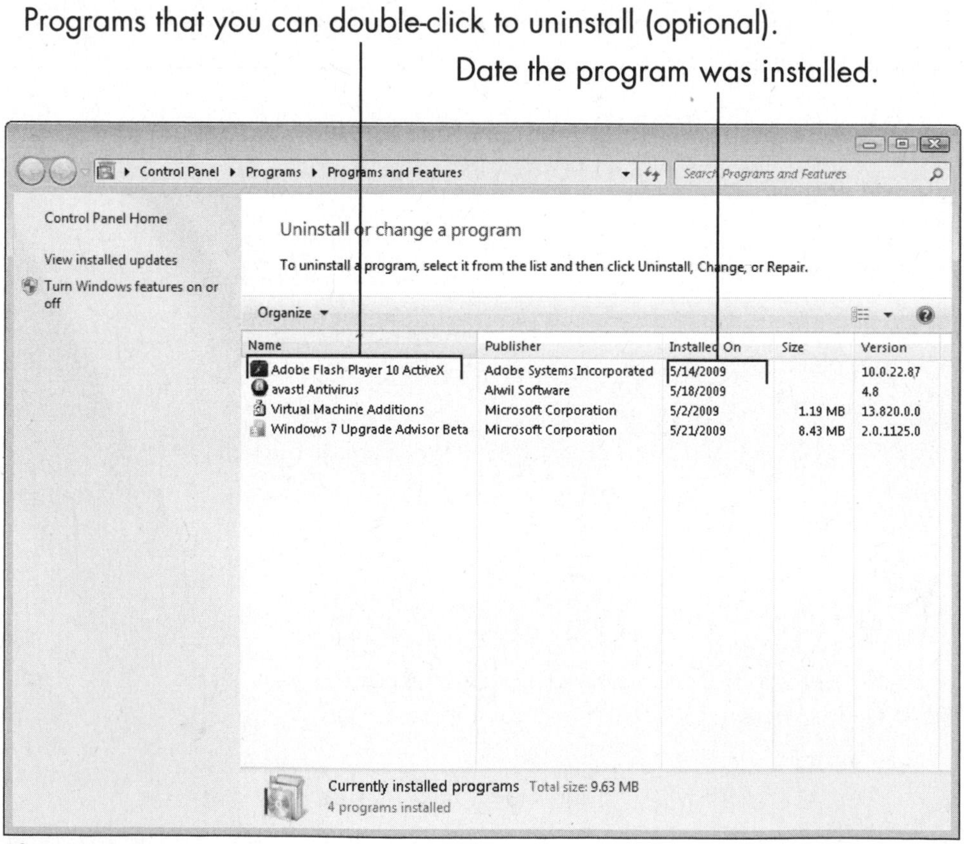

Programs that you can double-click to uninstall (optional).

Date the program was installed.

Figure 6-7

Just because you *can* uninstall a program doesn't mean you *should*. You can ignore programs you don't use. Look at program names, publisher, and date installed to determine whether you actually use a program.

2. Double-click the program you want to remove. A confirmation dialog box appears (see **Figure 6-8**).

Change or repair options

Click Yes to uninstall the program.

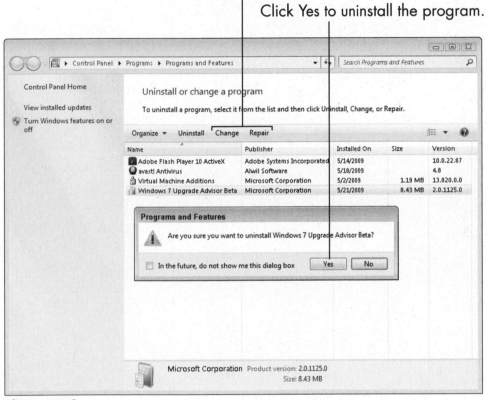

Figure 6-8

 Some confirmation dialog boxes are larger than the one shown in Figure 6-8 and may have other options, such as Repair or Change. Choose one of those options if you decide that you want to keep the program but are having a problem with it. A series of dialog boxes will lead you through the repair or change process.

3. Click Yes to remove the program. Uninstallation may take anywhere from a few seconds to several minutes. When the process is complete, the program no longer appears in the All Programs menu (refer to "Determine Which Programs Are on Your Computer," earlier in this chapter).

4. If Windows 7 tells you to restart the computer after it uninstalls a program, you can restart now or later, at your convenience.

 Before you uninstall a program that you may want to reinstall later, make sure that you have a copy of it on a CD or DVD (or that you know where to download it from the Internet again). You have no undo option when you uninstall a program.

Working with Printers and Other Add-On Devices

*E*very computer has a screen, a keyboard, and a mouse or other pointing device. Computers accept add-on devices for additional functionality — devices such as printers. You can also add a second display, a mouse, or another hard drive. Specifically, you may want to add a mouse or replace the one that came with your computer. Other devices you may add to your computer include an external hard drive that you can use to back up precious files.

Perhaps the idea of using two displays intrigues you. Laptops have built-in support for two displays — an external display in addition to the laptop screen — and Windows 7 makes it very easy to use a second display. Most desktop computers also support a second display, although there is a little more setup than with laptops.

For any add-ons — which tech-folk call *peripherals* — Windows 7 has a trick up its sleeve to help you. Thanks to *Plug and Play* technology, which automatically identifies add-on devices, connecting new devices to your computer can be quite easy.

Trust USB Plug and Play for Add-Ons

There are many kinds of add-on devices you may find useful:

→ A **printer** lets you, well, print documents or photos. Your choices for printers include black and white versus color, and ink jet versus laser printer. Consider a multifunction printer that includes a copier, scanner, and fax machine.

→ A **scanner** enables you to make digital images of old photos or documents so that you can view them onscreen.

→ An **external hard drive** stores backup copies of your most precious files.

→ An additional or replacement **pointing device** (your mouse is a pointing device), including a trackball or a pen with a tablet, may be more comfortable to use than what came with your computer. Switching between pointing devices helps you avoid repetitive stress.

→ A **microphone** is crucial for communicating by voice with your computer, through speech recognition, or with your friends over the Internet. A combination headset with microphone may sound the best.

→ A **video camera** (or *webcam*) is essential for video phone calls *a la* the Jetsons.

The majority of these devices connect using USB (Universal Serial Bus) technology. When you connect a device to your computer using a USB cable to the USB port (see **Figure 7-1**), the device identifies itself to the computer. This identification process is called *Plug and Play*. Ideally, you connect your device, and it simply works.

USB port   USB cable

Figure 7-1

Windows 7 uses a *device driver* to communicate with an add-on device. The driver is really a program that tells Windows 7 how to run the device. When you connect a device, such as a printer, Windows 7 looks for a driver (specifically, a printer driver, in this case). That driver may be built into Windows 7, or it may come on a disc that's packaged with the device. Or, the driver may need to be downloaded from the Internet, either automatically by Windows 7 or manually by you.

Every computer has at least a couple of USB ports. Some are harder to reach in the back of the computer, and some are in front. If your computer doesn't have enough ports, you can buy a USB hub, which is a small box with two to four USB ports, to add more ports. If a port is hard to reach with a device's cable, you can buy a USB extension cable.

Bluetooth is a wireless technology for adding devices to your computer. If your computer has Bluetooth, you can use Bluetooth in addition to USB, to add some devices, especially a microphone or headset. The process differs from connecting a USB device; you pair the device and computer via a dialog box.

View the Printer and Other Devices on Your Computer

1. Maybe you're curious and just want to see all the devices that are attached to your computer. Luckily, you can see most of them from one screen, the Devices and Printers window (also called the Device Stage). And to get there, choose Start⇨Devices and Printers.

2. The Device and Printers window appears (see **Figure** 7-2) and shows you all the devices attached to your computer, including the computer itself, the display (or monitor), external add-on devices, such as a hard drive, flash drive, or memory card, and the mouse. Your screen will look different.

 Windows 7 automatically installs the Microsoft XPS Document Writer, which doesn't print, but creates printable files, as your default printer. When you connect a real printer, the new printer becomes your default printer automatically. See the next section, "Connect a Printer to Your Computer."

3. Double-click the device you want to examine. This action opens the device's properties either in a full-screen dialog box with options or in a smaller dialog box with limited information and options. (Older devices have more limited information.) When you're finished reviewing the information, if a small dialog box popped open, close it. If a full-screen dialog box opened, use the Backspace key or click Devices and Printers in the address bar of the window to return to the previous screen.

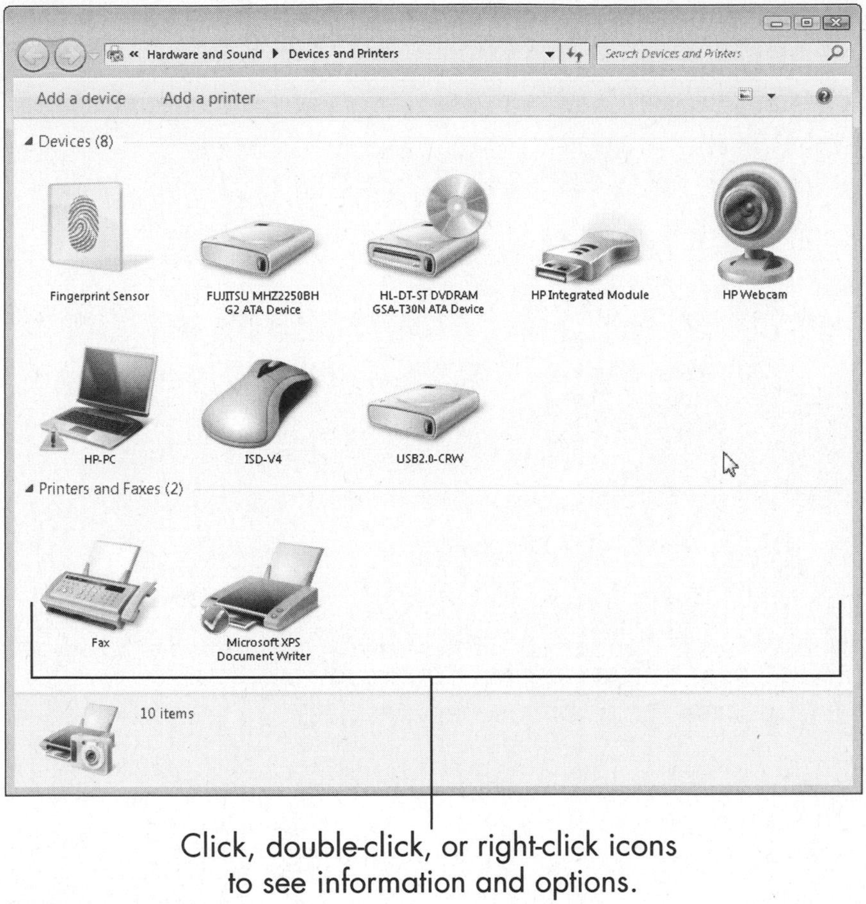

Click, double-click, or right-click icons
to see information and options.

Figure 7-2

4. Right-click any device to open a context menu of other options, including access to settings, options, or properties for that device. For example, your printer options include seeing what's printing, which is especially useful if nothing comes out of your printer. If you're having problems with a device, click the Troubleshoot option on the context menu to open a guided troubleshooting program to walk you through options for resolving problems with the device.

Although you see buttons to Add a Printer or Add Device in the command bar of the Device and Printers window, you need to use those buttons only if Windows 7 doesn't automatically detect and install your device. With USB and Plug and Play, most devices install automatically.

Connect a Printer to Your Computer

1. Take your printer out of the box. Keep all the packing material together until you know you won't need to return the printer. Arrange all the components for easy access. In addition to the printer, you'll probably find ink cartridges or a toner cartridge, a power cable, and a CD with printer software. Read the setup instructions that come with your printer.

2. Remove all tape from the printer. Most printers ship with the print mechanism locked in place to prevent it from moving during shipping. Look for brightly colored tape, paper, or plastic indicating what you need to move or remove to release the print mechanism.

3. Put the printer within cable length of your computer. Insert the ink or toner cartridge before you turn on the printer for the first time. Place some paper in the paper drawer or tray. Connect the printer to the power supply. Plug the printer cable into the printer and into the computer.

 Your printer may have come with a disc with a printer driver and other software. You don't need to use that disc unless Windows 7 fails to correctly install a driver automatically.

4. Turn on the printer. You may see some informational dialog boxes or pop-up messages as Windows 7 handles the configuration.

5. To confirm that your printer is installed properly, choose Start⇨Devices and Printers. You should see an icon for your new printer onscreen in the Devices and Printers window (refer to Figure 7-2).

6. Double-click your printer icon to see information about your printer. Click on Customize Your Printer to open a separate Properties dialog box, as shown in **Figure 7-3**. At the bottom of the General tab, click the Print Test Page button.

 If a test page doesn't print, check that both ends of the cable are plugged in properly and make sure the printer is turned on. Double-check all the preceding steps and try to print a test page again. Contact the printer manufacturer, the location you bought the printer from, or the Web for more help.

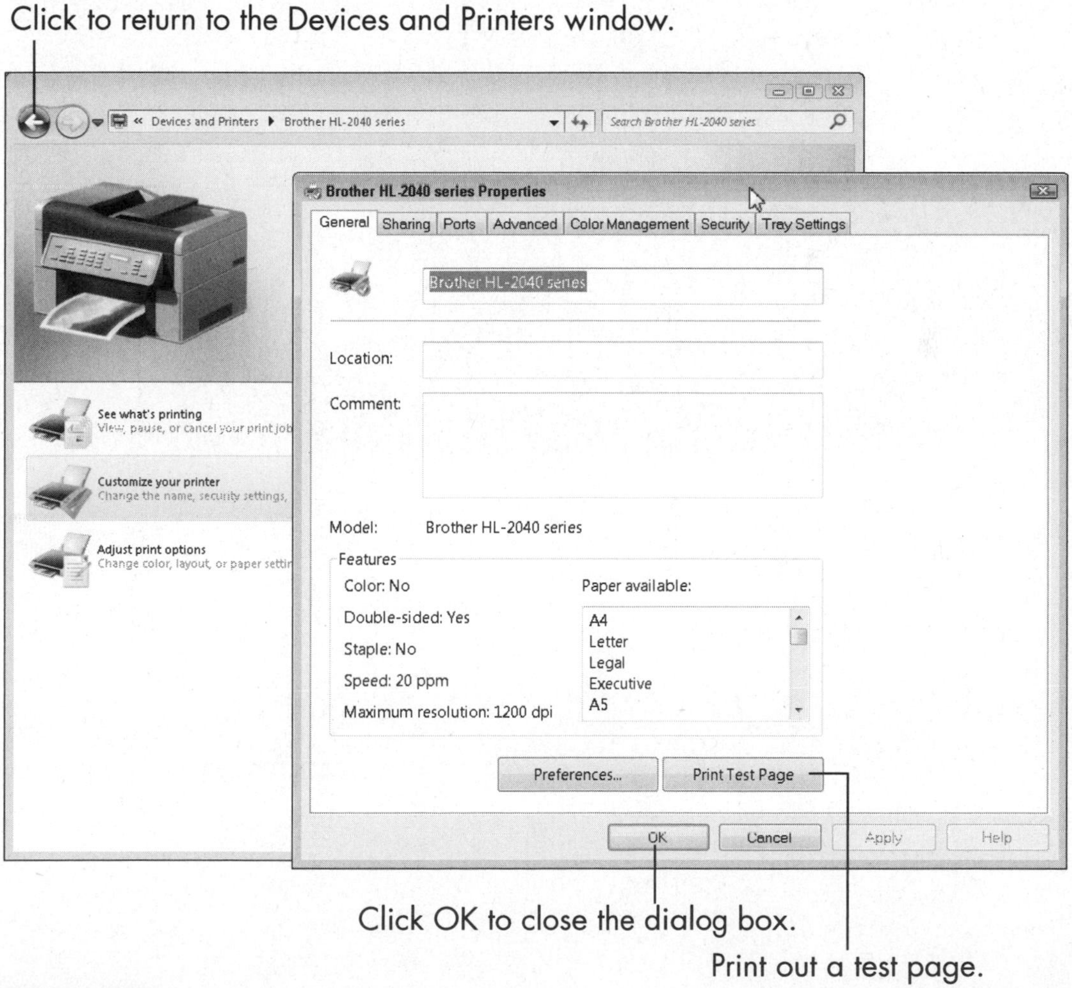

Click to return to the Devices and Printers window.

Click OK to close the dialog box.

Print out a test page.

Figure 7-3

7. After you successfully print your test page, click the Back button or close the dialog box showing the properties. Confirm that your new printer is identified as the default printer, which is the one Windows 7 assumes you intend to use whenever you print something. In the Devices and Printers window, right-click over the printer. If there isn't a check mark next to Set as Default Printer, click that option.

8. Start a program and create or open a document. (See Chapter 3.) Print from any program by choosing File⇨ Print, clicking a Print button (usually a printer icon), or pressing Ctrl+P.

 When you print from a program, a Print dialog box appears and gives you options for changing how your printer prints any specific document. In most cases, you can just click the Print button without changes.

Add an External DVD or Hard Drive

1. Your computer has a built-in hard drive storing Windows 7, all of your programs, and the files you create — your *data*. There's always a possibility that you'll lose your data through accident or theft. To make an extra copy, or back up a large amount of data (or all of your computer files and programs), attach an external USB hard drive. Although you can also back up files to an external DVD drive, you're more likely to want one to record and play DVDs for entertainment.

2. Plug the external drive into a power source and into a USB port. Turn on the drive. Windows 7 installs a device driver automatically. You may see pop-up notifications near the clock in the taskbar as the driver is installed and when the device is ready for use. Windows 7 may automatically open the AutoPlay dialog box shown in **Figure 7-4**.

An external device brings up the AutoPlay dialog box.

Close

Click to view files on the device

Figure 7-4

 Choose Start⇨Computer (or press the Windows key and E) to explore your new hard drive or disc drive. See Chapter 19 for information on backing up your data. Also, Chapters 12 and 13 tell you what you need to know about copying your photos and music to disc.

Add a Second Display for Twice the Fun

1. Before you buy a second display (also called a *screen* or *monitor*), you should find out whether your computer is ready for a second display. Right-click the desktop and then choose Screen Resolution from the pop-up menu. You arrive at the Screen Resolution window, as shown in **Figure 7-5**.

Using two computer displays at once may sound excessive, but in fact, two displays give you twice as much space to see everything you want to see and work with at one time. For example, you can position your e-mail program on one display while you use the other for games or real work. Your e-mail will always be visible as you go about doing other things. Trust me: Once you try this, you'll see that two displays are twice the fun.

2. Click the Detect button and then click the drop-down list next to Display. On the first line, you see 1. followed by the name of the computer's default display (such as 1. Mobile PC Display in Figure 7-5). If you see a second line in the menu (possibly worded Available Display Output), your computer is ready for a second display; you may also see an icon representing a second display. If only one display is listed, you can't add a second display without replacing the graphics card, which is more work and expense than you may want to get into now.

3. When you're ready, if you don't have a display leftover from another computer, buy an LCD display at an office supply or discount electronics supply store.

4. To add a second display, shut down Windows 7. With the computer off, plug your second display into the wall or power strip and connect the display cable to your computer. See **Figure 7-6** for an example of a typical display cable and plug (this is not USB). On a desktop computer, the plug is behind the computer. Your first display will be plugged in near the plug for the second. On a laptop computer, the plug is probably located along the back edge, near the hinge.

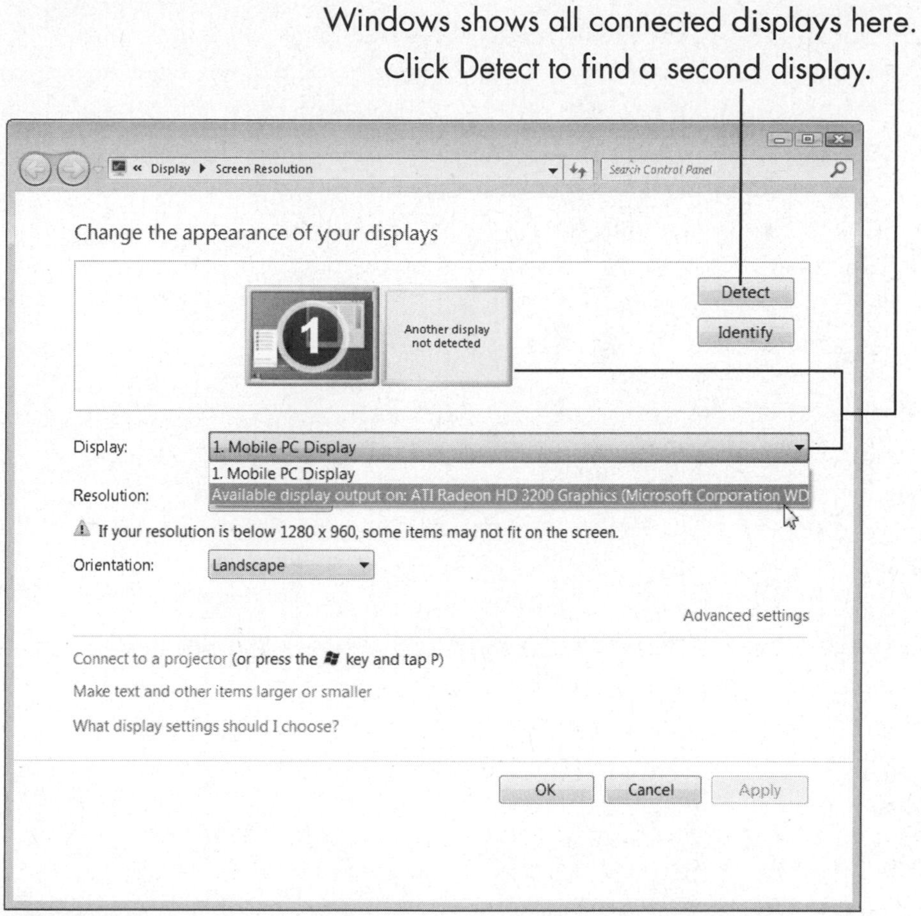

Windows shows all connected displays here.
Click Detect to find a second display.

Figure 7-5

5. Turn the new display on and turn the computer on. If you're using a laptop computer, press ⊞ (the Win key; see the Introduction) and the X key simultaneously to open the Windows Mobility Center, shown in **Figure** 7-7. (The Mobility Center is not available on desktop computers.) Click the Connect Display button. In the next dialog box, click Extend, which allows you to use the two displays separately. If both displays show the desktop, skip to Step 9.

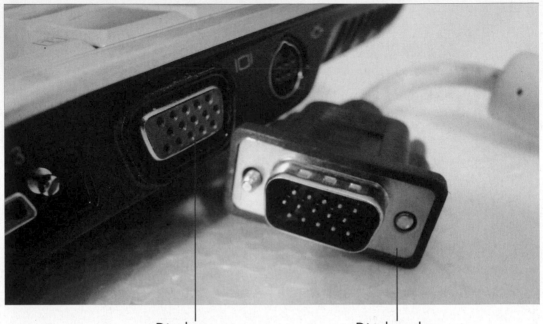

Display port   Display plug

Figure 7-6

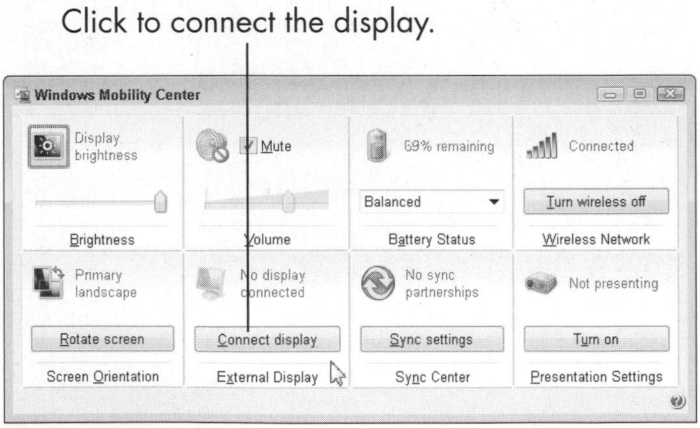

Click to connect the display.

Figure 7-7

6. To activate the second display on a desktop computer, right-click on the desktop and then choose Screen Resolution from the pop-up menu. Once again, you arrive at the Screen Resolution window (refer to Figure 7-5).

7. Open the Multiple Displays drop-down list and choose Extend These Displays to enable the new display. Click Apply. Click Identify; each display should briefly show a huge number 1 or 2.

8. If both screens display the desktop, close the Screen Resolution dialog box.

 If the second display still isn't working, check all the cable connections and the display power switch. Repeat Step 7. Confirm that two lines appear in the Display drop-down list and two numbered icons appear near the top of the dialog box.

9. If both displays work, you can drag a window that is neither maximized nor minimized from one display to the other, where you can maximize it or size and place it, as you wish. The taskbar and Start menu appear only on the original display. Now you have some room to work with.

Part III
Discovering the Internet

The 5th Wave   By Rich Tennant

It started as a wrap-around porch, and then Stuart found a section on medieval architecture on the Internet.

Connecting to the Internet

*T*he *Internet* is a global network of computers. Any computer can connect to any other computer through the Internet. Your Internet connection is the gateway to communication via e-mail and to browsing the World Wide Web for information and entertainment.

Windows 7 makes connecting to the Internet easy. At its easiest, you turn on the computer and you're connected. Because there may be more to connecting than that, you work with two different types of connections in this chapter: wireless and wired.

A wireless connection has the benefit of providing you with mobility and no cables to get tangled. Furthermore, Windows 7 is designed to find wireless connections and simplify connecting. Public connections — such as those you can find in hotels, coffee shops, fast food joints, public libraries, and airports — will surely be wireless, but you may find wireless best for home, as well, especially with a laptop.

A wired connection involves more setup steps than wireless, not to mention wires. A desktop computer running at home may use a wired connection, especially if your desk is conveniently located next to the connection — either your cable service access or phone line. Wired connections are often referred to as *Ethernet* connections, which use a cable-like thick phone cord.

There are three components to an Internet connection:

➡ **Hardware** in the form of a wireless or a wired adapter built into every new computer

➡ **Software** in the form of Windows 7

➡ **Access** provided by an Internet service provider (ISP), such as your phone company, cable TV provider, or a public connection in a coffee shop or library

Connect to the Internet Anywhere

1. If you have a laptop computer and carry it with you, you can connect to the Internet in many public locations. Many of these locations provide free, easily accessed connections, commonly called *hotspots*. To follow these steps, take your laptop to a library or coffee shop that offers a hotspot.

 Most free, public connections don't require passwords or special permission to connect. If you have trouble connecting to a hotspot, it may be part of a private network or require a password to connect. Ask for the log-in requirements at the front desk or counter.

2. Turn on your laptop. After the Windows 7 desktop appears, wait a moment while Windows 7 searches automatically for available wireless connections, including private ones. You may see a notification in the taskbar for available connections or an icon with five vertical bars. Click the message or the icon for a list of available connections (see **Figure 8-1**). If you see a list, skip to Step 5.

Click a network to select it.

Click the Connections icon to see
a list of available connections.

Figure 8-1

3. If you don't see a list of available connections, press +X
for the Windows Mobility Center, as shown in **Figure 8-2**.
(The Windows Mobility Center is not available on desktop
computers.)

4. In the section — or *tile* — labeled Wireless Network, if
the button says Turn Wireless On, click it. (If the button
says Turn Wireless Off, don't click — it's on already.)
Above the button, if you see the word *Connected,* you're
done and ready to use the Internet. If you don't see
Connected, click the button with five gray bars to open
the Available Networks dialog box shown in Figure 8-1.

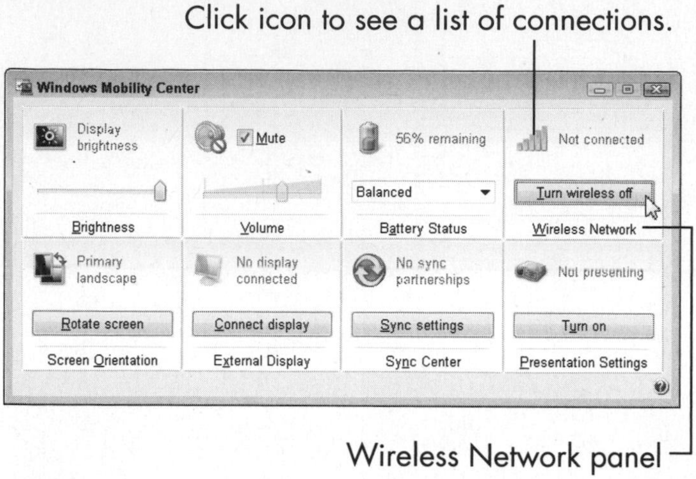

Click icon to see a list of connections.

Figure 8-2

Wireless Network panel

If wireless is off but you can't click the button, you may have a separate switch on the laptop that turns wireless on and off. Turn that wireless switch on; then repeat Step 4.

5. The Available Networks dialog box lists all networks in range of your computer, including private networks you can't access. Network names are often technical or whimsical. Look for the name of the establishment you're in. If more than one network looks promising, choose the one with the most green bars, indicating the best connection.

Stay away from networks with weird names like DeathTrap or Warez. (A network named FluffyBunny could be just as dangerous, of course.) A network connection is a two-way street. Be careful who you connect to.

6. Click the name of the network you intend to connect to (see **Figure 8-3**). If you plan on connecting to this network again in the future, you can select the Connect Automatically check box to make reconnection easier. If this is a one-time connection, deselect the Connect Automatically check box. Click the Connect button.

Click a network to select it.

Refresh the list.

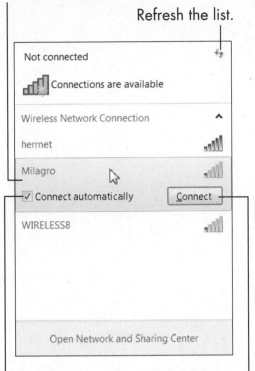

Click Connect to use this network now.

Check here to automatically connect.

Figure 8-3

7. If the network you're connecting to requires a security key or passphrase (password), you see the dialog box shown in **Figure** 8-4. Hotels often require this information, even on an account that's free to guests. If you know the required information, enter it here and click OK to connect. Otherwise, ask someone for help or try a different network.

8. If the network connection doesn't require a password or you've entered one, Windows 7 prompts you to identify the type of network connection you want. Your choice here sets security for the connection.

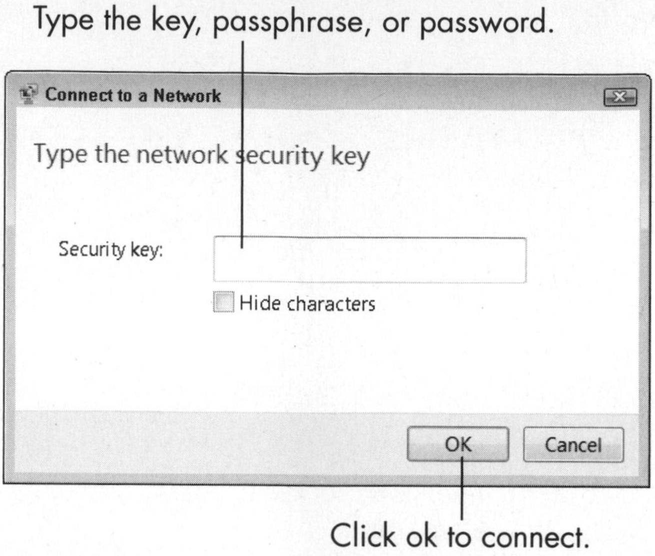

Type the key, passphrase, or password.

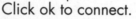

Figure 8-4

- **Home:** You may connect wirelessly to your own home network, in which case, identifying that connection as Home makes it easy for other computers you have at home to share documents and resources, such as a printer.

- **Work:** You may connect to an office network with this option.

- **Public:** Use this option for all other connections or when in doubt. Identifying this as a public network automatically sets many security options to be more secure.

 Speaking of *security*, you need it when accessing the Internet. Windows 7 does many things automatically to secure your machine, protecting you from intruders and other trouble. See Chapter 18 for information about what steps you need to take to stay secure.

9. The Wireless Network tile of the Windows Mobility Center (get there by pressing +X) indicates Connected, as shown in **Figure 8-5**. If not, start over and select a different network. Repeat as many times as necessary or read the next section for some trouble-shooting tips.

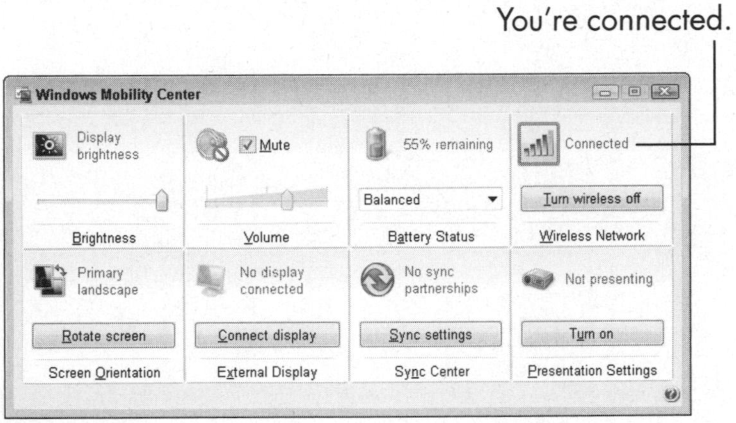

You're connected.

Figure 8-5

10. Test your Internet connection: Start Microsoft Internet Explorer. (See Chapter 9 for information on using Internet Explorer, or IE.) Click in the address bar at the top of IE and type **www.google.com**; then press Enter. If a screen appears with the Google logo and a search box, you're connected to the Internet. If you still don't have a connection, repeat these steps using a different wireless network.

Bring the Internet Home

If you have a laptop that you use at home, try the steps in the previous section first. You may already have a wireless connection available at home if your Internet service provider provided you with a wireless router (look for antennas), or you live in a facility with wireless provided to residents.

1. To bring the Internet home, you need an account with an Internet service provider (ISP), such as your local telephone company or cable TV service. An ISP provides you with the hardware for a physical (wired) connection to the Internet, as well as an account for access. Your ISP may send you the hardware or deliver and install it. The hardware consists of a box (sometimes called a *modem*) that connects to your phone line or TV cable. In turn, your computer connects to this box with a wire or wirelessly.

> If you have a laptop, you can't beat wireless for ease of connection and mobility. If you see an antenna on the ISP box, it supports a wireless connection. If your ISP box doesn't have built-in wireless support, you can add it using a device called *a wireless router*. Details are beyond the scope of this book. See *Using the Internet Safely For Seniors For Dummies*, by Linda Criddle and Nancy Muir (Wiley Publishing, Inc.), for more on wireless network security.

2. With the Windows 7 desktop onscreen, insert the disc that comes with your hardware. (If you don't have such a disc, skip to Step 5.) If the setup program doesn't start automatically, choose Start⇨Computer. Double-click the disc icon. Double-click on Setup or Install. Follow the instruction screens, which tell you how to connect the hardware and set up your Internet access. At some point during this process, you'll enter the username and password the ISP provides.

3. When you're done with the setup program, test your Internet connection: Start Microsoft Internet Explorer. (See Chapter 9 for information on using Internet Explorer, or IE.) Click in the address bar at the top of IE and type **www.google.com**; then press Enter. If a screen appears with the Google logo and a search box, you're connected to the Internet. Skip the remaining steps.

4. If you don't have a disc from your ISP or you don't have an Internet connection at this point, proceed with the following steps.

5. Connect your computer to the ISP box using an Ethernet cable (which looks like a thick phone wire) if you haven't already done so. Plug the Ethernet cable into your computer's Ethernet port and into a port on the ISP box. See **Figure 8-6**. Turn on the box's power. Lights blink on the box.

Ethernet port (with the cable plugged in)

Ethernet cable

Modem

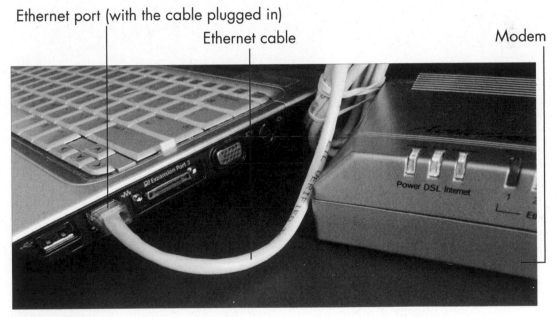

Figure 8-6

6. Test your Internet connection: Click in the address bar at the top of IE and type **www.google.com**; then press Enter. If a screen appears with the Google logo and a search box, you are connected to the Internet. If you receive any error messages, click in the address bar at the top of IE. Type the address for your connection; your ISP provides this numeric address, and 192.168.0.1 is very common. The configuration screen for your ISP connection appears, as shown in **Figure 8-7**. (Your screen may look different.)

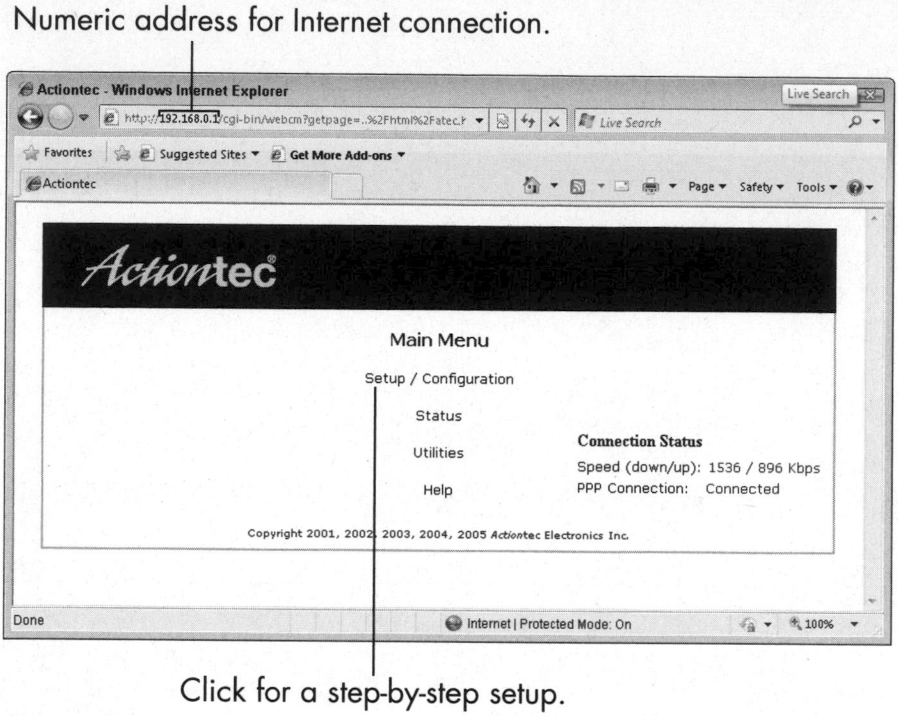

Numeric address for Internet connection.

Figure 8-7

7. Click the option for setup or configuration. You proceed through a series of screens with instructions. At some point, you enter the username and password provided by your ISP.

8. When you're done with the setup steps, test your Internet connection: Click in the address bar at the top of IE and type **www.google.com**; then press Enter. If a screen appears with the Google logo and a search box, you're connected to the Internet. If you still don't have an Internet connection, turn the ISP box on and off, and restart your computer. Test your connection again and, if you still aren't connected, call your ISP for assistance.

Finding What You Need on the Web

*T*he World Wide Web (simply, the Web, from here on) provides quick access to information and entertainment worldwide. One part library, one part marketplace, and one part soapbox, the Web makes everything equidistant: From down the block to halfway around the world — even out into space — everything is one click away. News, shopping, and the electronic equivalent of the town square await you.

You explore the Web using a *Web browser*, a program designed to make *browsing* the Web easy, enjoyable, and safe. In this chapter, I show how you can use Microsoft Internet Explorer to step beyond your computer into the global village.

You browse *Web pages*, which are published by governments, businesses, and individuals — anyone can learn to create Web pages. Each Web page can consist of a few words or thousands of words and pictures. A Web page is part of a larger collection called a *Web site*, which consists of a group of related Web pages published on a topic by an organization or individual. Companies and individuals create Web sites to organize their related pages.

Regardless of topic, pages and sites on the Web have some common characteristics:

➠ **Unique addresses,** which are formally called *URLs* (URL stands for Uniform Resource Locator, in case you're ever on *Jeopardy!*). The address of each Web page appears in the browser's address bar at the top of the screen.

➠ **Connecting links** that move you from page to page when you click them. These *links* (also called *hypertext links* or *hyperlinks*) often appear underlined and blue. Pictures and other graphic images can also be links to other pages.

Get Familiar with Microsoft Internet Explorer

1. Start Microsoft Internet Explorer (IE) by clicking on the blue *e* icon in the taskbar. The first time you run IE, one of the following will happen:

• The default Web page, known as the browser's *home page,* appears. The manufacturer of your computer may have chosen this page as your default. (Don't worry, you can change it later.)

• The Set Up Windows Internet Explorer dialog box may appear. On that screen, click the Ask Me Later button.

• An error message may appear if you don't have access to the Internet. See Chapter 8 for information about getting connected to the Internet.

2. Examine IE. Locate each of the following (see **Figure 9-1**):

Favorites Bar

Title

Address bar   Tabs

Command Bar

Search box

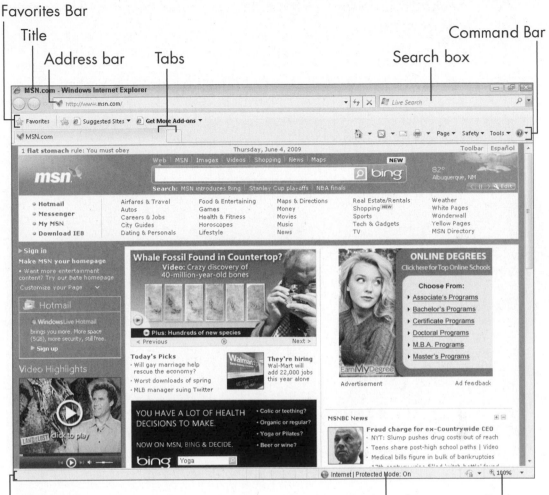

Status bar

Protected mode is on.   Zoom

Figure 9-1

- The **title** of the current Web page appears in the title bar and on a tab a few lines lower. Tabs allow you to open more than one Web page at a time.

- The **address bar** displays the Web page address for the page currently shown in the browser. As you follow links, the address changes. If you know the Web address of a page you want to visit, you can type it here and then press Enter to get there.

For a Web address that begins with www. and ends with .com, such as www.amazon.com, you can type the middle part of the address — for this example, **amazon** — and then press Ctrl+Enter to have the browser add the beginning and the end of the address: **amazon** with Ctrl+Enter becomes www.amazon.com.

- The **search box** allows you to type in topics or search terms for which you want to find matching Web pages. See the section "Search for Anything," later in this chapter.

You can also find new Web pages and sites by following links from other sites. When you discover sites that you intend to visit again, you can find your way back by marking those sites as favorites.

- The **Favorites Bar** displays links to frequently visited sites. See "Mark Your Favorite Places on the Favorites Bar."

- The **Command Bar** appears below the address bar and to the right of the tabs.

- The **Web page** appears in the main part of the IE window. If the page is longer than one screen, you can scroll down the page by clicking in the scroll bar area on the right edge of the window.

- **The status bar** displays information about the page, including Done, if the page is complete. Look in the status bar for the message Protected Mode: On, which indicates that IE is protecting your computer from some hazards. At the right end of the status bar, zoom in and out by clicking on 100% or using the down arrow for a drop-down menu of zoom levels.

Scroll down a page by pressing Page Down or the spacebar. Scroll back up by pressing Page Up or Shift+spacebar. Use the up and down arrows to scroll up or down one line at a time.

Browse for News

1. You have to start browsing for something, so why not the news? There's no need to delete whatever is currently in the address bar if you click once in the address bar and see everything there is highlighted. Type **www.newseum. org** in your browser's address bar and press Enter. IE automatically adds `http://` to the front of whatever you type — you never have to type that part of a Web address. Your browser has a home page — the first page you see when you start the browser. Each Web site you visit also has a home page, the first page you see at that site. The home page for the Newseum, an online collection of newspapers, appears in **Figure 9-2**.

 See "Install an Add-On in Internet Explorer," later in this chapter, if you see a message about installing Flash.

2. Click the button for Today's Front Pages, which is possibly on the right side of the screen. It can be tricky to find the link or button you want on a Web page, but links are usually underlined or a different color from regular text. The mouse pointer turns into a hand with a pointing index finger when you hover over something you can click. Most Web sites arrange major links horizontally near the top and vertically along either side of the page. Keep in mind that Web pages are subject to change any time, so what you see onscreen may be different from the pages you see in this chapter.

Click Today's Front Pages.

Figure 9-2

 Some Web pages are wider than the browser window, in which case you have to scroll right and left by clicking in the horizontal scroll bar or by pressing the right- or left-arrow keys.

3. On Today's Front Pages (see **Figure 9-3**), scroll down the page and up again. Look at the thumbnails of front pages from newspapers around the world. Use any of the blue, underlined links:

- **Next:** This link shows you more front page thumbnails.

- **Previous:** After you click Next one or more times, this link returns you to pages you've already seen.

- **Show 40 80 100 All per page:** Use one of these numbers or All to change the number of thumbnails that appear on one Web page.

- **Sort Papers by Region:** This link displays thumbnails grouped by international region, such as U.S., Europe, or Africa. The current display (See All Papers) is alphabetical by newspaper name.

Click to sort by area.

Choose how many front pages to see at once.

Click a front page.   Click to see more front pages.

Figure 9-3

4. To see one newspaper, click the thumbnail of the front page or the underlined text (the link) beneath that thumbnail.

5. The next page (see **Figure** 9-4) displays the front page of the paper you just selected. Scroll down the page to look at the front page and then scroll up again. Click one of these links above the front page:

- **BACK** returns you to the previous page of thumbnails.

- **Web Site** takes you from the Newseum site to the Web site for that particular newspaper.

Click Back to return to the list of front pages.

Click Web Site to see this newspaper's Web site.

Figure 9-4

6. Click in the address bar. Type **news.google.com** (no www) and press Enter. Google News displays headlines as links to news stories from around the world. Click any link to go to the story, as reported by any one of thousands of sources. Click the Back button or press Backspace to return to `news.google.com`.

Use Tabs to Browse Multiple Web Pages at Once

1. IE provides *tabs* to open more than one Web page at the same time. Click the narrow New Tab button to the right of your current tab, below the address bar. (As an alternative to clicking the New Tab button, you can press Ctrl+T.) A new tab appears (see **Figure 9-5**) next to the tab you were using.

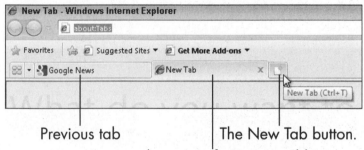

Previous tab   The New Tab button.

A new tab is open for a new address.

Figure 9-5

2. Type **www.newseum.org** in the address bar, replacing about:Tabs. As you type, IE displays matching addresses you can pick with the mouse or with the down arrow and Enter (see **Figure 9-6**).

3. Click the tab to the left of the new one to return to your previous tab — it's still open and available. Return to the newest tab by clicking it.

As you type, IE looks for matches.

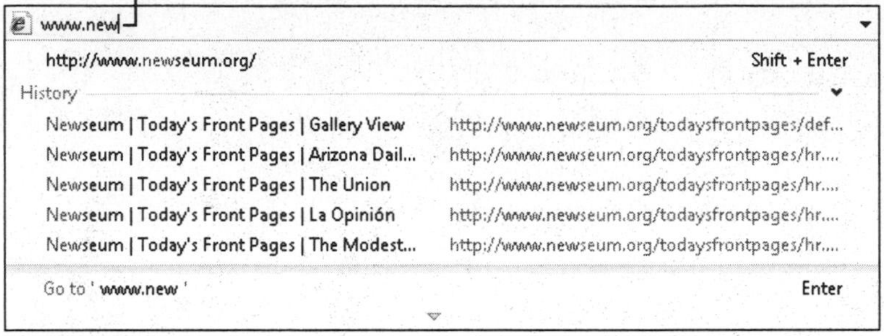

Figure 9-6

 Another way to open a Web page in a new tab is to right-click over a link on a page. Click Open in New Tab. You can open as many tabs as you need. I use multiple tabs so that I don't lose my place on one page as I move on to the next.

4. Click the Quick Tabs (or press Ctrl+Q) button to the left of your first tab to display thumbnails for all open tabs (see **Figure 9-7**). Click on a thumbnail to switch to that tab. Click the down arrow to the right of Quick Tabs for a list of open tabs.

Click the Quick Tabs button or arrow.

Click the X button to close the tab.

Click a thumbnail to switch to that tab.

Figure 9-7

5. Close an open tab by clicking the X to the right of that particular tab (or press Ctrl+W).

Change Your Browser's Home Page

1. When you start your Web browser, the browser's default Web page — its home page — appears. You can make the browser's home page one you want to see every time you start the browser. A news Web site or any other might be a better home page for the browser than the default page the browser chooses.

 Whenever you're wandering the Internet, you can quickly return to your browser's home page without restarting IE. To the right of the browser tabs, on the same bar, click the Home Page button. It's an icon that looks like a house with a chimney. The browser's home page appears.

2. To change your browser's home page, browse to the page you want to use as home. Click the down arrow next to the Home Page button. Click Add or Change Home Page, and the corresponding dialog box appears (see **Figure 9-8**) with two options:

- **Use This Webpage as Your Only Home Page** replaces the previous home page with the current page.

- **Add This Webpage to Your Home Page Tabs** creates a group of home page tabs, all of which open when IE starts.

3. Make your choice and click Yes. After you do, clicking the Home Page button opens your choice (or choices). Each time you start IE, this page opens, as well.

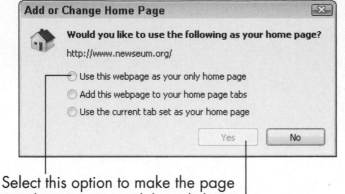

Select this option to make the page
your home page, and then click Yes.
Figure 9-8

Mark Your Favorite Places on the Favorites Bar

1. In IE, the Favorites Bar appears directly below the address
bar. You can add links here to take you back to pages you
want to return to, such as your favorite news site or your
bank's Web site. Browse the Web page for this book:
Type **www.mjhinton.com/w7fs/** in the address bar and
press Enter.

2. On the Favorites Bar, click the Add to Favorites Bar
button, which has a green arrow over a gold star.
Without any fanfare, the title of the current Web page
appears to the right of the Add to Favorites Bar button
(see **Figure 9-9**).

Click a favorite to see that page.
Click to add the current page to the Favorites Bar.
Figure 9-9

3. To return to a site using the Favorites Bar, click on the
link.

4. Rename a Favorites Bar link by right-clicking over that link. Choose Rename. For this book, you could type **Windows 7 book**. Then click OK. Shorter names allow you to fit more links on the Favorites Bar and make those links easier to recognize.

5. Delete a link from the Favorites Bar by right-clicking over that link and choosing Delete from the resulting menu. A dialog box asks whether you're sure. Click Yes (if you are).

 Use the Favorites Bar for the Web sites you visit most often, and delete links you don't often use.

Add More Favorites

1. You can bookmark any Web page as a favorite place to make it easy to return to that page later. Browse to a site you like to visit (for example, the Web page for this book): Type **www.mjhinton.com/w7fs/** in the address bar and press Enter.

2. To mark the Web page that appears as a favorite, click the Favorites button below the address bar. See **Figure 9-10**. The Favorites panel displays any page titles already marked as favorites, as well as folders used to organize favorites into groups.

3. Click the Add to Favorites button. The Add a Favorite dialog box appears with the title of the current Web page showing in the Name box. You can change that name, if you want. See **Figure 9-11**. Favorites is the name of the main folder for these links. You can select a different folder or create a new folder. Don't feel you have to be so organized. Click the Add button.

 Pressing Ctrl+D opens the Add a Favorite dialog box directly. You can press Ctrl+D to get the Add a Favorite dialog box at any time, even if the Favorites panel isn't open.

Click to add the current page to the Favorites panel.

Click Favorites to see the Favorites panel.

Figure 9-10

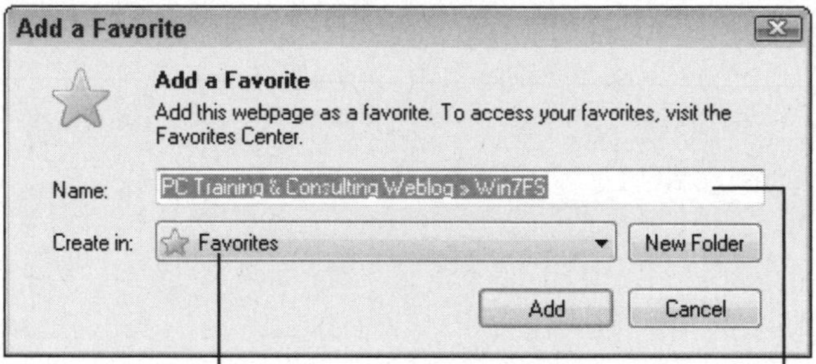

Place the favorite in a different folder (optional).

Change the name of the favorite (optional).

Figure 9-11

4. To return to a Web page you previously marked as a favorite, click the Favorites button. Click on the title of the page you previously marked. If you put the favorite in a folder, click on the folder and then on the title.

You can also return to a previously viewed Web page by typing the address or the title in the address bar for a list of matching pages. Or, choose Favorites⇨ History and click on the heading for the date you visited the Web page.

Search for Anything

1. With IE open, click in the Search box to the right of the Address bar (or press Ctrl+E). Type **travel**. As you type, a list of suggested search terms appears. You can continue to type your search terms or choose from this list, as shown in **Figure 9-12**. A search results page appears after you choose from the list or press Enter after your text. The results come from www.bing.com, the default *search engine* for IE. A search engine is simply a Web site that allows you to find other Web sites. A search engine provides links to Web pages that match your search. That definition ignores the complex process going on behind the scenes.

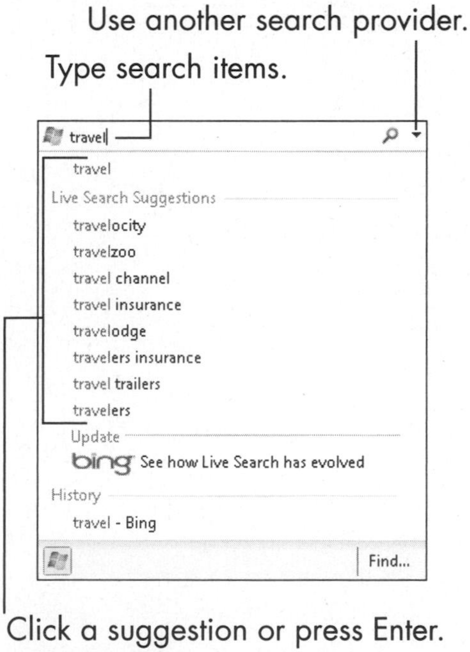

Use another search provider.

Type search items.

| travel | | 🔍 | ▾ |

travel

Live Search Suggestions

travelocity

travelzoo

travel channel

travel insurance

travelodge

travelers insurance

travel trailers

travelers

Update

bing See how Live Search has evolved

History

travel - Bing

Find...

Click a suggestion or press Enter.

Figure 9-12

2. Scroll down the page of search results. Click on any link you want to follow. Click Next at the bottom of the page for more search results.

Browsing your search results is often a good time to use multiple tabs for browsing. (See the section "Use Tabs to Browse Multiple Web Pages at Once," earlier in this chapter.) Simply right-click a search result's link and choose Open in a New Tab. Doing this several times enables you to pursue several results at once in different tabs.

3. If the search results aren't what you're looking for, you can refine your search. Just add to or change your search terms in the search box near the top of the results page. Press Enter to perform the refined search.

 Different search engines may turn up different results even if you use the same search terms. Two other popular search engines are Google (www.google.com) and Yahoo! (www.yahoo.com). By entering those addresses in the address bar, you can use either search engine for exploring the Web. You can also change the default search engine IE uses by clicking the down arrow at the end of the Search box (refer to Figure 9-12) and choosing Find More Providers (other search engines).

Shop Online Using Amazon

1. You can shop, pay bills, do your banking, and even invest your money online. Your bank and brokerage firm have Web sites, as do many companies that sell almost anything you may want to buy. So first, how about shopping? Enter **www.amazon.com** in the address bar. Amazon is the largest online retailer in the world.

2. You can use the menu under Shop All Departments to look for specific categories of products, or you can use the Search box at the top of Amazon's home page. Click in the Search box and type **bird watching**. As you type, Amazon automatically suggests potential matches. You can select from the suggestions or continue typing and click the Go button. Search results appear along with links to Related Searches (in this case, those related to *bird watching*), specific departments within Amazon, and brand names. See **Figure 9-13**.

Click any related searches that interest you.

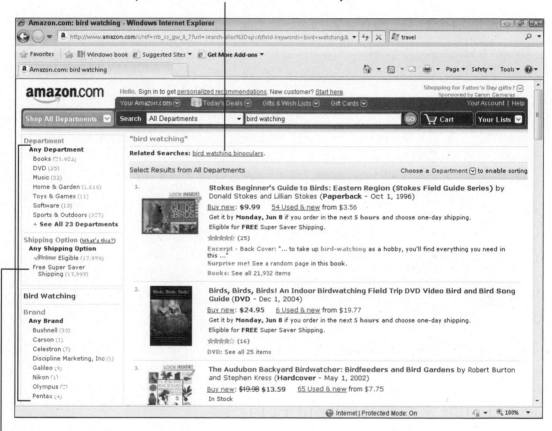

Explore or refine results.

Figure 9-13

3. Click on the link or picture of one of the items listed to see its product page, similar to the one shown in **Figure 9-14**. Amazon's product pages are chock-full of information and links to more information. Scroll down the product page and look at price, description, and ratings and reviews from buyers.

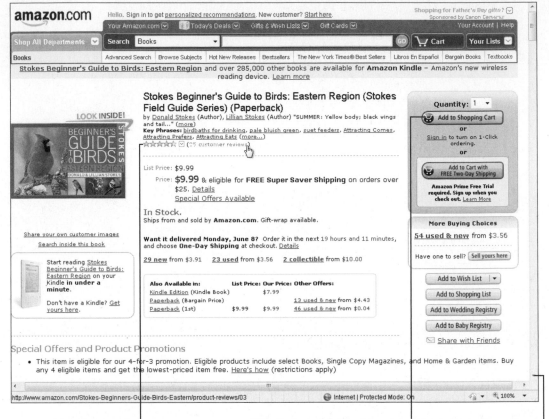

Note the star rating. | Click to add the item to your shopping cart.

Scroll down for more information.

Figure 9-14

4. Repeat the preceding steps a few times to look at products that interest you. Before you continue, you can pick a product you actually want to buy.

5. To purchase a product, click the Add to Shopping Cart button on the right side of a product page. A new page appears, offering other products (see **Figure 9-15**). You can continue shopping for more products, but when you're ready, click Proceed to Checkout. (You may want to select the check box next to Show Gift Options During Checkout.)

Click when you're done shopping.

Figure 9-15

6. The Amazon sign-in screen appears with options for new or returning customers. Enter your e-mail address (see **Figure 9-16**). See Chapter 10 for information on setting up an e-mail account and getting an address. Click the Sign In Using Our Secure Server button.

 Security in the browser comes in many forms. In this case, the Web address now begins with `https`; the `s` indicates a secure connection, as does the presence of a padlock icon next to the address. You want a secure connection like this for all online financial transactions.

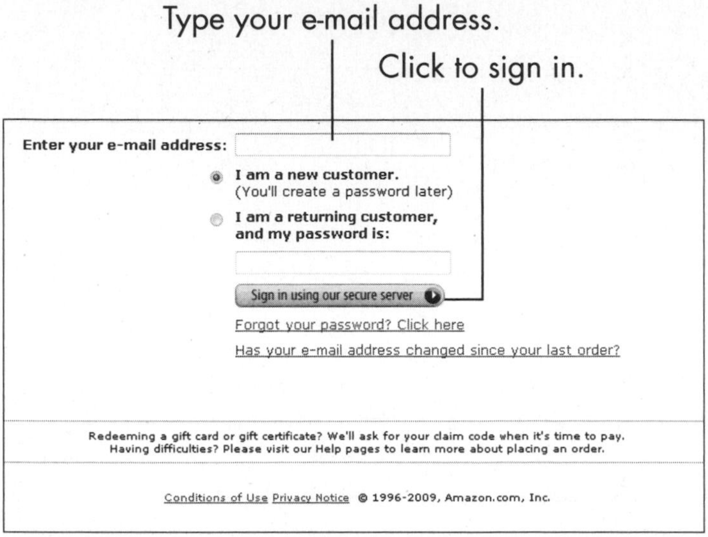

Type your e-mail address.

Click to sign in.

Enter your e-mail address:

○ **I am a new customer.**
(You'll create a password later)

○ **I am a returning customer,
and my password is:**

[   ]

[Sign in using our secure server ⊙]

Forgot your password? Click here

Has your e-mail address changed since your last order?

Redeeming a gift card or gift certificate? We'll ask for your claim code when it's time to pay.
Having difficulties? Please visit our Help pages to learn more about placing an order.

Conditions of Use Privacy Notice © 1996-2009, Amazon.com, Inc.

Figure 9-16

7. On the next screen (see **Figure 9-17**), enter your full
name. Reenter the e-mail address in the space provided.
Type a new password into the two boxes provided. Your
password should be easy for you to remember but hard
for someone else to guess. Amazon requires at least six
characters in a password. Click the Create a New Account
button.

 When you create a password, don't use the words
password or *secret* and avoid using the names of your
spouse, children, close friends, or even your pets.
Start with a memorable phrase, such as, "I like
shopping on Amazon." Reduce that to initials: **ilsoa**.
Add punctuation: **ilsoa!** To make a better password,
capitalize some letters: **iLsoA!** Turn letters into
numbers: **1Ls0A!** No one will guess that password,
but it's relatively easy to remember. If you choose to
write down passwords, hide your notes well.

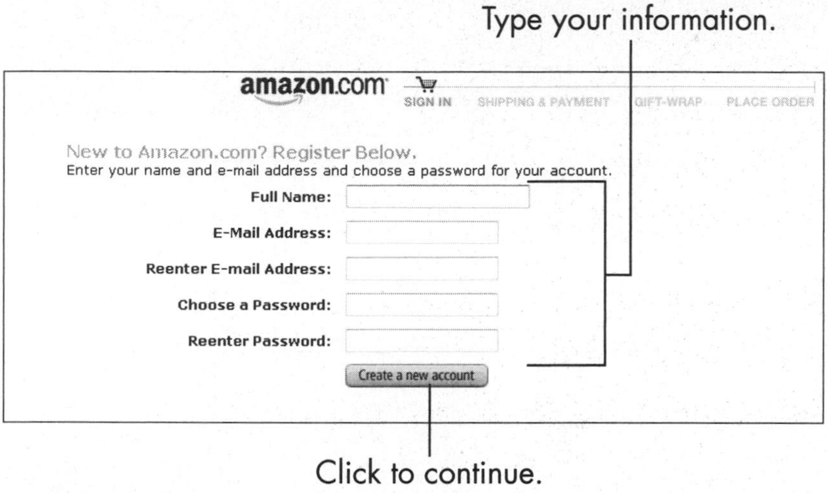
Type your information.
amazon.com
SIGN IN
SHIPPING & PAYMENT
GIFT-WRAP
PLACE ORDER
New to Amazon.com? Register Below.
Enter your name and e-mail address and choose a password for your account.
Full Name:
E-Mail Address:
Reenter E-mail Address:
Choose a Password:
Reenter Password:
Create a new account
Click to continue.

Figure 9-17

8. The next screen (see **Figure 9-18**) provides a form for your address, even if you are purchasing a gift. Fill in the form appropriately, select Yes as the answer to the billing address question, and click Continue. If any of the information you enter is incomplete, you may see this page again with a message describing the problem, such as a missing zip code.

Don't click the Back button on any of these screens; the process requires you to move forward, except where you see a link or button on the screen itself that indicates you can go back to change something. You'll have an opportunity later to review and revise information or cancel your order or account.

9. On the next screen, choose a shipping speed. Standard shipping usually takes four business days. Select the check box for gift option if this is a gift; you'll enter a gift address, later. Click Continue.

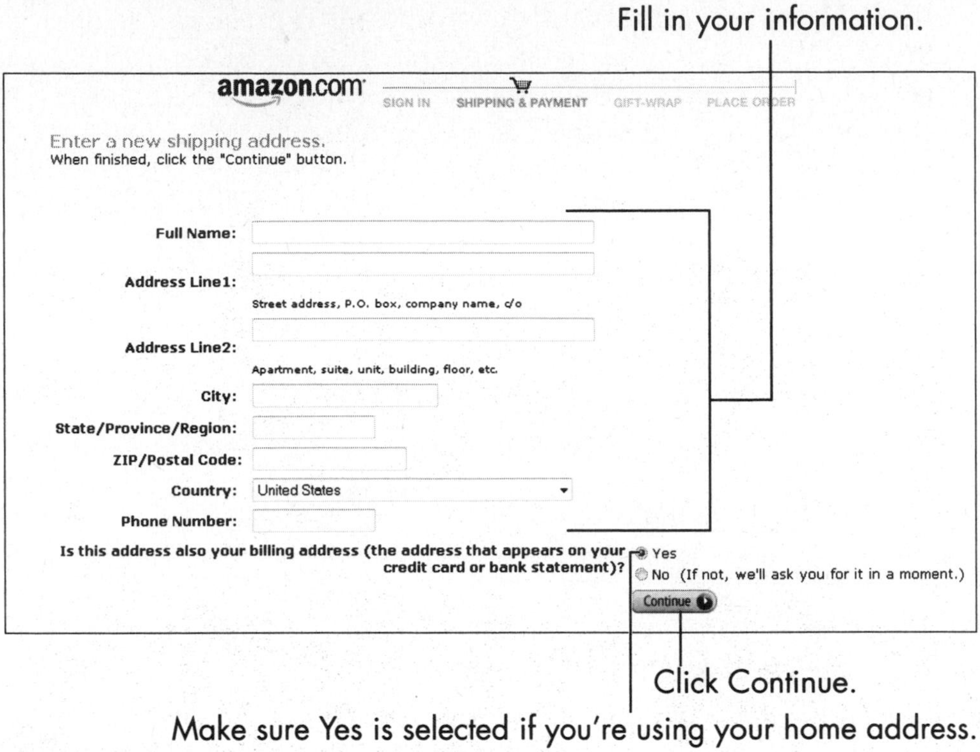

Fill in your information.

amazon.com

SIGN IN   **SHIPPING & PAYMENT**   GIFT-WRAP   PLACE ORDER

Enter a new shipping address.
When finished, click the "Continue" button.

Full Name:

Address Line1:

Street address, P.O. box, company name, c/o

Address Line2:

Apartment, suite, unit, building, floor, etc.

City:

State/Province/Region:

ZIP/Postal Code:

Country: United States

Phone Number:

Is this address also your billing address (the address that appears on your credit card or bank statement)?

○ Yes

○ No (If not, we'll ask you for it in a moment.)

Continue

Click Continue.

Make sure Yes is selected if you're using your home address.

Figure 9-18

10. If you didn't select the gift option in the previous step, skip to Step 11. The Add Gift-Wrap and Write a Free Gift Message screen appears. Select gift wrap for a fee, if you choose. Type a short message in the gift note box, if you want. Prices for gift items will not appear on the packing slip sent with the gift unless you uncheck the check box next to Don't Print Prices. You'll still get prices on your receipt, regardless.

11. On the Payment page, to use a credit card, click the Add a New Card button. A form appears below that button. Enter your card number (with or without dashes) and your name as it appears on the card. Use the drop-down lists to pick the month and year your card expires. Click Select Card Type to choose your card. With all fields complete, click the Add Your Card button. Your credit card information now appears on this same screen. Click Continue.

12. You may see a screen to Choose a Billing Address. If the correct address appears onscreen, click the Use This Address button just above that address. If the address displayed is not the correct billing address, enter the correct information on this screen and click the Continue button.

13. The review screen (see **Figure 9-19**) displays your shipping address, shipping speed, purchase details, and an Order Summary with any shipping, handling, and tax. Review your order. To ship a gift to a different address, click the Change button next to Shipping To. Select a different shipping speed, if you want. Click buttons to Change Quantities or Delete part of the order, to Change Gift Options, to Change Payment Method, or to Change Billing Address. To proceed with the order, click Place Your Order.

 If you don't want to continue with an order, at this point, click the Change Quantities or Delete button. On the next screen, set quantities to zero and click the Continue button. The next screen indicates you have nothing in your shopping cart.

14. A thank you screen appears with links to track or cancel the order. If you're done, you can close this browser tab.

Click to complete your order.

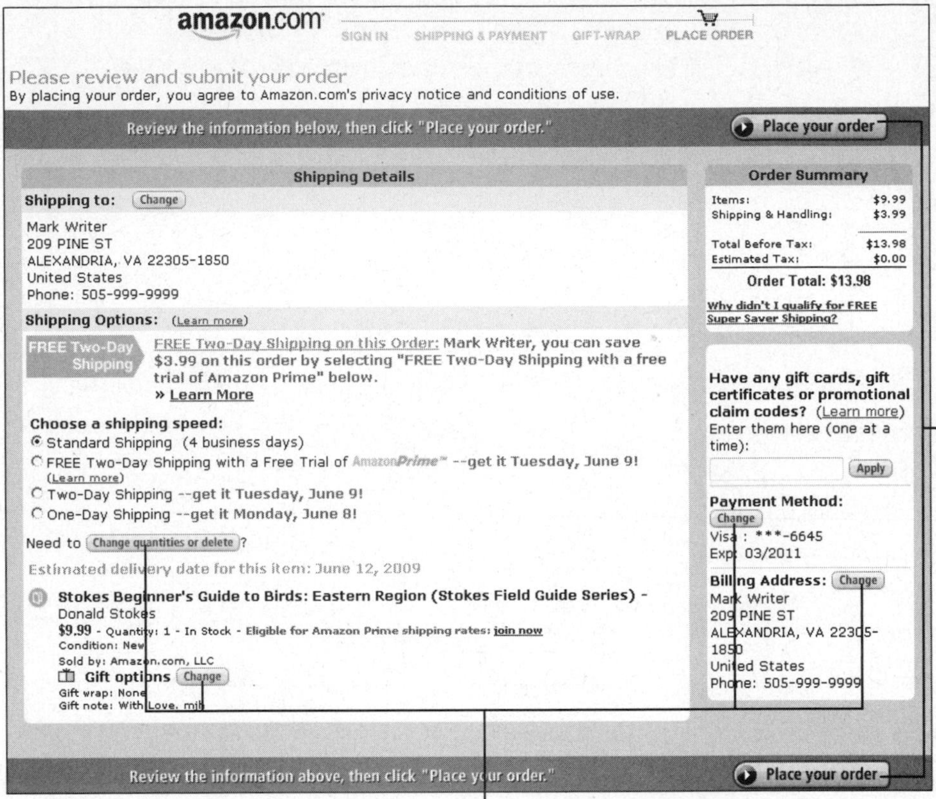

If needed, click a Change button to change information.

Figure 9-19

15. Amazon, like most online retailers, sends e-mail with your order information and again when your product ships. The shipping e-mail includes a tracking number, or you can find shipping information by typing **www. amazon.com** in your browser's address bar and clicking Your Account. Click the View Recent and Open Orders button. Type or confirm your e-mail address and type your password. Click the Sign In Using Our Secure Server button. The Order History screen displays sections for Open Orders and Completed Orders, if any. For open orders — those that haven't shipped — click the View or

Change Order button. You can change or cancel an order on the next screen. For completed orders, click the View Order button to see details of your order or click the Track Your Package button, if your order hasn't been delivered yet.

When you enter a password on a Web page, the AutoCompete Passwords dialog box appears. If you click Yes, IE will save your password for this site and enter the password automatically when you return to this site. If you click No, IE will not save the password for this site. The Yes option is convenient, although it means anyone with access to your computer can log in to those sites for which IE has saved passwords. Don't select Don't Offer to Remember Any More Passwords — you may want IE to remember passwords in the future.

Close Internet Explorer

1. When you're done browsing the Web with IE, close it like you do any other program: Click the X in the upper-right corner of the window. If you have more than one tab open, IE displays a message with buttons to Close All Tabs, which closes IE completely, or to Close Current Tab. If you don't intend to close IE or the current tab, click the X in the dialog box.

2. This dialog box protects you from accidentally closing tabs you don't intend to close. However, you can check Always Close All Tabs to prevent this dialog box from appearing again in the future.

Sending and Receiving E-Mail

Chapter 10

E-mail has largely replaced notes and letters of previous centuries. Every day, billions of e-mail messages circle the globe, conveying greetings, news, jokes, even condolences.

To send and receive e-mail, you need an account with an e-mail service. Your Internet service provider (ISP) probably gave you an e-mail account and address when you signed up for Internet access. You can use the account provided by your ISP with any number of e-mail programs you can install on your computer.

But my suggestion — for convenience and ease of use — is that you sign up for a Web-based e-mail account. After you do, you can access your Web-based e-mail from anywhere in the world using any computer connected to the Internet. New e-mail pops into your inbox 24 hours a day. With a bit of typing and a click, you can send your reply. Who needs postage stamps?

E-mail also provides a way to send and receive *attachments,* such as documents or photos. Who needs faxes or postcards?

With the good comes the bad, including unsolicited junk e-mail, referred to as *spam*. These messages may be only a distraction, or they may include efforts to trick you into trouble. Stay clear and stay safe.

In this chapter, I show you how to set up an e-mail account with Google Gmail, a shining example of e-mail service. You also find out how to send and receive e-mail, send attachments or handle ones you've received, organize your contacts, and dispatch the junk.

 Gmail places advertisements to the side of each screen. That's what pays for your account.

Set Up an E-Mail Account

1. To create a free e-mail account with Google's e-mail service, known as Gmail (Google Mail, in Europe), start Internet Explorer (IE) and type **mail.google.com** (no www) in the address bar at the top. The Welcome to Gmail page appears.

 As an alternative to Gmail, you can create a free e-mail account with another Web-based service, such as AOL (www.aol.com), MSN Hotmail (www.hotmail.com), or Yahoo! (www.yahoo.com). The steps for creating accounts with those services should be fairly similar to creating an account for Gmail.

2. On the Welcome page, click Create an Account. The Create a Google Account page appears, as shown in **Figure 10-1**.

3. Fill in the boxes (called *fields*) for your first and last name. In the Desired Login Name field, type the e-mail username you want. Your e-mail address will be this name followed by @gmail.com, such as mhinton47@gmail.com. (Typically, the login name is some variation on your first and last name.) Click the Check Availability button to see whether your desired name is available. If it isn't, try another name.

Fill in each field.

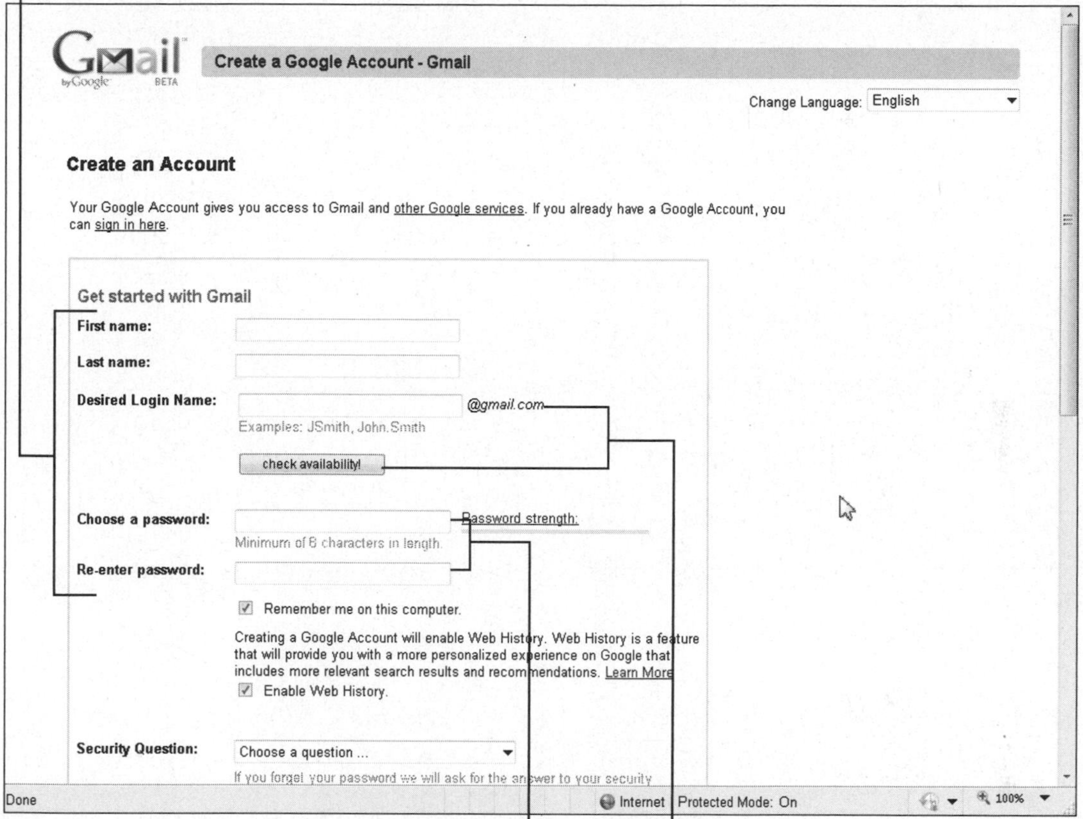

Enter your password twice.

Enter the login name you want, and click Check Availability.

Figure 10-1

 Adding numbers to your desired name increases your chance of finding an available name.

4. In the Choose a Password field, type a password of eight characters or more. Your password should be easy for you to remember but hard for others to guess. As you type the password, the Password Strength meter to the right displays a rating of your password from fair to strong. Reenter your password in the next field.

When you create a password, don't use the word *password* or *secret* or the names of people or pets. Start with a memorable phrase, such as "I use Gmail for e-mail." Reduce that to initials: **iugfe**. If a longer password is required, add punctuation and numbers: **iugfe99!** To make a better password, capitalize some letters: **iUgFe99!** Turn letters into numbers or numbers into letters: **1U9Fegg!** No one will guess that password, but it's relatively easy to remember. If you choose to write down passwords, hide your notes well.

5. Leave these check boxes selected:

- **Remember Me on This Computer:** When a check mark appears next to this box, the Gmail program will automatically remember you (and you don't have to type your username and password) whenever you use this same computer to access your e-mail account.

 Don't use Remember Me on This Computer if you're not using your own computer, but instead a friend's or a public computer.

- **Enable Web History:** When this box is checked, Google tracks information about your activity, including searches you perform.

6. Scroll down the Create Account page a bit to see the bottom half of the page, as shown in **Figure 10-2**.

7. Select a Security Question from the drop-down list and then enter an answer to the question in the Answer field. If you ever forget your password, Google will use this question and the answer you provide in the next field to verify that you are who you say you are.

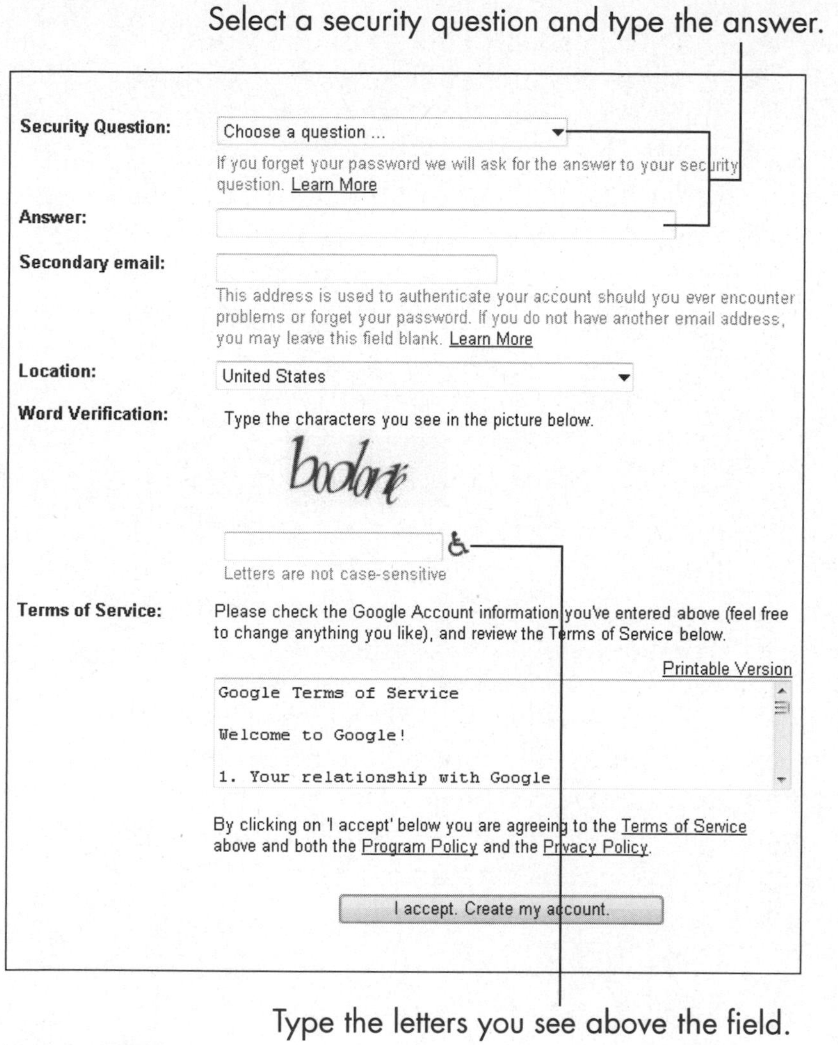

Select a security question and type the answer.

Security Question:	Choose a question ... ▼
	If you forget your password we will ask for the answer to your security question. Learn More
Answer:	
Secondary email:	
	This address is used to authenticate your account should you ever encounter problems or forget your password. If you do not have another email address, you may leave this field blank. Learn More
Location:	United States ▼
Word Verification:	Type the characters you see in the picture below.
	boolont
	Letters are not case-sensitive
Terms of Service:	Please check the Google Account information you've entered above (feel free to change anything you like), and review the Terms of Service below.
	Printable Version
	Google Terms of Service
	Welcome to Google!
	1. Your relationship with Google
	By clicking on 'I accept' below you are agreeing to the Terms of Service above and both the Program Policy and the Privacy Policy.
	[I accept. Create my account.]

Type the letters you see above the field.

Figure 10-2

8. If you already use another e-mail address, enter it in the Secondary E-Mail field. This provides Gmail with an alternative for contacting you. You may leave this field blank.

9. Select your country from the Location drop-down list.

10. In the Word Verification field, type the letters you see displayed above the field. This is a test to separate humans from programs designed to create e-mail addresses. (Seriously, it is.) If you can't read the letters, click the wheelchair icon to have Gmail read the letters out loud.

11. Be the first person ever to read the Terms of Service, which describes the relationship you and Google are entering into. Google promises very little and requires little of you.

12. Click the "I Accept. Create My Account." button (refer to Figure 10-2). The Congratulations screen appears. Click on Show Me My Account.

 If you decide to use Gmail for your e-mail, the account is Web-based — meaning you access it through any browser from any computer connected to the Internet. Although there are e-mail programs you can install on your computer (for example, Thunderbird), you don't have to bother with such a program if you're happy with access through the browser.

Check Your Inbox for New E-Mail

1. In Internet Explorer, go to http://mail.google.com. You may need to sign in with your username (e-mail address) and password. If Google remembers you from a previous sign-in, you go straight to your Inbox (see **Figure 10-3**). E-mail sent by others appears automatically in your Inbox, which is the first screen you see after signing in. The Inbox displays the sender's name, the subject line of the message, and the date or time the message was received. E-mail you haven't read yet appears in bold.

The links show different screens.

Messages you haven't read are in bold. Click a message to read it.

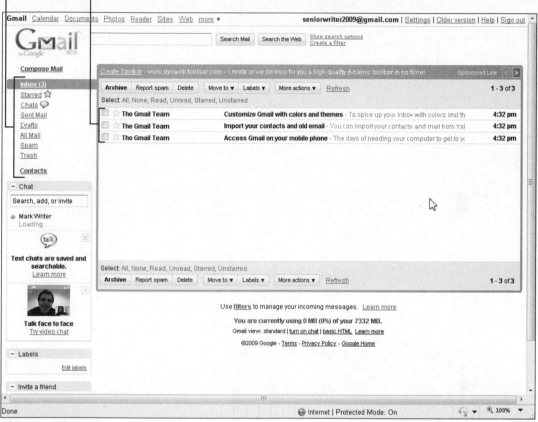

Figure 10-3

2. Click any message in your Inbox. The message appears onscreen (see **Figure 10-4**). Scroll, if necessary, to read the entire message.

 If the incoming e-mail contains any photos or other graphics, Gmail doesn't automatically display them. If you trust the sender of the e-mail, click the Display Images Below link near the top of the message.

The description of the buttons and the links below is based on looking at a single message — I assume you're not in the Inbox in this section. If you are in the Inbox, most of these buttons require that you select messages beforehand by clicking on the check box left of each message.

Click to reply to the message.

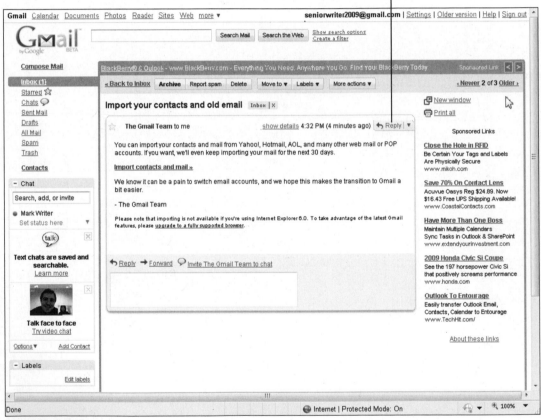

Figure 10-4

3. Use the buttons above the message (refer to Figure 10-4) to accomplish various tasks:

- **Archive:** Moves the selected message out of the Inbox. Use this if you want to keep this message but move it out of the Inbox. Click All Mail on the left to see archived and sent e-mail.

- **Report Spam:** Moves the selected message to the Spam folder for junk e-mail. See "Avoid Spam and Other Junk Messages," later in this chapter.

- **Delete:** Moves the selected message to the Trash folder.

- **Move To:** You can use labels to categorize your e-mail. (For example, you can label all financial e-mail as **investments**.) The Move To button archives the selected message and labels it using the label that you select from the drop-down list or one you create using this button.

- **Labels:** Use this button's drop-down list to add labels to e-mail without moving it out of the Inbox.

 Don't worry about labels, but they can be very valuable for finding messages later. The labels you use appear on the left side of the screen. When you click on a label on the left, all the e-mail you labeled that way appears in a list.

- **More Actions:** You can do much more with any e-mail message. Mark a message as unread so that it appears new and boldfaced in the Inbox. Add a star to a message to emphasize it. Create a task based on the message using Gmail's Tasks function. Create an event using Google Calendar. Create a filter to automatically label, archive, or delete incoming e-mail.

4. Click the links on either side of the buttons above the message to navigate through your mail:

- **Back to Inbox** (logically) takes you back to the full view of the Inbox with all your most recent messages showing.

- **Newer or Older** links take you to another message, if you are still viewing one message. On the other hand, if you're looking at the Inbox, these links page through groups of messages. After you get too many messages, you can't see them all together on one page. And so Gmail orders your messages by date and gives you these links to move through them.

 Gmail's fast search function — it's Google, the king of search engines — makes it a great choice for e-mail. Click in the search box on any screen to type text that is in any message you want to open. A list of messages containing that text appears. Click any message to open it.

Reply to E-Mail

1. Click any message in your Inbox. The message appears onscreen (refer to Figure 10-4). After you read the message, click the Reply button in the upper-right corner of the message or the Reply link at the bottom of the message.

 If the message you're replying to went to more than one person and you want everyone to see your reply, click the down arrow next to the Reply button and then select the Reply to All option. You can select Forward from this same menu to send this message to someone who did not receive it already.

2. A new compose mail box appears below the message you have open, as shown in **Figure 10-5**. The address of the sender of the message appears in the To field. You can add to that or change it. The cursor appears in the message box. The entire message you received appears below the cursor.

Click Reply and type your message in the compose box.

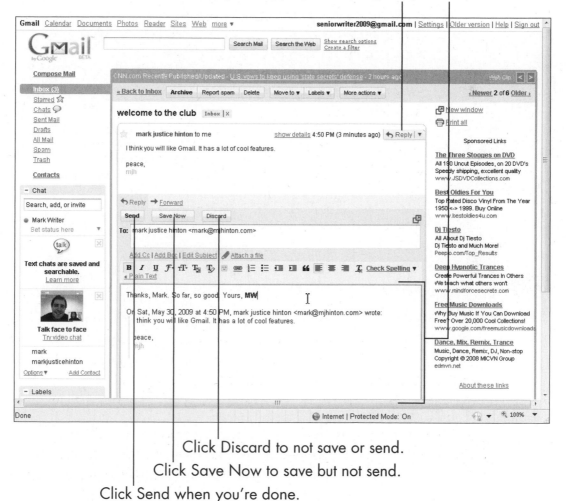

Click Discard to not save or send.
Click Save Now to save but not send.
Click Send when you're done.

Figure 10-5

To send the same e-mail to more than one person at a time, you can add a comma after the first e-mail address and type another. Click Add Cc (for *courtesy copy*) for another way to send this message to other recipients. Click Add Bcc (for *blind courtesy copy*) to add a recipient address other recipients won't see.

3. (Optional) The subject line doesn't appear — replies usually keep the same subject. However, you can click the Edit Subject link if you want to change the subject line. When you've edited your subject, click in the blank area at the top of the big box below.

 Gmail creates *conversations* out of e-mail message exchanges with the same subject line. This makes it easy to read all of the messages exchanged on that subject, by clicking on any message listed in the conversation. A reply to your e-mail will automatically link to all the other related messages, unless you change the subject line of a reply.

4. Type your response. Use the Save Now button if you don't want to send it immediately. Clicking the Save Now button creates a draft message you can revise and send later. (Click Drafts on the left, to see draft messages.) Click the Send button if your message is ready to go. After your reply is sent, click the Archive button to remove this message from your Inbox. (Click All Mail on the left to see mail you have archived or sent, including this message.) Return to your Inbox.

Create a New E-Mail

1. Click Compose Mail in the upper-left area of the Gmail page. The Compose Mail form appears. The From field displays your Gmail address.

To move from one field to the next on any Web form, such as the Compose Mail form, press the Tab key or click in the field.

2. In the To field, type an e-mail address you intend to write to. (You can use your own address for practice.) Don't type the person's name here, just the e-mail address. If you've written other e-mail, Gmail may display e-mail addresses for you to use along with that person's name (see **Figure 10-6**).

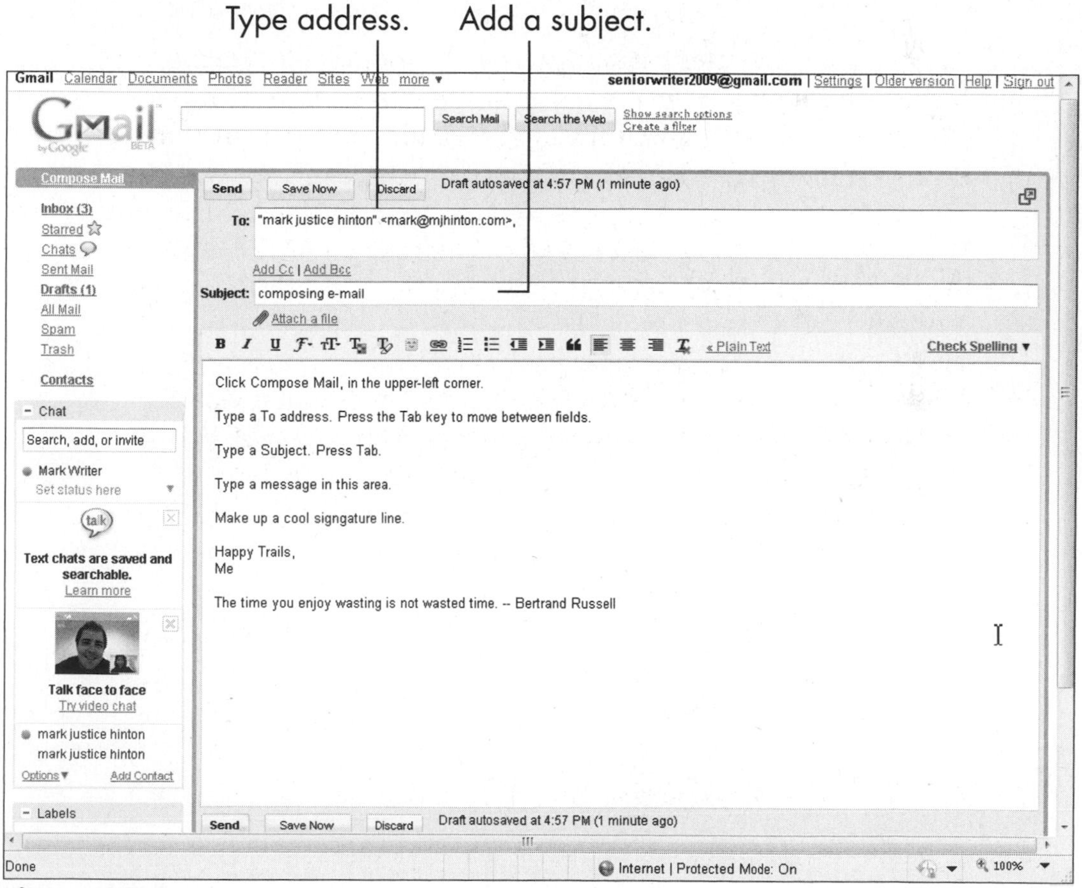

Type address.   Add a subject.

Figure 10-6

To send the same e-mail to more than one person at a time, you can add a comma after the first e-mail address and type another. Click Add Cc (for *courtesy copy*) for another way to send this message to other recipients. Click Add Bcc (for *blind courtesy copy*) to add a recipient address other recipients won't see.

3. In the Subject field, type a subject line (something short but descriptive).

4. In the message area, type your e-mail. A salutation, such as **Hi, Mark,** is optional, but common. Avoid using all capital letters, which some people interpret as yelling. You don't need to press Enter at the end of lines within a paragraph — as your words reach the end of a line, the cursor automatically goes to the next line of the paragraph.

5. (Optional) If you want to change the look of the text, select the text you want to modify and click any of these tools in the toolbar above the message area:

- **B** turns text **bold** (darker). Click the B icon a second time to remove bold from selected text, if necessary.

- *I* turns text *italics*. A second click removes italics.

- U <u>underlines</u> text.

- F allows you to select a specific font (a style of text or typeface) from a drop-down list.

- TT allows you to increase or decrease the size of the selected text from a drop-down list.

See Chapter 3 for information on formatting text.

The easiest way to include a clickable link in e-mail is to copy that link from the browser address bar and paste it into your e-mail. You can also type in a Web address, with or without http:// at the beginning, such as **www.google.com**.

6. End your message with your name or initials as a signature.

7. Click the Send button when you're ready to e-mail your message.

8. Click the Sent Mail link on the left to see the e-mail you've sent or click the All Mail link for e-mail sent or received.

 You can compose e-mail to send later. As you write, Gmail automatically saves your e-mail in the Drafts folder. You can also click the Save Now button to create a draft. Later, click on the Drafts link on the left and click on the e-mail you started earlier. Discard drafts you don't intend to send.

Attach a Document or Photo to E-Mail

1. Send a photo or any file to family and friends. On the Compose Mail form (explained in the preceding section), click the Attach a File link below the Subject line. The Choose a File to Upload dialog box appears.

2. Locate the file you intend to send with the e-mail and click it. (See Chapter 4 for information on using Windows Explorer to locate files.) The filename appears below the Subject field (as shown in **Figure 10-7**). You can remove this attachment with the Remove link, if you change your mind.

Gmail | Calendar | Documents | Photos | Reader | Sites | Web | more ▼   seniorwriter2009@gmail.com | Settings | Older version | Help | Sign out

Gmail by Google BETA

[ ] Search Mail | Search the Web | Show search options / Create a filter

Compose Mail

Send | Save Now | Discard

Inbox (2)
Starred ☆
Chats ○
Sent Mail
Drafts
All Mail
Spam
Trash

Contacts

To: "mark justice hinton" <mark@mjhinton.com>,

Add Cc | Add Bcc

Subject: attaching a photo

C:\fakepath\Koala.jpg remove

Attach another file

B *I* U F ⫶T⫶ T⫶ ☰ ☰ ⚏ ⚏ ☰ ⚏ 66 ☰ ☰ ☰ T « Plain Text   Check Spelling ▼

Attached file   Click if you want to attach another file.

Figure 10-7

3. Gmail begins to upload the file before you click the Send
button. For large files, you see a progress bar indicating
how much more time is required to complete the upload.
Be patient when attaching files.

4. Click the Attach Another File link and repeat Steps 2 and 3
for any other files you want to send.

5. To remove an attachment, click the Remove link next to
that attachment's filename.

6. Complete your message and click the Send button when
you're ready. Your message and the attachment(s) will be
delivered to the recipient.

Although you can attach any type of document to an
e-mail message, avoid sending video files, because
they are so large and take too long to send and
receive. Gmail refuses to send or receive program files
(executables) because such files are commonly used to
attack a computer.

View or Open Attachments

1. If incoming e-mail includes an attachment, Gmail displays the attachment's filename and links for handling the attachment. See **Figure 10-8**. (If the attachment is a picture, you get to see a preview of the image.)

Photos show previews.

Click View to see this photo in a new browser tab.

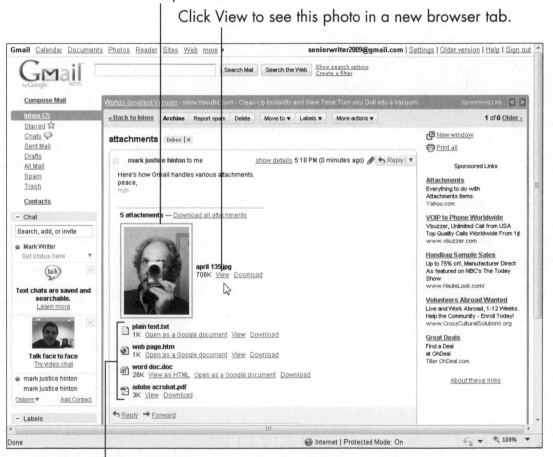

Different types of files have different links.

Figure 10-8

Ignore attachments from unknown senders. Never download or open these. Even if an attachment comes from a trusted source, be aware that attachments may contain content that can infect your computer with viruses, worms, or other rotten stuff. See Chapter 19 for information on keeping your computer safe.

2. The links Gmail displays for attachments vary depending on the type of attachment. Links include

- **View:** This link displays the contents in a new tab in the browser. Use this to view attached photos.

- **View as HTML:** This link displays the document's contents as a Web page in a new tab in the browser. This display may not look exactly like the original document — some formatting may not show.

- **Open As a Google Document:** This link opens the attachment as a new document in Google Documents, an online version of word processing, spreadsheets, and more. Use this option if you want to be able to edit the document without downloading it.

- **Download:** This option downloads the attachment to the Downloads folder under your username. Choose the Start⇨Computer command and select the Downloads folder to see this file. If you can't open a downloaded attachment, you may not have the necessary software. If the content is important to you, inform the sender and ask her to send the attachment in a different format, such as rich text format (RTF) or plain text (TXT).

Gmail stores all of your sent and received e-mail online. There's no option to save a message to your computer. If you want to save a copy of e-mail, click the down arrow next to the Reply button and choose Print. In the Print dialog box that appears, select Microsoft XPS Document Writer to create a file you can save to your computer. When you click the Print button, a Save As dialog box appears for you to enter the name and location to save this e-mail.

Keep an Electronic Address Book

1. Gmail automatically remembers e-mail address as you send or reply. As you type in the To, Cc, or Bcc fields, Gmail displays matching addresses, if any. To keep track of e-mail address and other information, click the Contacts link on the left. **Figure 10-9** shows the resulting Contacts screen.

2. Under My Contacts on the right, click the View Suggestions button. Gmail displays addresses you've used but not added to My Contacts. To add any of these to your contacts address book, click the check box next to each address you want and then click the Move to My Contacts button.

3. To add a new address, click the New Contact button. A new form appears on the right, as shown in **Figure 10-10**. Fill in the Name field — first name and last name. Title and Company are optional fields. Enter the e-mail address for this contact. For a contact with more than one e-mail address, enter the primary address first and then click the Add link next to Email for another e-mail field. There's a drop-down list on the right of the Email field for Home, Work, or Other so that you can categorize the e-mail address, but you don't have to use it. All other fields are optional and are included for your convenience.

New Contact

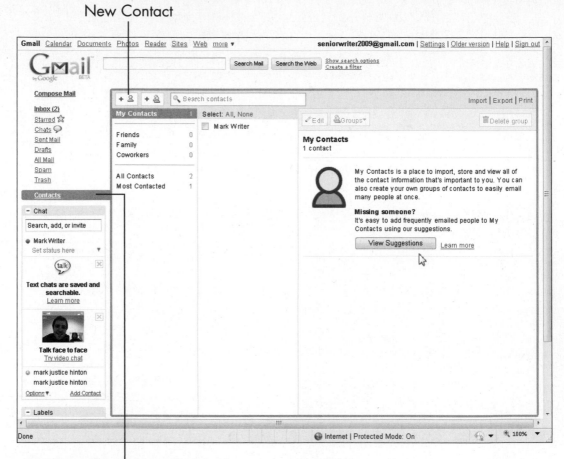

Click Contacts to view and add contacts.

Figure 10-9

4. Click the Save button to save this contact.

5. You can create optional groups in Gmail, if you want to organize contacts. To get you started, Gmail has groups for Friends, Family, and Coworkers. Click the New Group button next to the New Contact button (refer to Figure 10-9). Enter the name of the group, such as **teammates** or **classmates**.

6. To add contacts to any group, select the contact's check box and click the Groups button for a list of groups. One contact can be in as many groups as you want or in no groups.

Fill out the Name and Email fields.

New Contact   Click Save when you're done.

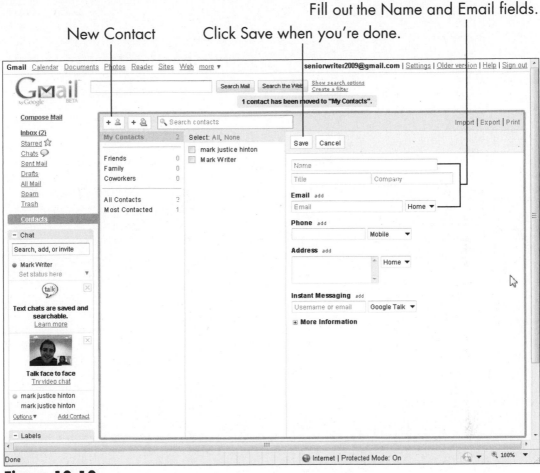

Figure 10-10

 You can send e-mail to everyone in a group. In the Compose Mail form, type the name of the group in the To, Cc, or Bcc fields.

Avoid Spam and Other Junk Messages

When you get e-mail from a source you don't recognize, don't open it. In your Inbox, click the check box next to the e-mail and then do one of the following:

➡ Click the Delete button to move the e-mail into the Trash. Eventually, Gmail *will* delete that e-mail.

➠ Click the Report Spam button for unsolicited junk mail, including advertising and solicitations. By using the Report Spam button, you help Gmail recognize spam automatically for all of its customers, not just for you. The spam you report or Gmail recognizes goes into your Spam folder.

 If someone sends you e-mail you never get, that e-mail may be in the Trash or Spam folder. You can check these folders, although you have no obligation to do so. Open e-mail in the Trash or Spam folder only if you're sure it's legitimate.

Avoid junk e-mail in the first place. Keep these practices in mind:

➠ Don't give Web sites, businesses, or groups your real e-mail address if you don't have to.

➠ On forms that require an e-mail address, look for options to opt-out of receiving e-mail.

➠ Don't respond to unsolicited e-mail. Don't even open it, because that may be all the sender needs in order to know the address works.

➠ Don't click on links in e-mail unless you're 100 percent confident about the person who sent the e-mail. Links may look like they take you to a legitimate site but, in fact, switch you to a fake site.

Part IV
Having Fun with Windows 7

The 5th Wave   By Rich Tennant

FANTASY CHESS

"See here, Tepperman. Playing chess online doesn't mean you can draft IBM's Deep Blue supercomputer as a midseason replacement!"

Playing Games

*I*f you're like me, everything you do on the computer is a game — for me at times, a frustrating game I can't seem to win. But you may find that you enjoy the diversion of playing the real games included in Windows 7. Windows 7 groups games under the Game Explorer on the Start menu.

Most of the games included with Windows 7 are based on widely familiar, traditional games. These fall into three categories:

⟹ **The card games:** FreeCell, Hearts, Solitaire, and Spider Solitaire.

⟹ **The board games:** Chess Titans, Mahjong Titans, and Minesweeper.

⟹ **The Internet games:** Backgammon, Checkers, and Spades. These are board or card games you play online against opponents around the globe. Internet games require an Internet connection. See Chapter 8 about connecting to the Internet.

With a little searching, you can find other games to play online or to install on your computer. Along with tradition-based games, such as those in this chapter, all manner of new games exist to place you in a virtual world. Have fun, but don't forget to come back to this world for a break.

Get ready to . . .

Each game in this chapter has a Help option in the top menu. Unfortunately, the help information tells about options in each game program and doesn't include help with rules, play, or strategy. Start with a game you already know how to play.

Use the Games Explorer

1. To play the games included with Windows 7, choose Start⇨Games to open the Games Explorer. The first time you do this, the Set Up Games dialog box appears. Click the option labeled Yes, Use Recommended Settings. The Games Explorer appears (see **Figure 11-1**).

 In the Preview pane on the right of the Games Explorer, you may see a note indicating that this computer's performance information has not been created. Although you can click the link to Rate This Computer to begin that process, I suggest that you ignore this option for now. The performance information — also called the Windows Experience Index — helps Windows 7 determine whether you can play certain games, but it isn't crucial at this time.

2. Click a game to find out more about it. The Details pane at the bottom of the Games Explorer displays some information about the selected game, including the date and time you last played the game (if ever). The Preview pane to the right displays tabs for the game, including rating, performance requirements, and statistics, if any.

 As with Windows Explorer, you can hide or display the Preview pane by clicking the button near the far-right side of the Command bar. You can also change the look of the icons for the games with the View button just left of the Preview pane button.

When you start a game, you may receive a warning about slow game performance. Don't be alarmed. Click OK to start the game.

Click to hide the Preview pane.

Preview pane

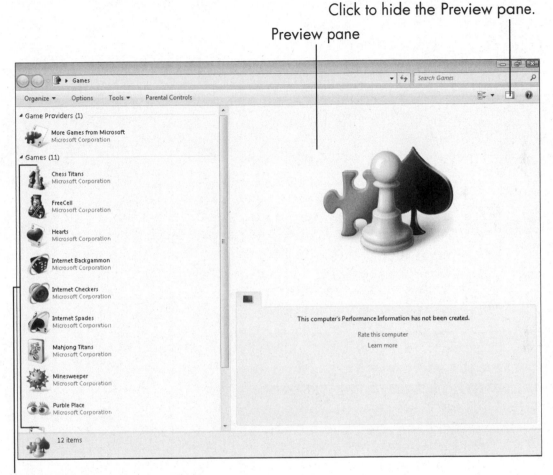

Double-click a game to play.

Figure 11-1

Play Solitaire

1. In the Games Explorer window, double-click Solitaire. The Solitaire window opens, as shown in **Figure 11-2**. For the record, the gist of solitaire is to drag cards into stacks of alternating red and black, placing lower-value cards on higher-value cards sequentially — for example, by dragging the eight of spades onto the nine of diamonds.

Click to turn over a card.

Click and drag to stack cards.

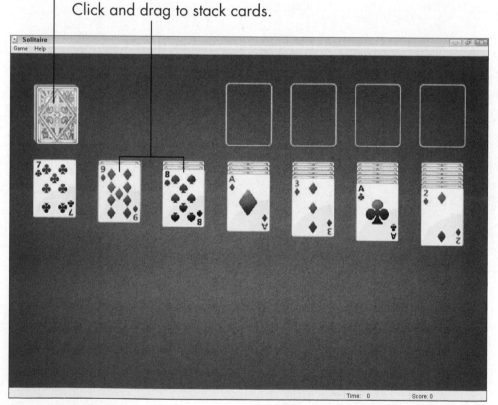

Figure 11-2

2. You can place a king in an empty column. Click face-
down cards in the stacked columns to turn them over;
click the face-down card pile in the upper-left corner to
access cards in the deck. Double-click cards to send them
to the top-right row (the *home row*), beginning with aces,
then two, three, and so on. Proceed through the game
until all cards are stacked by suit in the home row or
you're unable to move remaining cards.

3. Click Game. The menu allows you to start a new game,
undo a move (you can also press Ctrl+Z to undo), and
get a hint (during play, press the letter H). Choose
Options to open the Options dialog box, shown in
Figure 11-3, where you can change how cards are drawn
(draw one card from the deck or three) or scored (no
scoring, standard, or Vegas scoring). Click OK after setting your options.

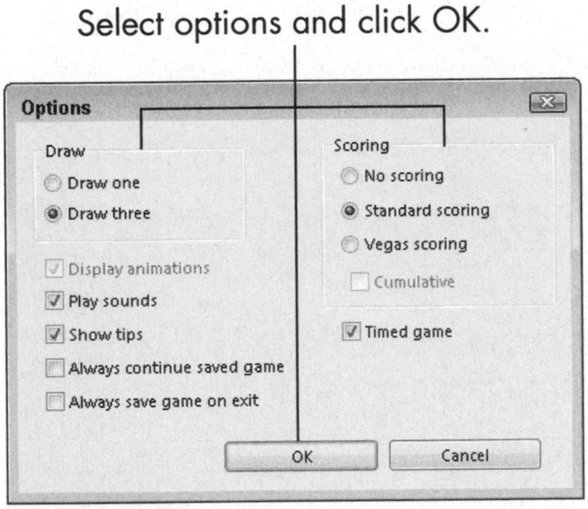

Select options and click OK.

Figure 11-3

4. Choose Game⇨Change Appearance to select a different
style of cards or background. In the Change Appearance
window, select a style for your deck and background, and
then click OK.

5. If you close the Solitaire window before completing the game, click Save if you want to resume the game next time. Click Don't Save if you want a new game next time.

Show Your Grandkids Purble Place

1. Purble Place (see **Figure 11-4**) is designed for young children. In the Games Explorer window, double-click Purble Place to start the game. There are three games within Purble Place:

- **Purble Pairs:** Click two tiles to reveal pictures. If two pictures match, you have a pair. You have to remember which pictures you've already seen to find matches. A gold symbol marks special tiles, including a joker for a free match or a bonus tile. At the end of the game, your final score appears. Click Play Again, Main Menu, or Exit.

- **Comfy Cakes:** Match an order for a cake by choosing pan, batter, frosting, and decoration. Move the cake down the assembly line with the right arrow.

- **Purble Shop:** Click to add eyes, nose, and mouth to a figure.

2. When you choose one of the games, the Select Difficulty dialog box appears. Choose from Beginner, Intermediate, or Advanced.

3. At any time, choose Game⇨New Game to start over. Choose Game⇨Main Menu if you want to switch from one of the three types of games to another.

4. Click the big red X in the lower-left corner to exit the main menu or the usual X in the upper-right corner of any window. You can exit Purble Place anytime. Your game is automatically remembered for the next time.

Click here for Purble Pairs...

...here for Comfy Cakes...

...and here for Purble Shop.

Figure 11-4

Play Internet Backgammon

1. In the Games Explorer Window, double-click Internet Backgammon. A dialog box informs you that you'll be matched with players online. Click Play. A dialog box displays Looking for Other Players and then Starting Game. The game board appears, as shown in **Figure 11-5**. The computer assigns you the white or brown pieces (the message at the bottom of the board tells which color you are playing). White gets to click Roll first.

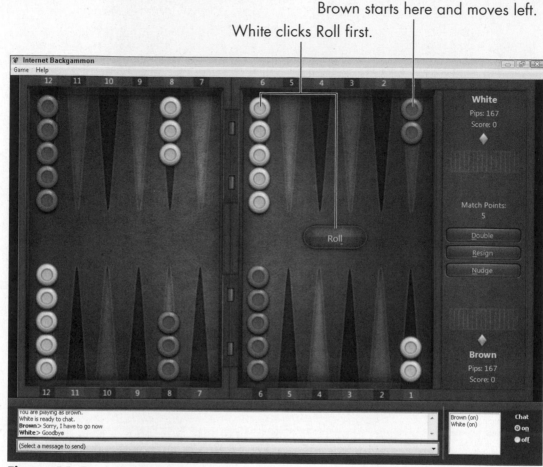

White clicks Roll first.

Brown starts here and moves left.

Figure 11-5

2. Internet games include options for chat or instant messaging. Internet Backgammon doesn't allow free-form chat. Instead, you can select from a list of available messages by clicking Select a Message to Send. Select Off (under Chat) if you don't want to exchange messages with your opponent.

3. Your goal is to move all your markers from your end of the board around to the other end in a sideways U. When you click Roll, use the numbers on the dice to determine how far you can move one (combined dice) or two of your pieces (one die per piece).

4. You can't land where your opponent has two or more markers. If one player lands on another player's single marker, that single marker goes in the middle, and the player whose marker is in the middle must roll to move the marker back to his starting area at one end of the board. For example, if white lands on a brown marker, the brown marker moves to the middle, and the brown player must roll to move the marker back to his starting area. You cannot move your other pieces until you move your pieces that are in the middle back onto the board. Roll, move, and chat.

5. If you don't want to continue play, click the Resign button in the right pane. The loss counts against your statistics.

 You start play as a beginner. Choose Game⇨Skill Level to select Intermediate or Expert from the submenu. The next time you start a game, you will be matched with an opponent with a matching skill level.

Get More Games from Microsoft and Others

If you like computer games, you're not alone. Use any of these methods to find more games:

➠ In the Games Explorer window, click More Games from Microsoft (refer to Figure 11-1). In the Preview pane, click any of the links under Microsoft games. These links start Internet Explorer and display different Web pages at zone.msn.com, the Microsoft online game Web site. You can find free and paid games to play online or download to your computer.

➠ Your computer's manufacturer may have placed other links under Games or Game Providers. Use those links to look for more games.

⇒ Facebook has games you can play against friends or strangers. From your Facebook page (if you have one), choose Applications➪Browse More Applications➪ Games (see **Figure 11-6**). Click an application, such as Scrabble. On that application's page, click the Go to Application button. Finally, if you want to play the game, click the Allow button to allow the game access to your profile. (Some people have concerns about giving applications access to the information in their profiles, but millions of Facebook users do it.)

Click here and then click a game to play.

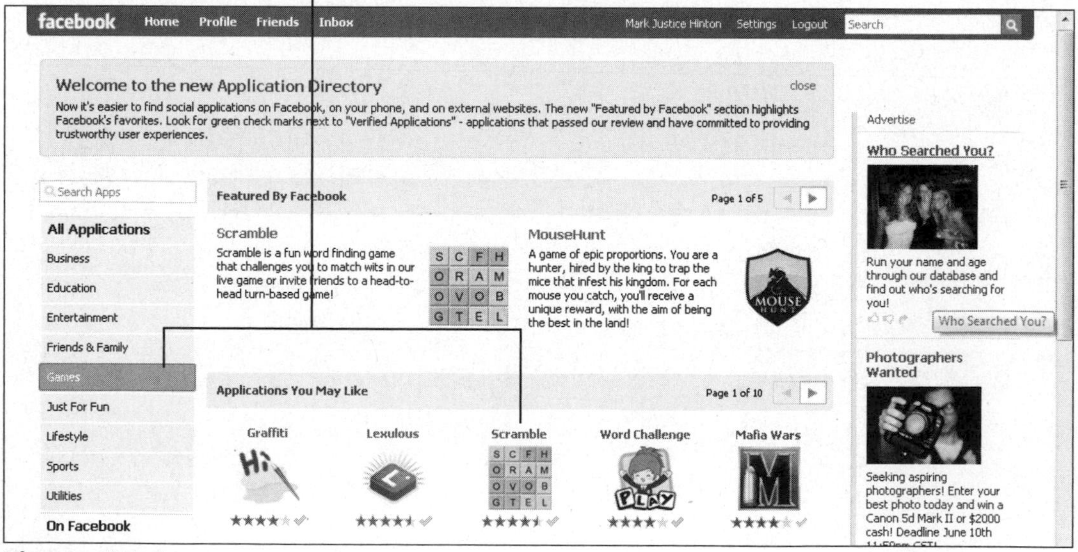

Figure 11-6

⇒ Use a search engine, such as www.google.com, to search for games.

 My Scrabble-expert wife recommends the Internet Scrabble Club (www.isc.ro) for an internationally popular online version of the game.

Enjoying Photos in Windows 7

*W*indows 7 makes enjoying digital photos easy. You can pick and choose photos to look at or display a group of photos in a slide show. Make a favorite photo your desktop background so you see it every time you start Windows 7. In this chapter, you do all these things using the photos Windows 7 includes as samples.

The Paint accessory enables you to resize a photo for e-mail or inclusion in a document. Use Paint to crop a photo to remove unwanted parts of the photo and draw attention to the subject.

If you have a printer, you can print photos for yourself or to send to someone. Even black-and-white prints of color photos may be nice.

Of course, if you want to take your own photos, nothing beats having a digital camera. Connect your camera to your computer to copy photos to the Pictures library for viewing and printing.

Get ready to . . .

In this chapter, you use the tools built into Windows 7 for working with photos. You may want the additional features of a digital photo organizer and editing program. See my other book, *Digital Photography For Seniors For Dummies* (Wiley Publishing, Inc.). That book has detailed steps on organizing, editing, printing, and sharing photos, as well as on using a digital camera.

View Photos in Windows 7

1. Choose Start⇨Pictures. This opens the Pictures library, which contains photos you copy from a digital camera and the Sample Pictures folder, included with Windows 7. (**Figure 12-1** shows the Pictures library.)

Double-click Sample Pictures.

Figure 12-1

2. Double-click Sample Pictures to see the pictures Microsoft includes with Windows 7, shown in **Figure 12-2**. Click the triangle next to the Views button on the Command Bar and choose Extra Large Icons for the largest thumbnails of these photos.

Click the triangle next to View and select Extra Large Icons.

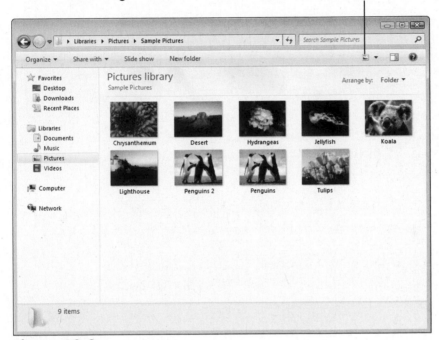

Figure 12-2

3. Double-click the first photo to preview it. The photo opens in one of these programs:

  • **Windows Photo Viewer** is the standard viewer for Windows 7. See **Figure 12-3**.

- **Windows Live Photo Gallery** is a free photo program from Microsoft. You can download Windows Live Photo Gallery from `http://download.live.com/photogallery`.

- **Picasa** is a free photo program from Google. You can download Picasa from `http://picasa.google.com`.

- **Another program** installed by the company that sold your computer, by the person who set it up, or by your digital camera.

 If the photo didn't open in Windows Photo Viewer, close the program that opened. In the Sample Pictures library, click a photo. Click the triangle to the right of Preview and choose Windows Photo Viewer.

4. In Windows Photo Viewer, these tools appear across the bottom of the window from left to right (see Figure 12-3):

- **Change the display size (Zoom):** Click the magnifying glass for a pop-up slider to zoom in and out of the photo.

- **Actual Size** and **Fit to Window:** These two tools alternate in the second position of the toolbar. Most photos are larger than computer screens. Actual Size shows the true size of the photo, but you can't see all of it at once. You can click and drag the photo to move it. This is called *panning* the photo. Use Actual Size to see details in a photo. Fit to Window allows you to see the entire photo at once.

- **Previous:** Click this tool to see the photo before the current one, depending on how the photos are sorted. You can also press the left-arrow key to see the previous photo.

- **Play Slide Show:** This button displays each photo in the folder at full screen for a few seconds before moving on to the next. See the task "See Photos in a Slideshow."

- **Next:** Click this tool to see the photo after the current one, depending on how the photos are sorted. Alternatively, press the right-arrow key to see the next photo.

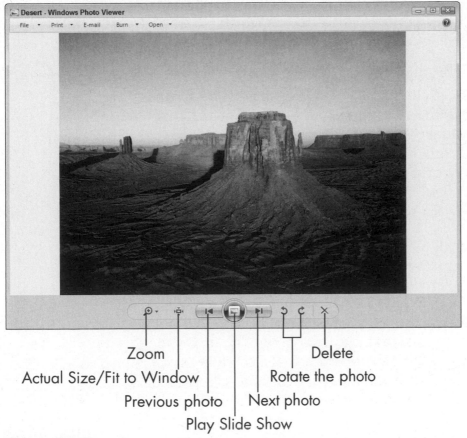

Zoom

Actual Size/Fit to Window

Previous photo

Play Slide Show

Next photo

Rotate the photo

Delete

Figure 12-3

- **Rotate Counterclockwise:** Each click of this button turns the photo 90 degrees to the left. Use this to fix photos that are turned sideways. See "Copy Photos from Your Digital Camera to Your Computer."

- **Rotate Clockwise:** Each click of this button turns the photo 90 degrees to the right. Use this button to fix photos that are turned sideways. See "Copy Photos from Your Digital Camera to Your Computer."

- **Delete:** Stop! Later, click this button to delete the current photo. However, you don't have many sample photos to work with, so don't test this button yet.

 A warning, really: The two Rotate buttons and the Delete button actually change the photo — the other tools don't make changes. These changes are saved automatically. It's easy to fix a Rotate problem by clicking the button repeatedly to get back to the original look. Delete is a little harder to undo. If you delete a photo and want it back, turn to Chapter 4 for the section on getting back a file you deleted.

5. Click Next to see each of the sample photos in Windows Photo Viewer. Close Windows Photo Viewer.

See Photos in a Slideshow

1. In the Sample Picture folder, click the Slide Show button on the Command Bar. A full-screen slideshow of all the photos in the Sample Pictures folder begins.

You can start a slide show from Windows Photo Viewer by clicking the Slide Show button or pressing F11. (Think *Fu11*.)

2. During a slideshow, each picture appears briefly before changing to the next picture. The slideshow repeats *(loops)* indefinitely.

3. During the slideshow, press the left arrow to see the previous photo and the right arrow for the next photo.

4. To pause the slideshow, press the spacebar once. Press the spacebar again to resume the slideshow.

5. During the slideshow, click the right mouse button for a context menu. The display of this menu depends on your computer. The menu you see may not exactly match **Figure 12-4**, but similar options appear on all menus:

   • **Play, Pause, Next, Back** (Previous) work as described with the keystrokes mentioned in Steps 3 and 4.

   • Click **Shuffle** to mix the order in which the photos appear. Initially, photos appear in the order they appear in the folder.

   • Click **Loop** to turn off the endless repeating of the slide show.

   • Vary the speed — the time each photo remains on screen — from among **Slow**, **Medium**, and **Fast**.

   • Click **Exit** to close the slideshow. You can also press Esc.

Selected options

Figure 12-4

 Your computer can automatically start a slideshow when you aren't using it. See Chapter 14 for information on setting up a screen saver.

Display a Photo on Your Desktop

1. In the Sample Pictures folder, click a photo to select it.

2. Click the right mouse button over that photo to open the context menu and choose Set as Desktop Background (see **Figure 12-5**).

Click here to make the photo appear on your desktop.

Figure 12-5

3. Click the Show Desktop button to the right of the time in the taskbar (or press +D). The photo appears as your desktop background, as shown in **Figure 12-6**.

4. Click the Show Desktop button again to see the Sample Pictures folder. These steps work with any picture or photo.

Figure 12-6

Edit Photos Using Paint

1. You can use the Paint accessory to make changes to a photo, including making a picture smaller. In the Pictures library, click a photo to select it. Click the triangle next to Preview and choose Paint from the menu. The selected photo opens in Paint, as shown in **Figure 12-7**.

 In Windows Photo Viewer, choose Open⇨Paint to open the photo you're previewing.

File menu button

Image panel

Figure 12-7

2. Before you make any changes to this photo, consider saving a copy so you have the original and the changed version. You may not need to do this for every photo, but this gives you some insurance against edits you can't fix. Click the File menu button to the left of Home. Click Save As. You can ignore the menu of file types that pops out to the side when you hover over Save As, unless you know you want a particular file type. The Save As dialog box opens (see **Figure 12-8**).

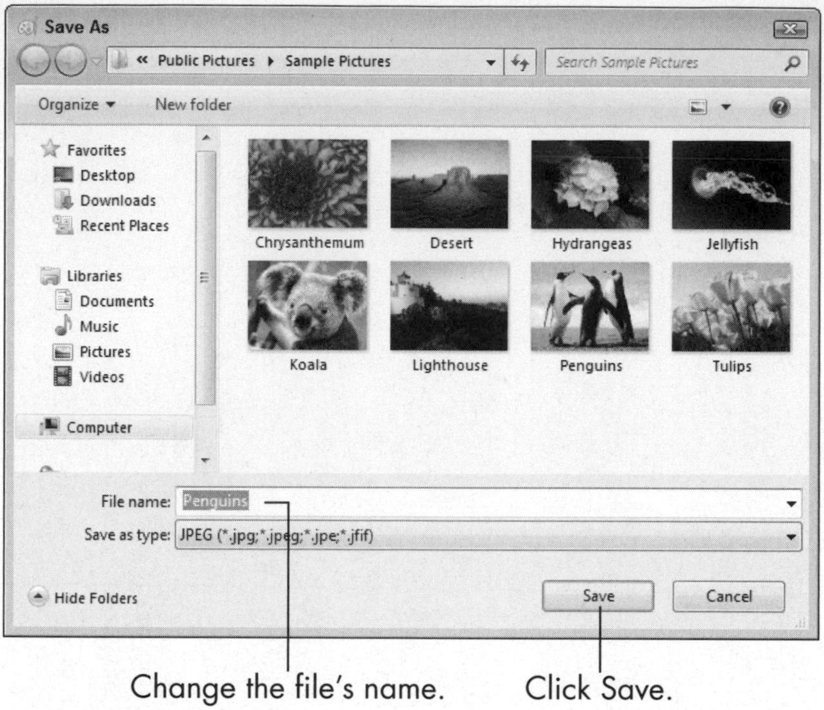

Change the file's name.   Click Save.

Figure 12-8

3. Change the name in the File Name field to create a new copy of this picture. Click Save. You're now editing the new copy, so the original file still exists under the original name and will remain unaltered.

4. Click Resize in the Image panel. In the Resize and Skew dialog box (see **Figure 12-9**), enter a percentage less than 100 (without the percent sign) in the Horizontal field. The value in the Vertical field changes automatically to the same number that you type. You're shrinking the width and height of the photo to this size. You can resize photos before inserting them into documents, such as in WordPad, or before attaching photos to e-mail. Click OK. The photo has been resized.

Enter less than 100 to make the photo smaller.

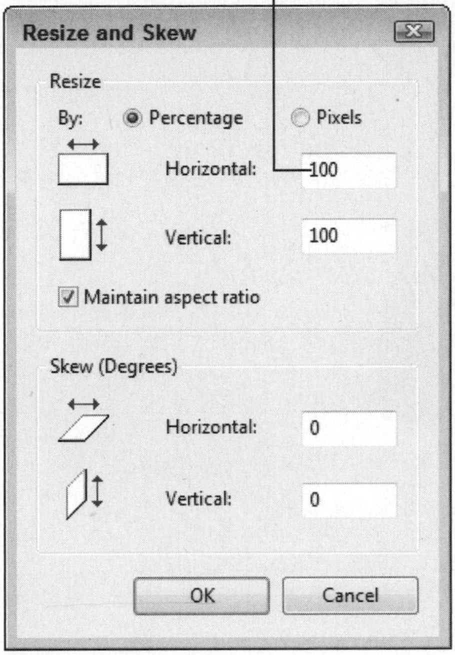

Resize and Skew

Resize

By: ⦿ Percentage   ○ Pixels

↔
☐   Horizontal: 100

↕
☐   Vertical: 100

☑ Maintain aspect ratio

Skew (Degrees)

↔
▱   Horizontal: 0

↕
▱   Vertical: 0

OK   Cancel

Figure 12-9

 You can undo each step by clicking the Undo button above the Home tab (or by pressing Ctrl+Z).

5. Many photos can be improved by cutting out distracting elements and keeping just part of the photo. This is called *cropping*. Crop photos to concentrate on the most important part of the photo. To crop, click Select in the Image panel above the photo. In the photo, click and drag a box over the area you want to keep — everything outside this box will be deleted. Click Crop. The selected area is all that remains, as shown in **Figure 12-10**.

6. If you want to save the changed photo, click the Save button. Close Paint.

See Chapter 5 for information on Paint's drawing and text tools, which you can use on photos.

Figure 12-10

Print Your Photos

1. In the Sample Pictures folder, click a photo to select it. Click the Print button on the Command Bar. The Print Pictures dialog box appears (see **Figure 12-11**).

 To print more than one photo at once, before you click Print, select additional photos by holding down the Ctrl key as you click on each photo.

2. You can simply click the Print button for prints of your photos filling one full-size page each. However, you can also use the options along the right side of the dialog box to specify the size of each print. The number of prints that can fit on one page appears in parentheses next to each size. (Your choice here doesn't change the photo files.) Select from these sizes:

- **Full Page Photo:** This option prints one photo per page. The photo fills most of the page.

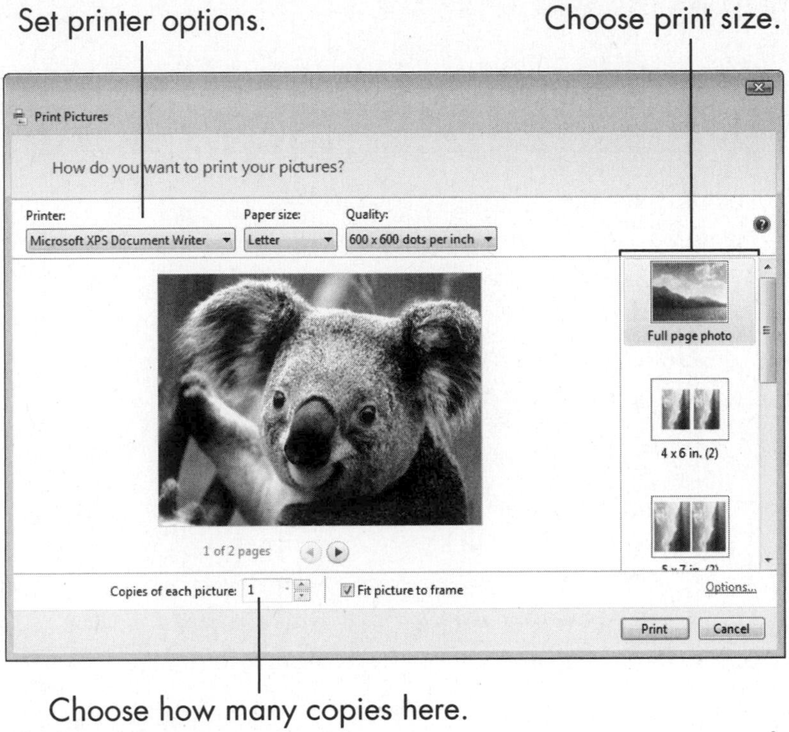

Set printer options.

Choose print size.

Choose how many copies here.

Figure 12-11

- **4 x 6 in. (2):** Use this to print two photos per page (if you select more than one photo or more than one copy). This is a standard print size for photos.

- **5 x 7 in. (2):** Prints two photos per page (if you select more than one photo or more than one copy). These prints are larger than those from the 4 x 6 in. option.

- **8 x 10 in. (1):** This option is the same as Full Page Photo, unless you've changed paper size in the printer options. (See Step 5 for more on this.)

- **3.5 x 5 in. (4):** This option prints four smaller photos per page (if you select more than one photo or more than one copy).

- **Wallet (9):** Use this option to print up to nine small photos per page (if you select more than one photo or more than one copy). Each print is 3 x 2¼ inches.

- **Contact Sheet (35):** Use this option to print up to 35 very small photos per page (if you select more than one photo or more than one copy). Each print is 1½ x 1 inches. The filename of each photo appears below the photo. This is a quick way to evaluate the print-worthiness of a large number of photos at once.

3. If you want more than one copy of each photo, enter a number or click the up and down arrows on the box beside the Copies of Each Picture option at the bottom of the dialog box. If you select more than one photo in Step 1, you print this number of copies of each photo. Two copies of three photos equal six prints, of course. That requires six sheets of paper for full-size prints but only one for wallet-size — with space for three more prints. Check page count under the preview to see how many pages this printing requires.

 If you intend to print on specialty paper, such as preprinted stationery or photo paper, print a test on regular paper, first. That way, you don't waste special paper as you get the options set the way you want them.

4. Deselect and re-select the Fit Picture to Frame option, watching how that changes the print preview. If selected, this option expands the shorter of width or height of the photo to fill the available space and eliminate any white space around the photo. As a result, the longer of width or height may extend beyond the edges of the print frame, and if so, will be cut off when printed. When you

deselected this option, the entire photo fits within the available space, but you may have blank space above and below or to both sides of the photo. (This space is shown as off-white around the photo in the dialog box.)

5. You may not need to change any of the printer options that appear across the top of the dialog box. These options are available:

   • **Printer:** Your current default printer (possibly your only printer) is listed automatically. If you have another printer, you can choose it here.

   • **Paper size:** Letter size is a standard 8½ x 11 inch piece of paper. If you're printing on other sizes, you may need to choose a different paper size from this list.

   • **Quality:** For the best prints, use the highest available quality (marked HQ in the drop-down menu). The numbers here refer to dots per inch — more dots make smoother images. You may be able to switch to a lower quality for drafts and quick prints.

6. When you're ready to print, click the Print button. The dialog box indicates a wait. Your prints should come out of the printer soon after. The more photos you select to print at once and the more copies you specify, the longer this step takes, as the Photo Viewer formats each print. If nothing prints a few minutes after the dialog box disappears, check to make sure that the printer is on and its cable is connected. See Chapter 7 for information on setting up and troubleshooting your printer.

 You can order high-quality prints at low cost from an online photo service or by taking photos to a local printing service. For specific steps, see my other book, *Digital Photography For Seniors For Dummies*.

Copy Photos from Your Digital Camera to Your Computer

1. Copying photos from your camera to your computer — also called *downloading* or *importing* — begins with one of two methods:

- Connect a cable from the camera to a USB port on the computer. Turn on the camera. Look for a menu on the camera's LCD screen. Choose the option to connect to or copy to a PC.

- Remove the memory card from your camera and insert it into a matching slot in the computer or separate card reader. Many laptops accept several different kinds of memory cards.

 The first time you connect your camera to your computer or insert the memory card, you may see a pop-up tip indicating that a *driver* is being installed to allow Windows 7 to access the device.

2. The AutoPlay dialog box appears the first time you copy photos (see **Figure 12-12**). Select the Always Do This for Pictures check box. Then click the Import Pictures and Videos Using Windows button unless you see a different program under AutoPlay you intend to use for pictures.

3. The first Import Pictures and Videos dialog box appears briefly as Windows 7 searches the device for photos. The more photos on the device, the longer this box displays, but the dialog box is replaced automatically by the next one.

Check this option.

Click to import your photos.

Figure 12-12

4. The next dialog box appears with a thumbnail of the first picture found, as shown on the left in **Figure 12-13**. Use the Tag These Pictures field to add *tags*, which are labels or categories, to all of the photos you import at this time. If all the photos have something in common — for example, all are from a vacation or celebration — enter a tag such as **vacation**, **graduation**, or **birthday**. You can separate multiple tags with semicolons: **vacation; New Mexico**, for example. Later, you can use tags to search for photos and group photos by tag instead of by location or date taken. If these photos have nothing in common, don't enter a tag. Click the Import button to continue.

Add an optional tag here.   See thumbnail here.

Click to import photos.   Click to erase after importing.

Figure 12-13

5. A thumbnail of each photo appears briefly as photos are copied, as on the right in Figure 12-13. If you have time, select the Erase After Importing check box. If Erase After Importing is checked, Windows 7 verifies each photo was copied successfully and then deletes those photos from your camera's memory card. Otherwise, you have to manually erase photos from your camera as a separate step using your camera's controls.

6. After the importing process completes, Windows 7 opens the Imported Pictures and Videos window to display your recently imported photos (see **Figure 12-14**). Double-click one of your newly copied photos to preview it.

7. Preview each photo you copied using Windows Photo Viewer (refer to Figure 12-3). If you want to delete a photo, click the red X in the toolbar. If a photo isn't upright, click one of the two Rotate buttons to reorient that photo. Use the Next button (right arrow) to step through all of the photos you just copied. When you're done, close Windows Photo Viewer.

Imported photos

Figure 12-14

Control How Windows 7 Names and Organizes Photos

1. Your photos are automatically copied into the My Pictures folder in the Pictures library. Each time you import pictures, Windows 7 creates a new folder under My Pictures and names the folder and pictures according to the Import Settings. You don't have to change these settings, but you may want to.

2. To access these settings, begin the steps to copy photos from your camera, as explained in the preceeding task. When you see the Import Pictures and Videos dialog box, click Import Settings (refer to Figure 12-13). This opens

the Import Settings dialog box, which offers you many
options, including where you import your files, how you
name the folders and files, whether you automatically
rotate pictures, and so on.

 Feel free to change your picture and video import settings to your heart's content. You can always restore
the original import settings by clicking Restore
Defaults. This button puts all options back the way
they were when you installed the program.

Listening to Music and Watching DVDs

Chapter 13

Windows Media Player plays media, as you would guess from the name. The term *media* on computers refers to something other than text: Audio and video are examples of media. *Audio* is a catchall term for music and other sound files, such as books on CD.

The delivery of music has come a long way from Edison's wax cylinder or even vinyl LPs. Nowadays, music is often entirely digital. Use Media Player to play the sample music included with Windows 7. If you have an audio CD handy, you can play it on your computer using Media Player. To make playing that CD even more convenient, you can copy the audio files to your computer.

With a library of music copied from your CD collection, you can create your own CDs, combining *tracks* (songs) at your whim. You can also copy your audio to an MP3 player.

When you're ready for a break from all the music, pop a DVD into your computer and enjoy the show. In this chapter, you do all of these things using Windows Media Player.

Play Music with Windows Media Player

1. To start Windows Media Player, click its icon (a white triangle on an orange circle on a blue square) in the taskbar. The first time you start Media Player, the initial settings screen appears, as shown in **Figure 13-1**. Click Recommended Settings and Finish.

Select Recommended Settings.

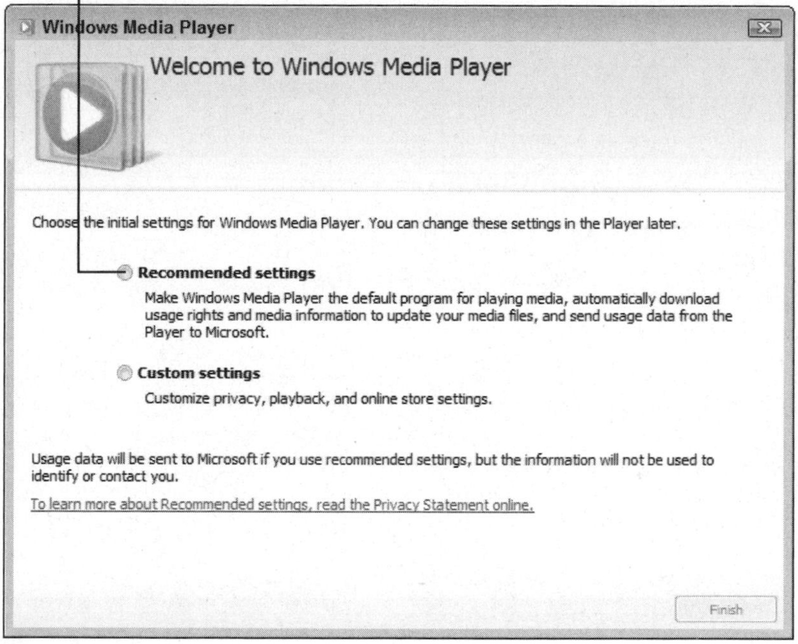

Figure 13-1

2. After a brief delay, the Media Player Library displays music that comes with Windows 7, shown in **Figure 13-2**, and any music already copied to your computer. The toolbar at the bottom of Media Player's window provides the following controls:

- **Shuffle:** Click this button to turn on *shuffle*, which randomly mixes the tracks you play. A second click turns off shuffle, and the tracks play in the order in which they appear onscreen.

- **Loop:** Click this button to turn on *loop* (repeat), which continuously plays all the tracks again after all have played.

- **Stop:** Click to stop a track.

- **Previous:** This button skips to the previous track.

- **Play/Pause:** Click the button with two vertical lines to pause play mid-track. Click the same button (now with a triangle pointing to the right) to resume playing from the point you paused.

- **Next:** This button skips to the next track.

- **Mute/Unmute:** Click this button to silence the player. Although the track continues to play, you won't hear it. When mute is on, a red circle and slash appear next to the speaker icon. Click the button again to hear the track.

- **Volume:** Click or drag the slider to decrease (to the left) or increase (to the right) the volume of the track. Your speakers may also have manual volume control. Windows 7 has a separate volume control in the taskbar, as well.

- **Now Playing:** Located far to the right of the toolbar, click this button to reduce the player to a small size.

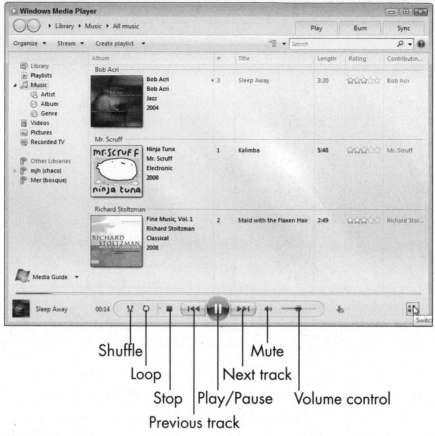

Shuffle
Loop
Stop
Previous track
Play/Pause
Next track
Mute
Volume control

Figure 13-2

3. Using these controls, click Play to play the music. Adjust the volume with the slider. Mute and unmute the music. Pause the music and resume playing. Stop the music. Play any music.

4. Click the Switch to Now Playing button to the right of the toolbar to shrink Media Player to a smaller window, as shown in **Figure 13-3**. To return to the larger window, click the Switch to Library button.

Switch to Library

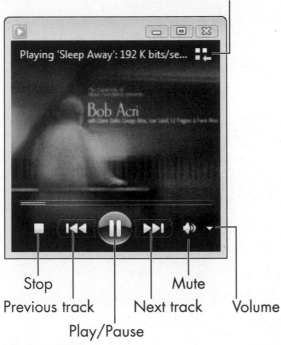

Playing 'Sleep Away': 192 K bits/se...

Bob Acri

Stop

Previous track   Next track   Volume

Mute

Play/Pause

Figure 13-3

 You can buy music online and download the tracks directly to your computer.

Select Music to Play

Initially, Media Player plays all the music in your Music library, which consists of the My Music and the Sample Music folders. There are many ways to select music to play:

➡ Click Music in the Navigation pane on the left to display all music. Click Artist, Album, or Genre to display the music by these categories. With the small collection of music Windows 7 includes for free, the difference in these selections may not be obvious. With a large library of music, you can play everything by one artist, one selected album, or all music in a particular genre. Or, use these categories to find the one album or song you want to hear.

➡ Type the name of an artist, song, album, or genre in the Search box (click in the Search box in the upper-right or press Ctrl+E). Media Player instantly displays matching items, if any. To test this with the sample files, type **jazz** or **tuna** in the Search box. Clear the search results by clicking Music in the Navigation pane.

➡ Choose Start⇨Music to open the Music library in Windows Explorer. Double-click Sample Music. Click the Play All button on the Command Bar (see **Figure 13-4**) or double-click one track to play just that track in Media Player.

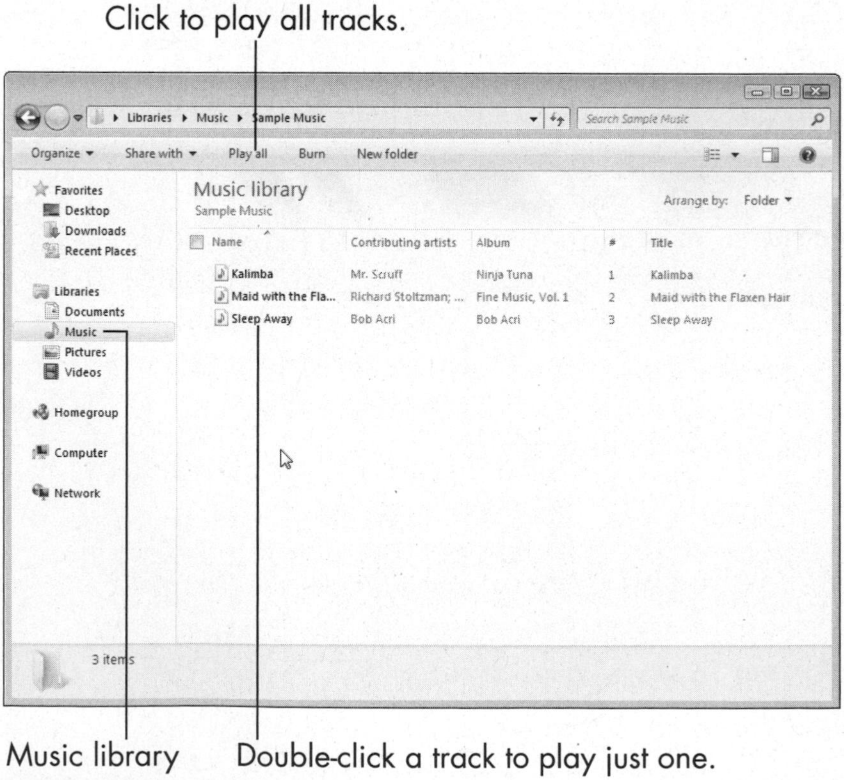

Click to play all tracks.

Music library   Double-click a track to play just one.
Figure 13-4

➡ In the Music library in Windows Explorer, click one track and hold down the Ctrl key as you click another. Keep holding down the Ctrl key as you select all the music you intend to play. Click the Play Selection button on the Command Bar to play just the selected tracks in Media Player.

 When you play music from Windows Explorer, Media Player starts in Now Playing mode (refer to Figure 13-3), which provides a smaller toolbar to stop, play/pause, skip, and mute/unmute. Click the Switch to Library button if you want to see the full-size Media Player (refer to Figure 13-2).

Play a CD on Your Computer

1. Your computer has a disc drive capable of playing CDs. On the front of a desktop computer or tower, look for a narrow door or cover. On a laptop, the CD tray may be on either side or in front. A button on or near the CD door opens the CD tray. Open the tray and position a music CD label-side up in the tray, which may have a spindle the CD snaps onto. With the CD in place, gently push the CD tray. If the tray doesn't close automatically, gently push it completely closed. Do not force the drive closed.

Some computers have a narrow CD-sized slot, instead of a door or tray. Insert a CD into the slot with the label up or facing left.

You hear the disc spin as the computer reads it.

 In case you were wondering, the word *disc*, with a *C*, is the preferred spelling for so-called *optical media*, such as CDs and DVDs, which use lasers. Disk, with a *K*, usually refers to magnetic media, such as hard disks and flash drives.

2. Windows 7 decides what to do based on the content of the disc you inserted. In the case of a music or audio disc, Windows 7 starts Media Player's small Now Playing window. If your computer is connected to the Internet, Media Player displays the name of the track, artist, and album title, as well as the album cover. If you don't have Internet access or the CD is unrecognized, you see Track 1 as the title and a generic music note icon. See Chapter 8 for information on connecting to the Internet.

3. Use the Now Playing toolbar to stop, skip to the previous track, pause or play, skip to the next track, mute/unmute, and adjust volume. (For details, see the earlier task "Play Music with Windows Media Player.")

4. You don't just have to sit there and listen to the CD. You can play a game, browse the Internet, whatever. Media Player plays in the background as you go about your business. Enjoy.

5. If you want the larger window of Media Player, click the Switch to Library button.

6. You can minimize the Now Playing window or the Library window. Hover over the Media Player icon in the taskbar for an even smaller toolbar with Previous, Pause/ Play, and Next, plus a brief pop-up note of the track currently playing.

7. To remove the CD from the computer, press the button on the computer that opens the disc tray or right-click the CD title in Media Player Library and click Eject (see **Figure 13-5**).

Right-click CD title.

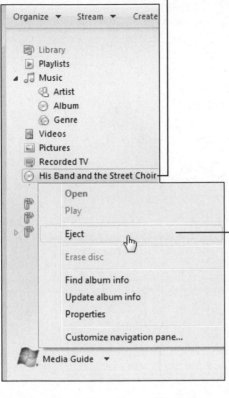

Click Eject.

Figure 13-5

Copy Music from a CD to Your Computer

1. You can copy music from a CD to your computer, both technically and legally (if you own the CD). Doing so allows you to play the music from the CD anytime without needing the disc. Copy all of your music CDs to the computer to create your own 21st century jukebox. (Be sure to refer to this as *ripping a CD* around your younger friends. But not the youngest, because they think CDs are way passé.)

2. Insert the CD you intend to copy. If Now Playing appears, click the Switch to Library button. The Rip CD screen appears automatically (see **Figure 13-6**). If you don't see this screen, click on the CD title in the Navigation bar on the left.

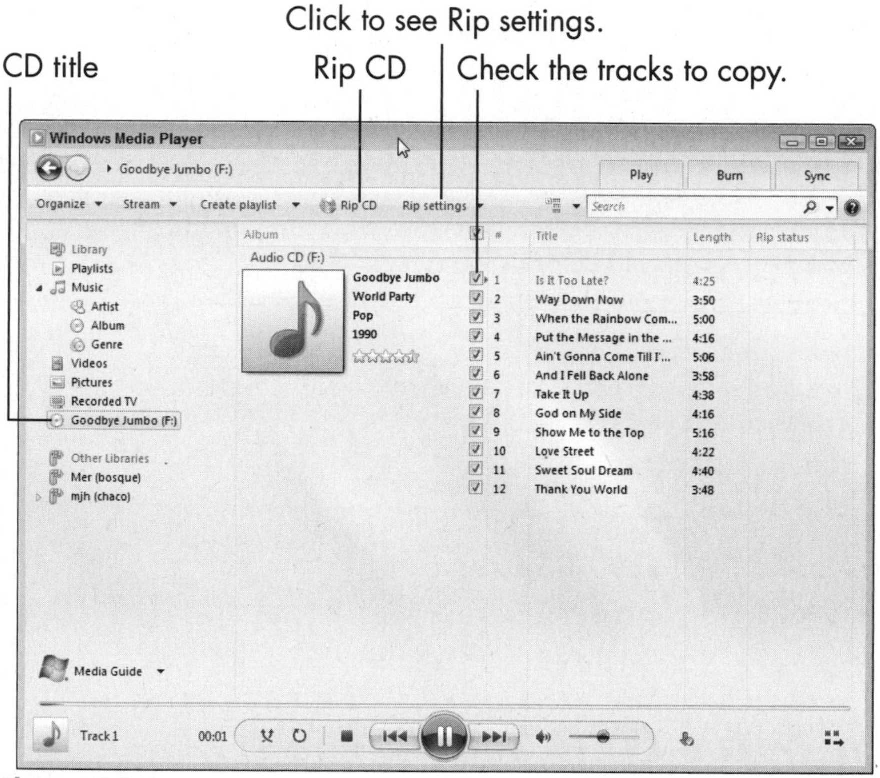

Click to see Rip settings.

CD title   Rip CD   Check the tracks to copy.

Figure 13-6

3. Check marks appear next to every track. Deselect tracks you don't want to copy, if any.

4. Before you start copying your first CD, select a few options under the Rip Settings button on the Command Bar:

- Audio Quality⇨192Kpbs (Best Quality) for the best possible recording quality

- Rip CD Automatically, if you want this process to be automatic for additional CDs

- Eject CD After Ripping, so the CD ejects automatically

This is a one-time step.

 If you have an MP3 player, determine whether it can play Windows Media Audio (WMA) files before you copy from a CD. To find this out, consult the MP3 player manufacturer's Web site or your manual. If the MP3 player can't play WMA or you're not sure it can, choose Rip Settings⇨Format⇨MP3 to create files you can copy to your MP3 player. See "Copy Music to an MP3 Player," later in this chapter.

5. When you're ready, click the Rip CD button on the Command Bar. If you're playing a track when you click the button, that track starts over. You can play the CD as you rip it or you can stop playing. To stop the copying — which you don't have to do — click the Stop Rip button.

6. In the Rip Status column, Media Player displays a `Pending` message next to tracks not yet ripped. A progress bar appears beside each track as that track is copied. `Ripped to Library` appears next to each track that is completed. See **Figure 13-7**.

7. You can finish listening to the disc, if you want. If the disc doesn't automatically eject, push the button on the tray or right-click the CD title in the Navigation bar on the left and click Eject.

Windows Media Player				

◄ ○ ▸ Goodbye Jumbo (F:)   Play   Burn   Sync

Organize ▾   Stream ▾   Create playlist ▾   ○ Stop rip   Rip settings ▾   ▦ ▾   Search   🔍 ▾ ❔

	Album		#	Title	Length	Rip status
	Library	Audio CD (F:)				
▸	Playlists					
▴ ♫	Music	Goodbye Jumbo	☐ 1	Is It Too Late?	4:25	Ripped to library
	Artist	World Party	☐ 2	Way Down Now	3:50	Ripped to library
	Album	Pop	☑ 3	When the Rainbow Com...	5:00	Ripping (20%)
	Genre	1990	☑ 4	Put the Message in the ...	4:16	Pending
	Videos	☆☆☆☆☆	☑ 5	Ain't Gonna Come Till I'...	5:06	Pending
	Pictures		☑ 6	And I Fell Back Alone	3:58	Pending
	Recorded TV		☑ 7	Take It Up	4:38	Pending
	Goodbye Jumbo (F:)		☑ 8	God on My Side	4:16	Pending
			☐ 9	Show Me to the Top	5:16	Ripped to library
	Other Libraries		☐ 10	Love Street	4:22	Ripped to library
	Mer (bosque)		☐ 11	Sweet Soul Dream	4:40	Ripped to library
▸	mjh (chaco)		☐ 12	Thank You World	3:48	Ripped to library

Media Guide ▾

Goodbye Jumbo   01:56   ⚡ ○   ■   ▌◀◀   ⏸   ▶▶▌   🔊 ───○───   ♪   ⏹⏹

Rip status

Figure 13-7

8. To see your newly ripped CD, click Music. The album you just copied appears in the library. (You may have to scroll down to see it.)

Delete tracks from your library by right-clicking and choosing Delete. In the dialog box, select the Delete from Library Only option to keep the music file on your computer or the Delete from Library and My Computer option to remove those tracks completely.

If you have vinyl LPs or 45s, you can digitize them using a USB turntable, though this takes some work. The details are beyond the scope of this book. Options include hardware from www.ionaudio.com and software from audacity.sourceforge.net.

Create a Playlist

1. Without any additional effort, you can play your music library in its entirety, by artist, by album, or by genre. If you want to play a mix of tunes from various CDs, create a *playlist*, a list of tracks to play together. In the Library, click the music category that shows the tracks you want to play.

2. Click the Play tab in the upper-right corner of Media Player to open the Play pane (see **Figure 13-8**).

Click to save your playlist.

Play tab   Playlist

Number of tracks and play time

Figure 13-8

3. To add a track to the playlist, drag and drop that track into the Play pane. Drag tracks up and down to rearrange the list order.

4. To remove a track from the playlist, right-click the unwanted track and choose Remove from List. To start over from scratch, click Clear List.

5. The total number of items (tracks) and total minutes of play appear at the bottom of the Play pane.

6. Click the Save List button to save this playlist for future play. The Unsaved list text above the tracks changes to Untitled playlist (see **Figure 13-9**). Type a name for your playlist and press Enter. The playlist title appears in the Play pane and in the Navigation pane under Playlists.

7. If you change the list by adding, moving, or removing tracks, click the Save List button again to preserve your changes.

8. When you're done creating the playlist, click the Play tab to close the Play pane.

9. To play the tracks on a playlist, double-click the playlist name under Playlists in the Navigation pane. Furthermore, you can right-click a playlist name and choose whether to Play, Rename, or Delete that playlist. Deleting a playlist doesn't delete any tracks.

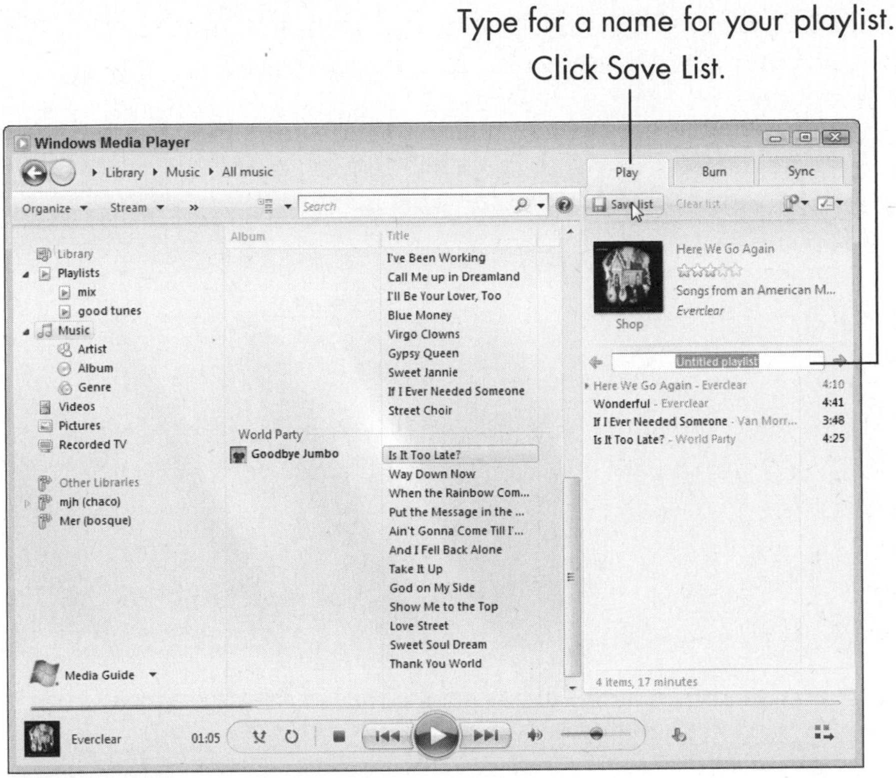

Type for a name for your playlist.
Click Save List.

Figure 13-9

Create Your Own CD

1. Creating your own CD with your favorite tracks is rather like creating the mixed tape of a generation ago. These days, you *burn* a CD, which means that you copy files to the CD. (As if the laser burns the disc, which it doesn't really do.) Click the Burn tab in Media Player to display the pane on the right side of Media Player, in which you can create a list of tracks to burn (your burn list). (See **Figure 13-10**.)

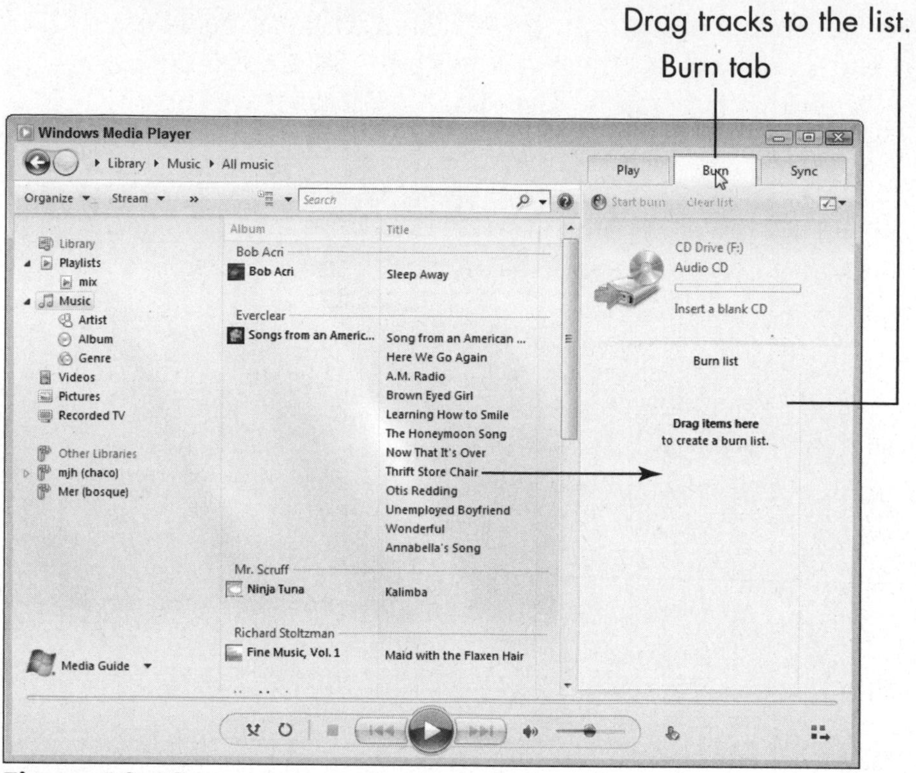

Drag tracks to the list.
Burn tab

Windows Media Player

◄ ► ► Library ► Music ► All music   Play | Burn | Sync

Organize ▼   Stream ▼   »   Search   🔍 ▼ ❓   ● Start burn   Clear list   ☑▼

	Album	Title
🎵 Library	**Bob Acri**	
▲ ▷ Playlists	🎵 Bob Acri	Sleep Away
▷ mix		
▲ 🎵 Music	**Everclear**	
👤 Artist	🎵 Songs from an Americ...	Song from an American ...
💿 Album		Here We Go Again
🎵 Genre		A.M. Radio
🎬 Videos		Brown Eyed Girl
🖼 Pictures		Learning How to Smile
📺 Recorded TV		The Honeymoon Song
		Now That It's Over
🗂 Other Libraries		Thrift Store Chair
▷ 🗂 mjh (chaco)		Otis Redding
🗂 Mer (bosque)		Unemployed Boyfriend
		Wonderful
		Annabella's Song
	Mr. Scruff	
	🎵 Ninja Tuna	Kalimba
	Richard Stoltzman	
🎵 Media Guide ▼	🎵 Fine Music, Vol. 1	Maid with the Flaxen Hair

CD Drive (F:)
Audio CD

Insert a blank CD

Burn list

Drag items here
to create a burn list.

Figure 13-10

2. Insert a blank recordable CD into the CD drive.

 Buy blank CDs at an office supply or electronics store. CD-Rs are good for music.

3. Click a playlist or music category to show the tracks you intend to copy to a CD.

4. Drag and drop a track, an album, or a playlist into the burn list. Drag tracks up and down in the burn list to rearrange them.

5. To remove a track from the burn list, right-click and choose Remove from List. To start over from scratch, click Clear List.

6. The number of minutes in the selected tracks appears in the burn list next to Disc 1 (see **Figure 13-11**). A CD holds about 75 minutes of audio. A bar graph and numbers indicate how many minutes are free of the total available. You don't have to fill a CD, although you may want to.

Click to start burning your CD.

Minutes free on the CD

Figure 13-11

 If you choose more tracks than will fit on one CD, Media Player starts a list for a second disc below the first. If you want to burn only one disc, remove one or more tracks from the list.

7. When you're ready to create a CD, click the Start Burn button on the Command Bar.

8. The burn progress bar appears near the top of the Burn list (see **Figure 13-12**). Let the burn complete before you go on to other tasks. If the disc doesn't automatically eject, push the button on the tray or right-click over the CD title and click Eject. Click the Burn tab to close the Burn pane.

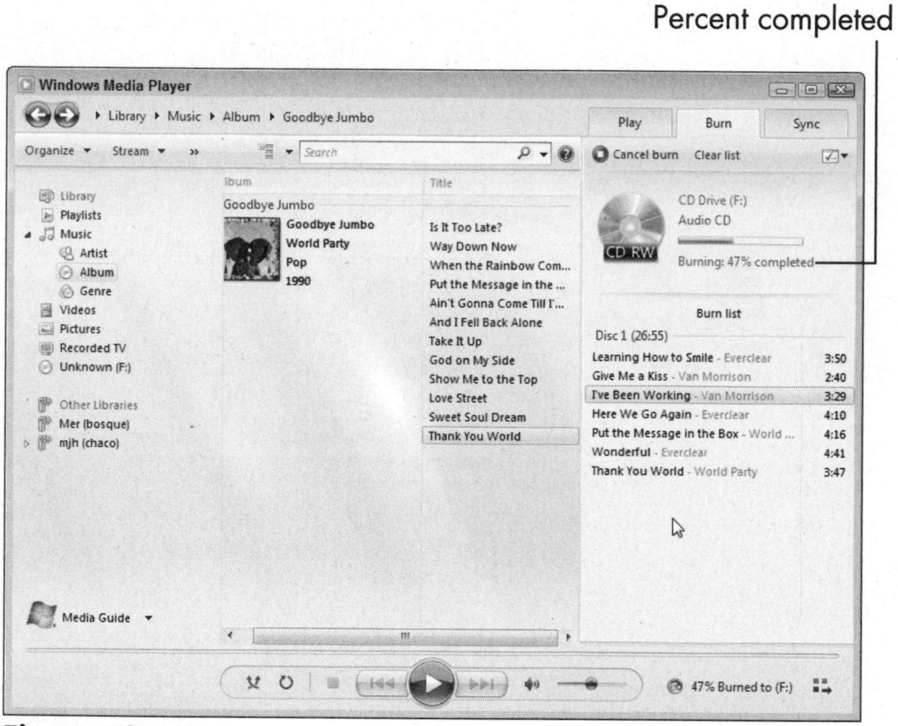

Percent completed

Figure 13-12

Although you can click the Cancel Burn button to stop mid-burn, odds are good that the disc will be unusable if you don't let the burn complete.

Copy Music to an MP3 Player

1. An MP3 is a music file. An *MP3 player* is a portable music player. You can copy tracks from your library to an MP3 player. That process is called *syncing*. In the Media Player Library, click the Sync tab to open the Sync pane on the right, in which you create the list of tracks to sync to your MP3 player (your sync list). (See **Figure 13-13**.)

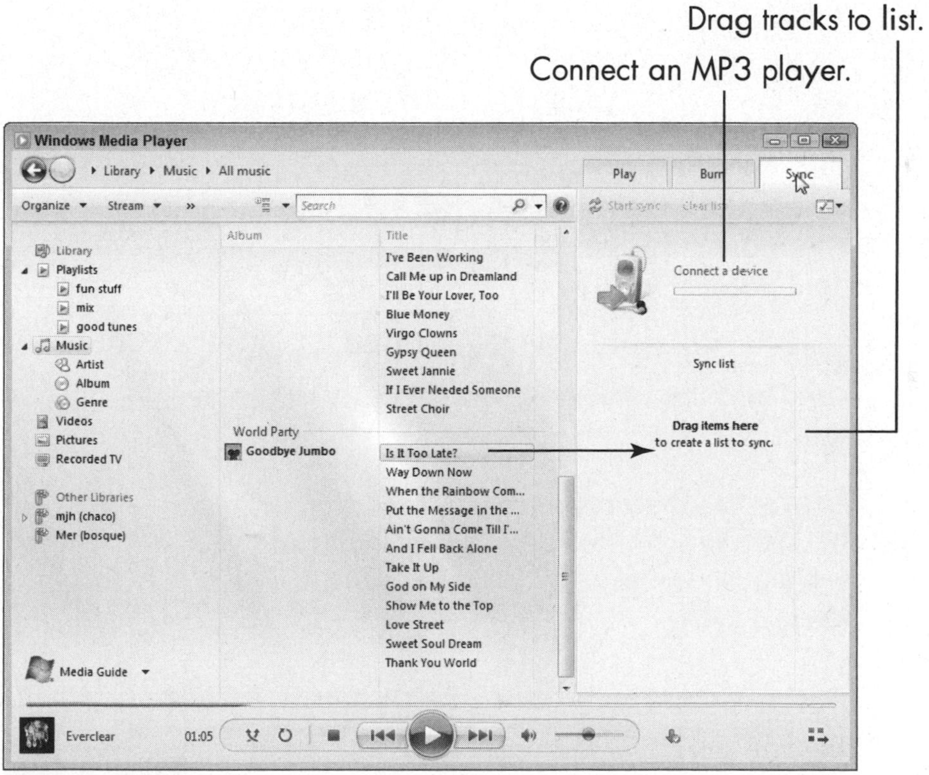

Drag tracks to list.

Connect an MP3 player.

Figure 13-13

2. Connect your MP3 player to your computer by using a cable (usually USB). Some MP3 players connect to a separate dock that's connected to your computer. Some MP3 players connect wirelessly. You may see two brief pop-ups the first time you connect a device as Windows 7 installs a driver for the device. After a few moments, the MP3 player appears at the top of the Sync pane. If the MP3 player already has tracks on it, those tracks are listed in the Sync pane.

3. Add tracks, albums, artists, genres, or playlists by dragging and dropping the items into the Sync pane's sync list. Drag tracks up and down in the sync list to rearrange them.

4. To remove a track from the sync list, right-click it and choose Remove from List. To start over from scratch, click the Clear List button at the top of the Sync pane.

5. A bar graph and numbers indicate the amount of space used and the free space left on your MP3 player (see **Figure 13-14**).

6. When you're ready to copy tracks to the MP3 player, click the Start Sync button. A progress bar and percentage indicate how much of the sync is done. (see **Figure 13-15**).

7. When the sync is done, a `Sync completed` message appears in the Sync pane. You can then disconnect your MP3 player.

Click to sync your MP3 player.   Free space

Figure 13-14

View Pictures in Media Player

Media Player shows more types of media than just music. In the Navigation pane on the left, click Pictures. (You may prefer viewing photos with the functions covered in Chapter 12.)

Using Media Player, you can

➠ Listen to music and look at pictures at the same time.

➠ Create playlists of pictures with or without music.

➠ Burn pictures to CD.

➠ Sync pictures to a media player, an MP3 player that also has a screen for pictures, such as a Microsoft Zune.

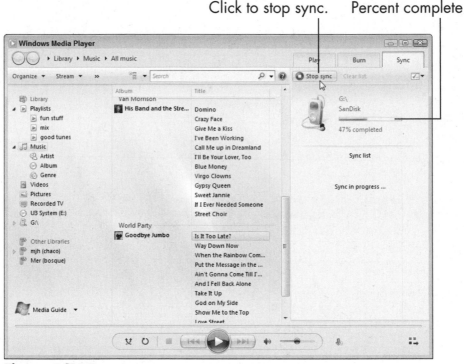

Figure 13-15

Watch a DVD

1. You can play DVDs on your computer. On the front of a desktop computer or tower, look for a narrow door or cover. On a laptop, the DVD tray may be on either side or in front. A button on or near the DVD door opens the DVD tray. Open the tray and position a music DVD label-side up in the tray, which may have a spindle the DVD snaps onto. With the DVD in place, gently push the DVD tray. If the tray doesn't close automatically, gently push it completely closed. Do not force the drive closed.

Some computers have a narrow DVD-sized slot instead of a door or tray. Insert a DVD into the slot with the label up or facing left.

You hear the disc spin as the computer reads it.

 DVD drives play both DVDs and CDs.

2. Windows 7 decides what to do based on the content of a disc. In the case of a movie, Windows 7 starts Media Player full screen. The opening screens of the movie appear automatically.

3. Move the mouse to display the Media Player toolbar at the bottom of the screen. The following buttons — many of which you also see in Figure 13-2 — are available (from left to right):

- **DVD:** This button displays the DVD menu with options to play the DVD or access special features, such as commentary.

- **Stop:** Click the Stop button to stop playing the DVD. A menu appears with options to Play DVD, Go to Library, or Play Previous List, which resumes playing the playlist prior to the DVD.

- **Previous:** This button skips to the previous chapter, as defined by the DVD. Click and hold this button to rewind.

- **Play/Pause:** Click the button with two vertical lines to pause play midstream. Click the same button (now with a triangle pointing to the right) to resume playing from the point you paused.

- **Next:** This button skips to the next chapter. Click and hold this button to fast-forward.

- **Mute/Unmute:** Click this button to silence the player, although the movie continues to play (you won't hear it). When mute is on, a red circle and slash appear next to the speaker icon. Click the button again to hear the movie.

- **Volume:** Click or drag the slider to decrease (to the left) or increase (to the right) the volume of the movie. Your speakers may also have manual volume control.

- **Exit Full-Screen Mode/View Full Screen:** Located far to the right of the toolbar, click this button to switch out of or into full-screen mode (alternatively, press F11). You can watch a DVD in a smaller window.

Move the mouse away from the bottom of the screen. The toolbar disappears.

4. Play the DVD. You deserve a break, don't you think?

5. To remove the DVD from the computer, press the button on the computer that opens the disc tray or click the Go to Library button in the top-right corner, right-click the DVD title in Media Player Library, and click Eject.

Part V

Having It Your Way with Windows 7

The 5th Wave
By Rich Tennant

SEVERAL HOURS PASSED BEFORE WAYNE DISCOVERED THAT HE WAS LOOKING AT HIS SCREEN SAVER AND NOT OUT THE SUBMARINE'S PORTHOLE

"It's incredible! I'm seeing life forms never before imagined!! Bizarre, colorful, almost whimsical!!!"

Making Windows 7 More Fun to Use

Chapter 14

*T*he nesting instinct is strong in human kind. We mark our territories in various ways (for example, with paint and decals). From refrigerator magnets to tattoos, we personalize things to make them our own. Why should Windows 7 be any different? The Personalization window gives you one-stop access to all the functions for changing the look of Windows 7.

➡ You see the Windows 7 desktop every time you start your computer. Put a photo — perhaps one of your own — on the desktop.

➡ Choose a favorite color for window title bars and borders. A different color scheme may be more soothing or easier to see.

➡ Change the sounds Windows 7 makes as you use it. Some of the Windows 7 sounds are nerve-wracking. Choose something more pleasant or eliminate a sound altogether.

➠ Set up a screen saver to display photos as a slideshow while Windows 7 is otherwise idle.

➠ Pick a mouse pointer that's easier to see.

Some people will dismiss personalization as *cosmetic*, ignoring the huge cosmetics industry. Make Windows 7 yours and, in the process, make Windows 7 more fun to use.

In this chapter, begin with a theme, which is a collection of all of these personalization options. You may be content with one of the choices Windows 7 provides. You can change the *look and feel* of Windows 7 as much or as little as you wish.

Personalize Windows 7 with a Theme

1. Right-click on the desktop. Choose Personalize from the shortcut menu. The Personalization window appears (see **Figure 14-1**).

 You return to the Personalization window often in this chapter. In many cases, the window stays open as you make choices. If you need to open this window again, repeat Step 1.

2. Scroll down through the themes displayed in the window. *Themes* are collections of Windows 7 settings, such as desktop background, color, sounds, and more. Explore the themes under these headings:

- **My Themes:** These are themes you customized and saved. If you haven't saved a theme (covered later in the "Save Your Theme" task), you see Unsaved Theme, which is your current setup.

- **Aero Themes:** These slick themes display beautiful photos as a changing desktop background and set transparent colors for windows. The Landscapes and Nature themes are particularly lovely. The Characters theme is whimsical.

Themes   Scroll for more themes.

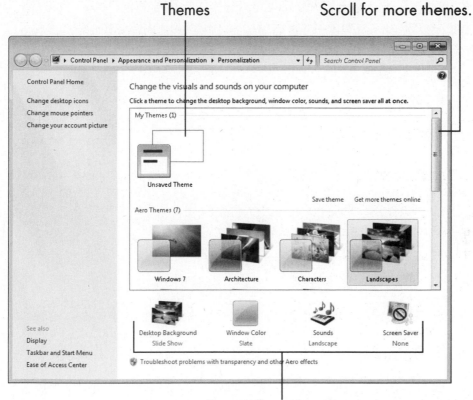

Personalization options

Figure 14-1

- **Basic and High Contrast Themes:** These are simpler, plainer themes, most with solid-color desktop backgrounds. High contrast may be useful for someone with a vision disability or for use in low light.

3. Click the Landscapes theme. You may not notice a change; if you can't see the desktop, click the Minimize button (or press +D) to see the new desktop background. See **Figure 14-2**. Other Personalization settings changed with this theme, as well.

4. Return to the Personalization window by clicking its icon on the taskbar. Try a different theme by clicking on it. To restore your original settings, click the Unsaved Theme under My Themes.

Personalization icon   Desktop background

Figure 14-2

Choose a Desktop Background

1. In the Personalization window, click the Desktop
Background option near the bottom. The Desktop
Background window appears, as shown in **Figure** 14-3.
The current background is part of the theme you
previously chose. If you chose the Landscapes theme
as I described in the preceding task, then under the
Landscapes heading in the list box of themes, photos are
marked with check marks. Each selected photo appears
one at a time as the desktop background.

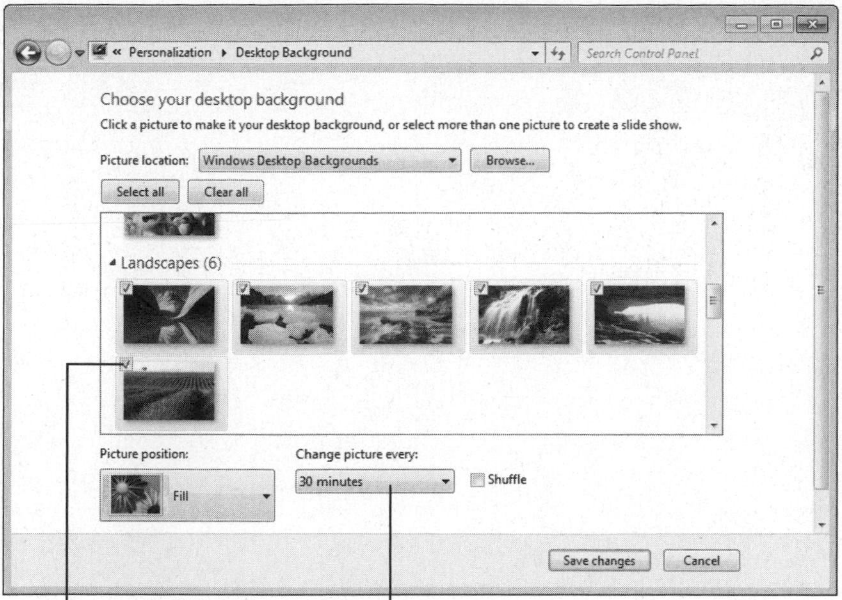

Choose how often the background photo changes.

Checked photos appear as the background.

Figure 14-3

2. Click on any photo to make that photo the only desktop background. Alternatively, select the small check box in the upper-left corner of a photo to add a photo to the photos that will appear, one at a time. Deselect a photo's check box to prevent it from displaying on the desktop. You don't have to select photos by theme — you can pick any photos.

 Click on a heading, such as Nature, to select all the pictures under that heading.

3. The Picture Position option is set to Fill, which fills the screen. Don't change this unless you want to display pictures that are much smaller than screen size.

4. Click the Change Picture Every drop-down list to change the amount of time that passes before the next picture displays. Intervals range from every 10 seconds to once per day. For a quick test of this feature, choose 10 seconds.

5. Select the Shuffle check box to mix the order in which photos appear.

6. Minimize the Desktop Background window. The desktop background changes every 10 seconds (unless you choose a different frequency or choose only one photo). Restore the Desktop Background window by clicking its icon on the taskbar.

 Pressing Alt+Tab allows you to cycle through open windows and the desktop. Keep holding down the Alt key and press the Tab key repeatedly until you see the window you want or the desktop. Release both keys to switch to the selected window.

7. In the Desktop Background window, click the Picture Location drop-down list and select the Pictures Library option. You see the pictures in the Pictures library, as shown in **Figure 14-4**. (These are the pictures discussed in Chapter 12, including your own photos if you copied some to the computer.) Deselect photos you don't want to see. Change the time each picture displays (as described earlier in Step 4). Minimize the window if you want to test your selections.

8. To keep the selections you make in the Desktop Background window, click the Save Changes button. To undo those selections, click Cancel. In either case, you return to the Personalization window.

Choose Pictures Library.

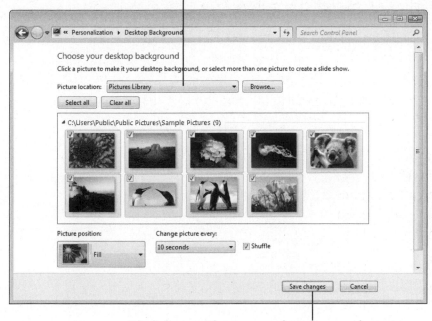

Click Save Changes to keep your choices.

Figure 14-4

Color Your Windows

1. You can change the color of the window title bar and border. In the Personalization window, click the Window Color option near the bottom. The next window or dialog box you see depends on your computer and on the theme you've chosen.

2. The Window Color and Appearance window in **Figure 14-5** appears if you select one of the Aero themes and your computer's graphics card supports *transparency*, which allows the background to show through the edges of a window. If you select a non-Aero theme or your computer doesn't support transparency, you see **Figure 14-6**, in which case, skip to Step 3.

Choose one of the color schemes. The color of the taskbar, title bar, and border changes immediately. If you want, you can adjust the Color Intensity slider to lighten (left) or darken (right) the selected color scheme. The inveterate tinkerer may choose Show Color Mixer for even more sliders to find just the right color and level of transparency. To keep your changes, click the Save Changes button. To discard your changes, click the Cancel button. Either choice returns you to the Personalization window.

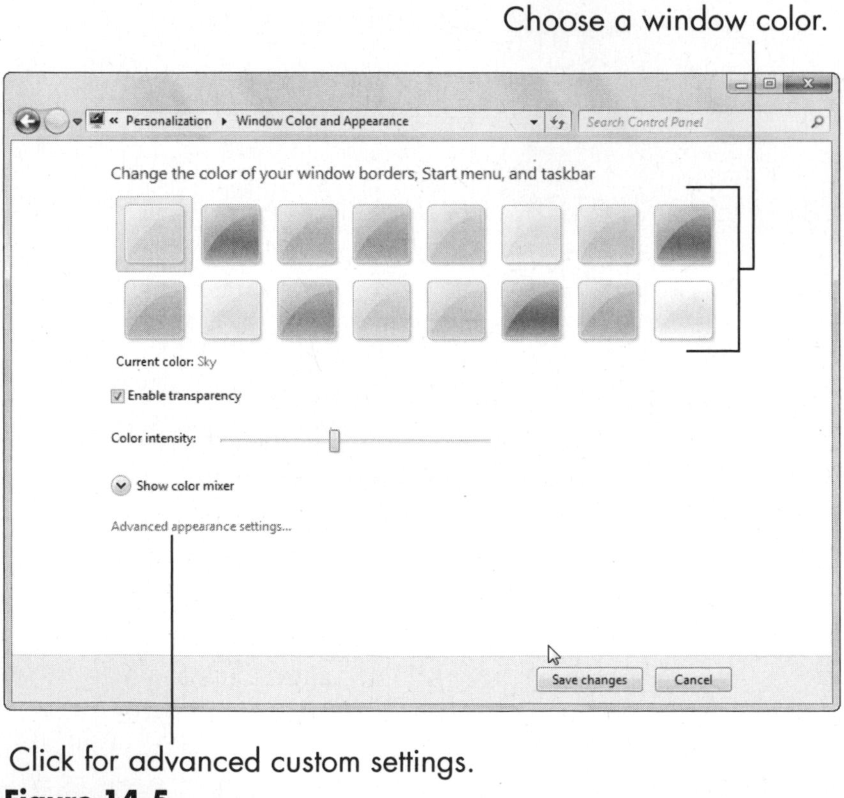

Choose a window color.

Click for advanced custom settings.

Figure 14-5

3. The Window Color and Appearance dialog box (see Figure 14-6) appears if your computer doesn't support transparency, if transparency is off, or if you click the Advanced Appearance Settings link shown in Figure 14-5.

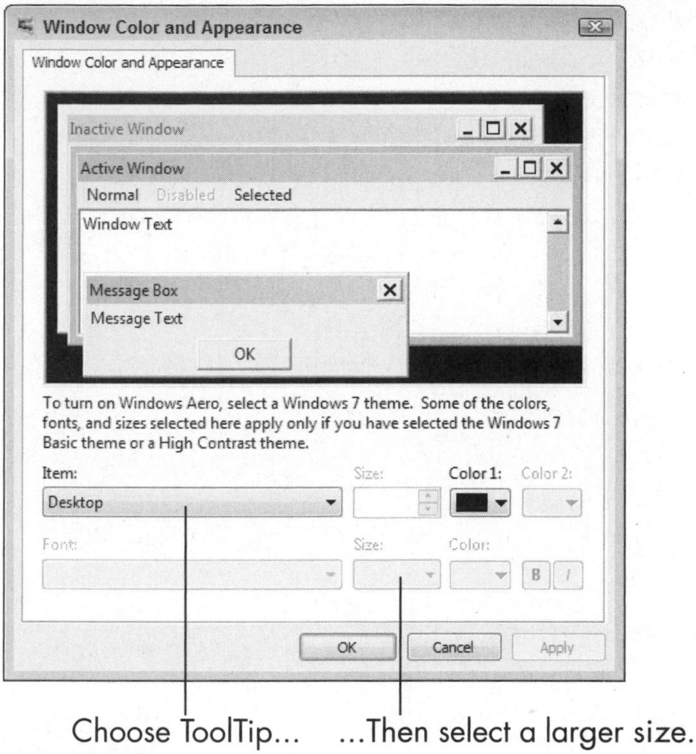

Window Color and Appearance

Window Color and Appearance

Inactive Window

Active Window

Normal   Disabled   Selected

Window Text

Message Box   ×

Message Text

OK

To turn on Windows Aero, select a Windows 7 theme. Some of the colors, fonts, and sizes selected here apply only if you have selected the Windows 7 Basic theme or a High Contrast theme.

Item: Size: Color 1:   Color 2:
Desktop

Font: Size: Color:

OK   Cancel   Apply

Choose ToolTip...   ...Then select a larger size.

Figure 14-6

This dialog box allows you to adjust the appearance of over a dozen parts of a window. These options are for the compulsive *tweaker* (no offense intended). However, there's one option in Advanced Settings that anyone may appreciate: It's the tooltip option, which determines the appearance of text in some of the pop-up boxes you see. Hover the mouse pointer over the Close button of this dialog box (don't click). That pop-up message Close is a tooltip. Follow these steps to make the tooltip text easier to read:

a. Click the Item drop-down list and select the ToolTip option.

b. In the Size drop-down list, select 14. This will increase the font size from 9 points to 14 points. (For reference, 72 points is about an inch tall.)

c. Change the background color (labeled Color 1) or the font color. Click the Color drop-down button (on the second line) and choose the blue square from the color picker that appears. Click the Apply button. A `Please Wait` message appears briefly, asking you to please wait.

d. Hover the mouse pointer over the Close button again long enough to see the changed tooltip, which should be larger and a different color. You may want to select different items from the background color (Color 1), Font, Size, and (Font) Color drop-down lists, as well as clicking the Bold button (but not Italics). Make any adjustments. Click Apply. Test again by hovering your mouse pointer over Close.

e. Feel free to look at the other options in the Item list. When you finish making adjustments, click OK to return to the Personalization window.

 If you want to return all of the Advanced Settings to their original settings, simply click any of the themes in the Personalization window (other than Unsaved Theme).

Change the Sounds Your Computer Makes

1. Windows 7 plays sounds in response to actions and events, including starting and exiting Windows 7. You can choose what sounds play or even to play no sounds. In the Personalization window, click the Sounds option near the bottom. The Sounds dialog box appears, as shown in **Figure** 14-7.

2. The current option showing in the Sound Scheme drop-down list is determined by the theme you choose. However, you can choose any sound scheme. Click the

Sound Scheme drop-down list and select one of the schemes, noting the current scheme before you do. In the Program Events list box, click Asterisk. When Windows 7 displays an alert, the sound associated with Asterisk plays. Click the Test button. Make sure your speakers are on, not muted, and the volume is high enough to hear.

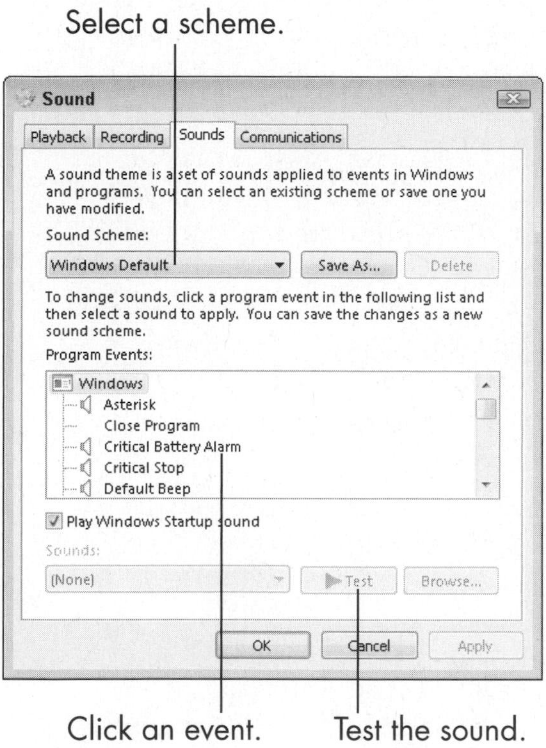

Select a scheme.

Figure 14-7

Click an event.   Test the sound.

 You can silence Windows 7 without silencing other programs, such as Media Player or IE. Choose No Sounds from the Sound Scheme drop-down list.

 Adjust all sounds by clicking the Windows 7 speaker icon in the taskbar. Click and drag the slider to adjust volume or click the pop-up speaker icon to mute or unmute Windows 7.

3. Select a different scheme from the Sound Scheme drop-down list. Click Asterisk in the Program Events list box and then click the Test button. Do you like this sound more or less?

4. Click Default Beep in the Program Events list box and then click the Test button. This is another sound you hear often.

5. Click the Sounds drop-down list to open it. The first option is (None). If you choose (None), any event that triggers the selected sound (Default Beep), won't make any sound, but other events will continue to produce sounds. You can pick any of the sounds listed as the sound you want to hear for the selected event. Test your selection by clicking the Test button.

6. If you want to keep the choices you made, click OK. Otherwise, in the Sound Scheme drop-down list, select the original scheme or Windows Default, and then click OK.

Set Up a Screen Saver

1. After a set period of time without mouse or keyboard activity, a screen saver displays changing images on your screen. You can choose which images appear and how much of a delay occurs before they appear. In the Personalization window, click the Screen Saver option. The Screen Saver Settings dialog box appears, as shown in **Figure 14-8**.

2. Click the Screen Saver drop-down list and select the Photos option. In the top half of the dialog box, you see what this screen saver looks like. The Photos screen saver plays a slideshow of photos in the Pictures library. For a full-screen preview, click the Preview button and then avoid moving the mouse or touching the keyboard for a few seconds. When you're done with the preview, press any key or move the mouse to return to the dialog box.

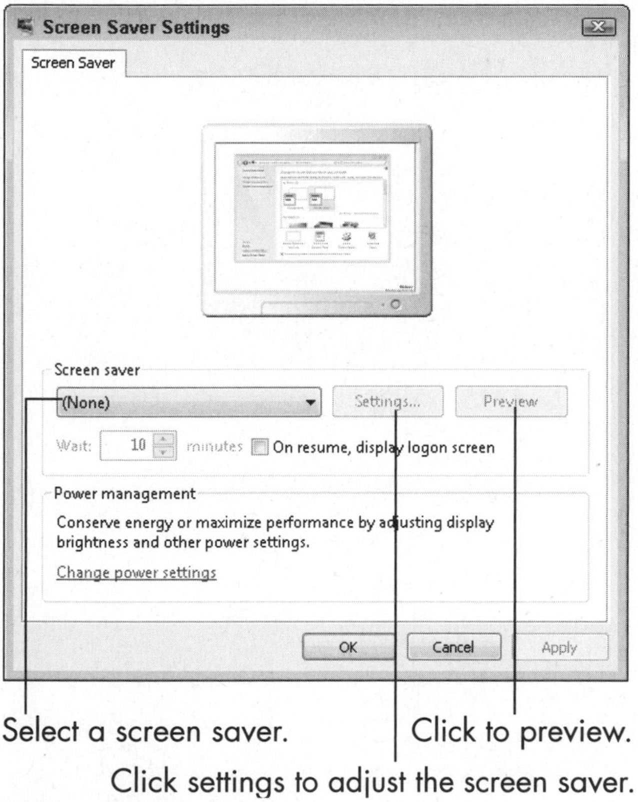

Screen Saver Settings

Screen Saver

Screen saver

(None)   Settings...   Preview

Wait: 10 minutes ☐ On resume, display logon screen

Power management

Conserve energy or maximize performance by adjusting display brightness and other power settings.

Change power settings

OK   Cancel   Apply

Select a screen saver.   Click to preview.

Click settings to adjust the screen saver.

Figure 14-8

The Photos screen saver is my favorite. You can try any of the other screen savers — Bubbles is great fun — but many screen savers don't run if the graphics card in your computer doesn't support them. A warning appears in the dialog box if you choose a screen saver you can't run, in which case you need to choose a different screen saver.

3. With Photos selected as the screen saver, click the Settings button. The Photos Screen Saver Settings dialog box appears (see **Figure 14-9**).

- If you want to see some pictures but not all — for example, just your recent vacation photos — click the Browse button and find the folder that contains those photos.

- Click the Slide Show Speed drop-down list to choose how frequently the photos change on screen (Slow, Medium, or Fast).

- Select the Shuffle Pictures check box to display photos randomly.

If you make changes here you want to keep, click Save. Otherwise, click Cancel. You're returned to the Screen Saver Settings dialog box.

4. Click the Preview button again to make sure you like your choices.

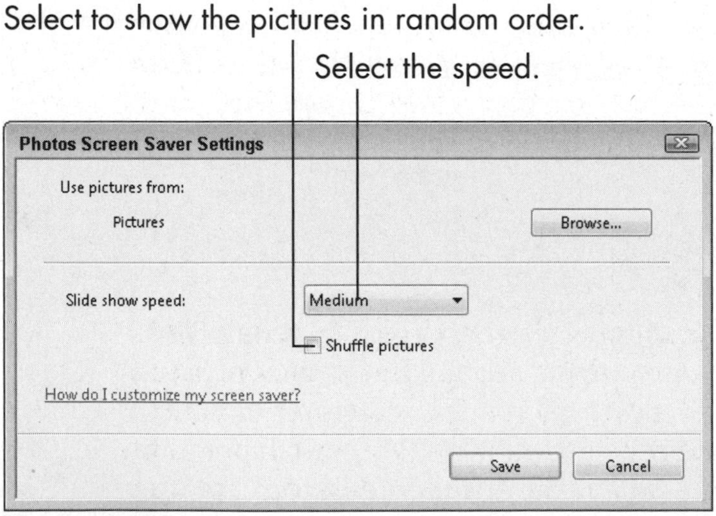

Select to show the pictures in random order.

Select the speed.

Figure 14-9

5. The Wait option displays the number of minutes of keyboard and mouse inactivity that must pass before the screen saver appears. You can change this number if you want more or less inactive time to pass before the screen saver starts.

6. Don't select the On Resume, Display Logon Screen check box, unless your account has a password and you want to require entering a password after the screen saver clears.

7. Click OK to keep your changes or Cancel to clear unapplied changes.

Save Your Theme

1. After you make various changes in the previous tasks, click the Save Theme link in the Personalization window. The Save Theme As dialog box appears.

2. Enter a name for your theme in the text box. Click Save.

3. Saving your current settings as a theme allows you to return to these settings. If you try other themes or settings and you want to go back to this theme, open the Personalization window and, in the large list box, click the name of the theme you saved under the My Themes heading. All settings are restored to their condition at the time you saved your theme.

Change Desktop Icons

1. Icons on the desktop provide easy access to certain files or programs. By default, the Recycle Bin is the only icon on the Windows 7 desktop. The manufacturer of your computer may add other icons. When you install programs, that process may also add icons to the desktop. You can choose a few Windows 7 icons to display on the desktop. In the Personalization window, click the Change Desktop Icons link in the Navigation pane on the left. The Desktop Icon Settings dialog box appears, as shown in **Figure 14-10.**

2. Select the check boxes next to the icons you want to add or deselect icons you want to remove. Click OK to keep your changes or Cancel to discard changes.

Select icons to display on the desktop.

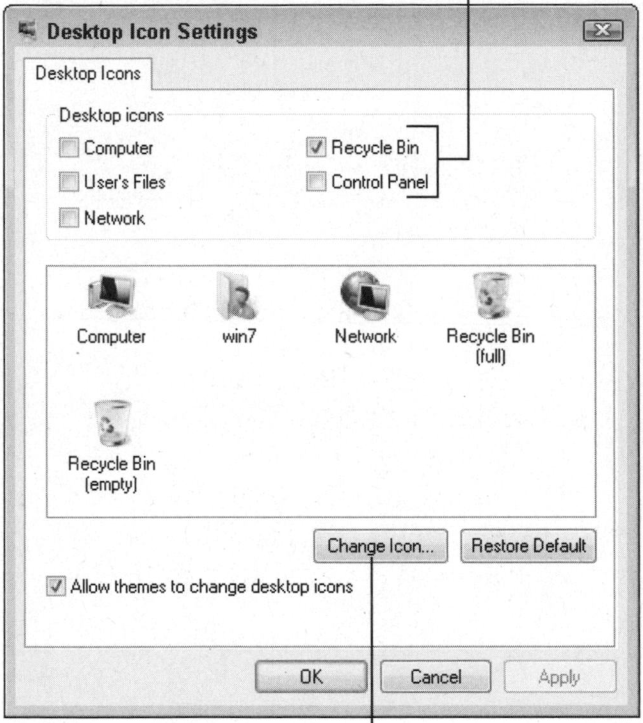

Desktop Icon Settings

Desktop Icons

Desktop icons

- ☐ Computer   ☑ Recycle Bin
- ☐ User's Files   ☐ Control Panel
- ☐ Network

Computer   win7   Network   Recycle Bin (full)

Recycle Bin (empty)

Change Icon...   Restore Default

☑ Allow themes to change desktop icons

OK   Cancel   Apply

Click to change an icon's look.

Figure 14-10

 Leave the Recycle Bin check box selected to make it easy to find when you need to undelete files. All of the other icons already appear on the Start menu and in Windows Explorer, so you may not need them on the desktop.

3. Minimize the Personalization window. To change the size of icons on the desktop, right-click the desktop. Choose View⇨Large Icons (see **Figure 14-11**). Repeat for Medium or Small Icons, whichever you prefer.

Some people consider desktop icons to be clutter that obscures the desktop background. You can hide all desktop icons by right-clicking the desktop and choosing View⇨Show Desktop Icons, which deselects and hides those icons. Repeat to bring the icons back.

Choose Large Icons.

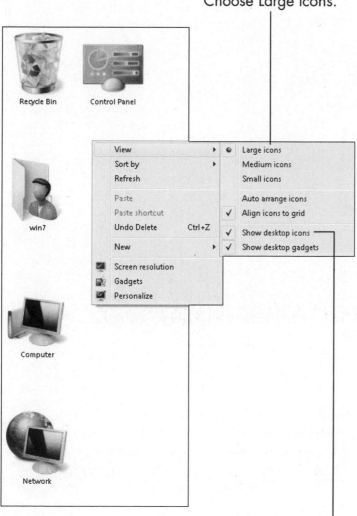

Click to hide desktop icons.

Figure 14-11

Pick Your Mouse Pointers

1. Changing the size, color, or shape of the mouse pointer may make it easier to see. In the Personalization window, click the Change Mouse Pointers link in the Navigation pane on the left. The Mouse Properties dialog box opens with the Pointers tab selected (see **Figure 14-12**).

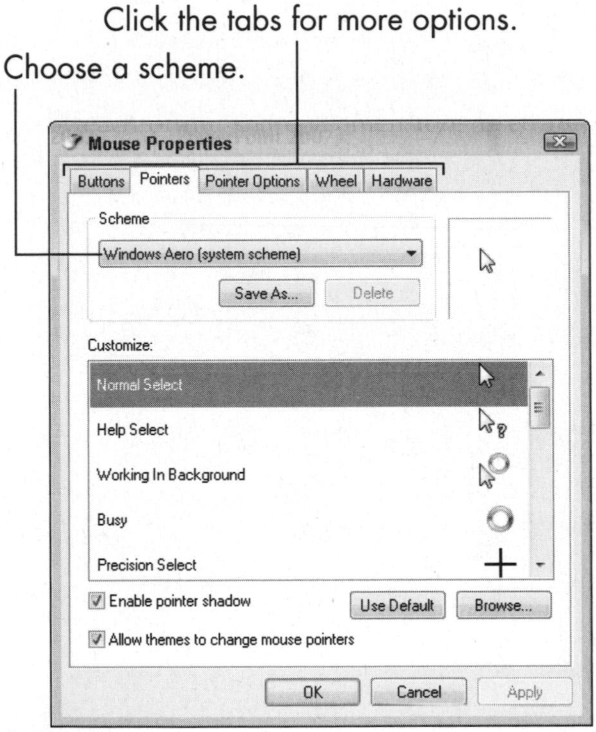

Click the tabs for more options.

Choose a scheme.

Figure 14-12

2. In the Scheme drop-down list note the current selection and then click it to see what options it has to offer. Each scheme provides different mouse pointers. Mouse pointers differ in size, color, and style:

- **Colors** include white, black, and inverted, which is transparent with an outline.

- **Sizes** are standard, large, and extra large.

- **Styles** include the modern-looking Aero, black-outlined Magnified, and the rest, which are variations on the standard.

 You may find additional styles installed by the computer manufacturer. You can also download mouse pointers from the Web.

3. Select Windows Black (Extra Large) from the Scheme drop-down list. In the preview to the right, the cursor appears black and larger. Click the Apply button to see this pointer size in action. Move the mouse around.

4. Select Windows Aero (Extra Large) from the Scheme drop-down list. This is the larger version of the default pointer scheme. Click the Apply button. Do you prefer one of these schemes?

 The rest of this section contains options you may find valuable, but it's okay if you skim to the next section.

5. Click the Buttons tab at the top of the dialog box. Consider these options (see **Figure 14-13**):

- **Button Configuration:** This option is intended for left-handers. Select the Switch Primary and Secondary Buttons check box to switch the functions of the left and right buttons. With this option selected, you single-click the right mouse button to select, double-click the right button to open, and left-click for the shortcut menu.

- **Double-Click Speed:** If you have trouble double-clicking, dragging this slider left or right may fix that. Double-click the yellow folder icon repeatedly. That icon should open or close each time you double-click. Adjust the slider slightly and repeat your test.

- **ClickLock:** Select the Turn On ClickLock check box to change click and drag. With this option selected, you don't have to hold the mouse button down as you drag. Click and drag becomes click, release, drag, click, release.

To keep your changes, click the Apply button.

Double-click here to test the speed.

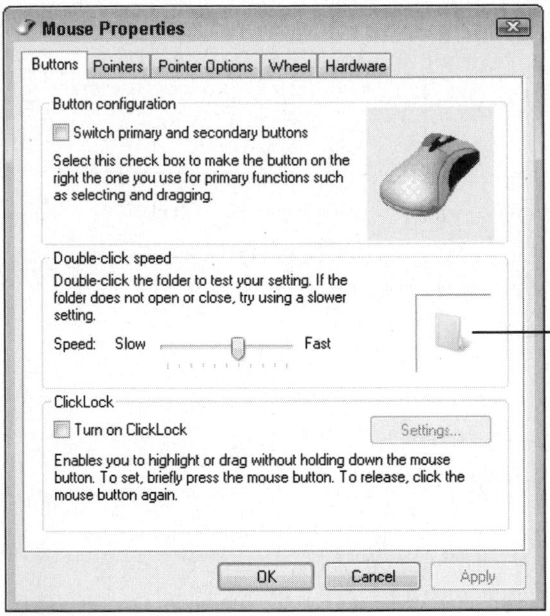

Figure 14-13

6. Click the Pointer Options tab (see **Figure 14-14**).

- **Motion:** If the mouse pointer seems to move onscreen too quickly or slowly for your tastes, try dragging the slider a little toward Slow or Fast to see if that helps.

- **Snap To:** If you select the Automatically Move Pointer to the Default Button in a Dialog Box check box, Windows 7 positions the mouse pointer over OK or Cancel, whichever is the expected option. This saves you from moving the mouse before you click.

- **Visibility:** Three options here to help you see the mouse pointer:

  Display Pointer Trails: Select this check box to exaggerate mouse pointer movements with a kind of slow-motion effect.

  Hide Pointer While Typing: Leave this check box selected so the pointer won't obscure the cursor position where you can type.

  Show Location of Pointer When I Press the Ctrl Key: If you select this check box, you can press the Ctrl key to create a radar or target effect around the pointer to help you locate it onscreen.

To keep your changes, click the Apply button.

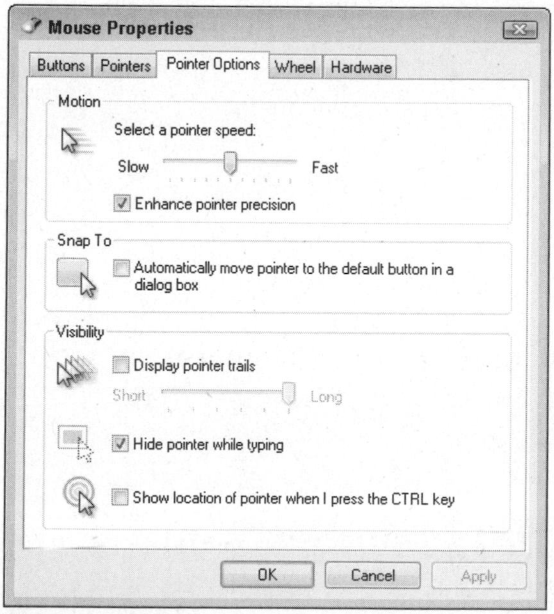

Figure 14-14

7. If your mouse has a wheel between the mouse buttons, you can use that wheel to scroll in longer windows, such as in IE. Click the Wheel tab (see **Figure 14-15**) to access these two options:

- **Vertical Scrolling:** By default, each time you turn the wheel slightly, the screen moves three lines up or down. To scroll down an entire screen requires turning the wheel about six times. Select the One Screen at a Time option to change that to one screen with each slight wheel turn.

- **Horizontal Scrolling:** Not all mouse wheels tilt left or right. If yours does, you can change how much the window scrolls horizontally as you press the wheel from either side to tilt it slightly.

Click Apply.

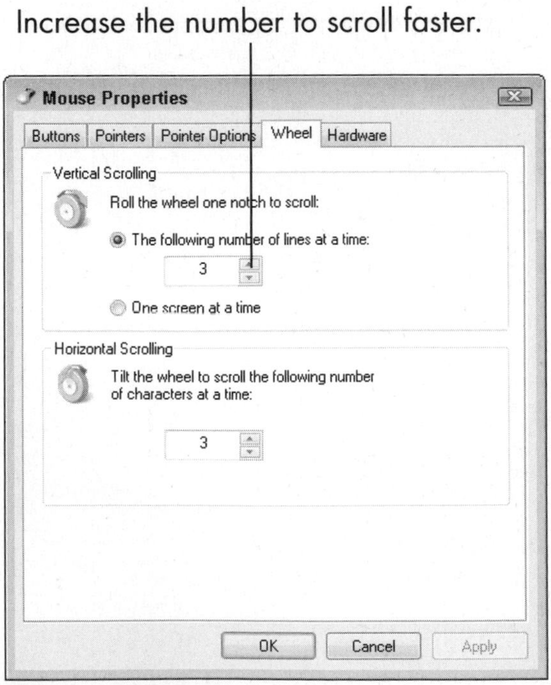

Increase the number to scroll faster.

Figure 14-15

8. When you're done with the Mouse Properties, click OK.

 See Chapter 16 for instructions on making single-click the way to open items and to add check boxes to Windows Explorer to select items.

Change Your Account Picture

1. Your account has a picture or an icon associated with it. This icon appears on the Welcome screen (if you see that screen to log in) and on the Start menu. In the Personalization window (refer to Figure 14-1), click the Change Your Account Picture link in the Navigation pane on the left. The pictures that Windows 7 provides appear in **Figure 14-16**.

Current user account picture   Choose a different picture.

Click to select your own photo.

Figure 14-16

2. Click one of the pictures and then click the Change Picture button. When you click the Start button, the new picture you chose appears at the top-right of the Start menu.

3. Back in the Personalization window, click the Change Your Account Picture link again. Click the Browse for More Pictures link below the pictures. In the Pictures library that appears, double-click a picture you want as your account picture. (You may have to open Sample Pictures, first.) Click the Start button. That picture appears on the Start menu. Repeat Step 1 if you want a different picture.

 Oddly, if you use the Browse option in Step 3, Windows 7 opens the User Accounts window instead of the Personalization window after you select a picture. Close the User Accounts window if it opens.

Using the Taskbar and Start Menu Smartly

*L*ooking at the taskbar, you see icons (buttons) for open windows. The taskbar also contains icons that are *pinned* to the taskbar, so that you can open those windows with just a click. The taskbar provides one way to switch between open windows as your attention shifts.

You can customize the location and appearance of the taskbar. Pin icons for programs you need immediate access to and unpin those you never use.

Throughout this book, you use the Start menu to run programs. You can determine just what appears on the Start menu to reduce clutter from icons you seldom use. As with the taskbar, you can pin or unpin programs depending on their value to you.

Both the taskbar and the Start menu provide a feature that is unique to Windows 7: *Jump Lists*. Jump Lists display recent and frequently used documents and options belonging to a specific program.

In this chapter, you customize the taskbar and the Start menu. You also take advantage of Jump Lists for quick access to important documents.

Tune Up Your Taskbar

1. Change the way the taskbar looks and acts. Right-click the taskbar and choose Properties. The Taskbar tab of the Taskbar and Start Menu Properties dialog box appears (see **Figure 15-1**).

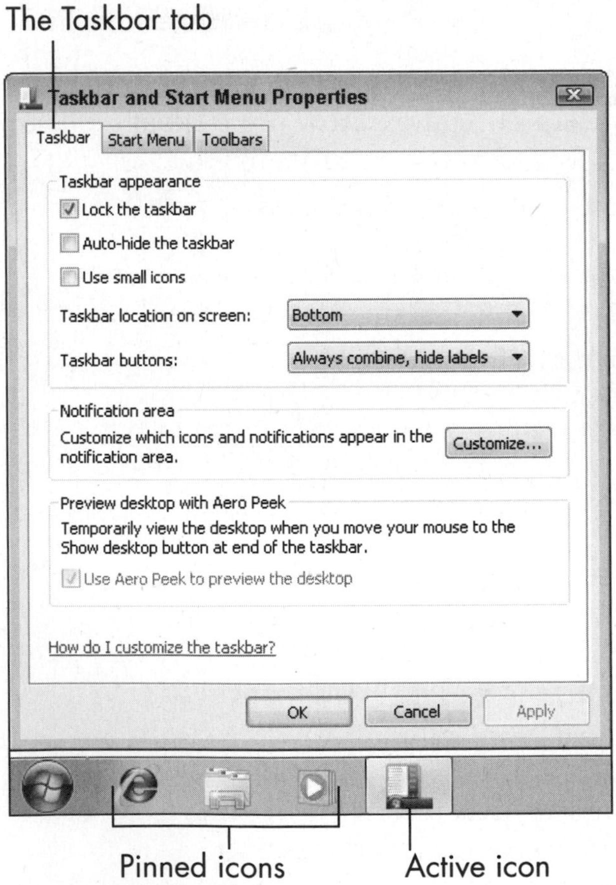

The Taskbar tab

Pinned icons   Active icon

Figure 15-1

These properties are not all equally important, so I skip a few.

2. Click the Taskbar Location on Screen drop-down list. Select the Top option and then click the Apply button. This moves the taskbar to the top of the screen. With the taskbar at the top, menus drop down instead of popping up. Because most windows have toolbars near the top of the window, you don't have to move the mouse as far between taskbar and toolbar. It's a small change you may have to use for a while to appreciate.

 On laptops and touchscreens, you may have an easier time using the taskbar at the top of the screen.

 For the rest of this chapter, figures show the taskbar at the top of the screen — if the world seems upside-down, that's why.

3. In the Taskbar and Start Menu Properties dialog box, click the Taskbar Buttons drop-down list. Select the Combine When Taskbar Is Full option and then click the Apply button. On the taskbar, the button for Taskbar and Start Menu Properties includes some text (see **Figure 15-2**), as in the previous version of Windows. With this option, you trade more information on the button for fewer buttons on the taskbar.

4. Under Preview Desktop with Aero Peek, the Use Aero Peek check box is unavailable if your graphics card doesn't support this feature. Aero Peek automatically turns all windows transparent when you hover over the Show Desktop button to the right of the clock on the taskbar — it's a narrow space that doesn't really look like a button. Aero Peek allows you to see the desktop background, icons, and gadgets without having to minimize windows. If this feature is grayed out or deselected, you have to click the Show Desktop button (or press +D) to see the desktop.

Places taskbar at top of screen

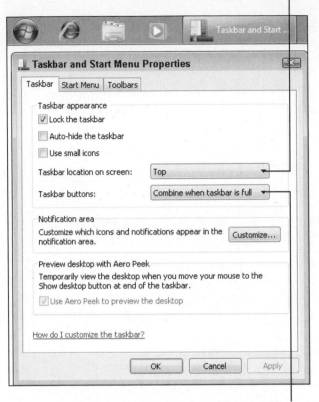

Expands the label on active icons

Figure 15-2

Control System Notification Messages

1. The notification area appears at the right end of the taskbar, to the left of the clock. This area displays icons for programs running in the background, for which there is no other icon on the taskbar. An example is the speaker icon. Use these icons to see the status of a program — through changes in the icon or pop-up *notifications* (messages) — or to access that program. The icons showing in the notification area in **Figure 15-3** indicate that

- I have an Action Center alert.

- The laptop battery is nearly fully charged.

- A wireless network connection is established.

- The speakers are muted. (The red slash over that fourth icon disappears when mute is off.)

2. If other icons are hidden from view in the notification area, as in this case, click the down arrow for a small window displaying those hidden icons.

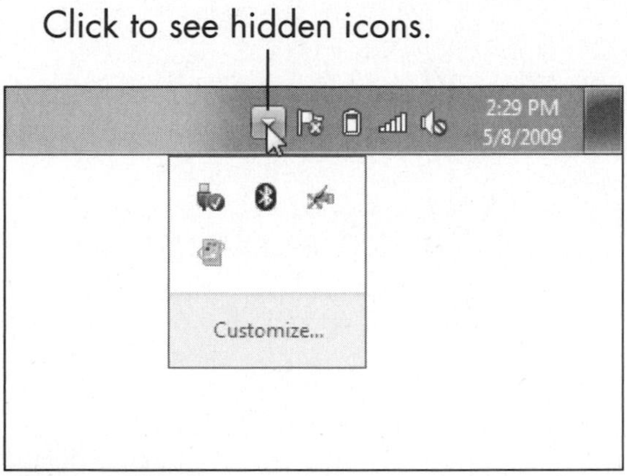

Click to see hidden icons.

Figure 15-3

See Chapter 18 for information about using the Action Center to tend to your computer.

3. Hover your mouse pointer over icons in the notification area to display tooltips (text). Click an icon to access a default option (or double-click, if needed). Right-click an icon for additional options.

4. You have some control over which icons appear in this area. In the Taskbar and Start Menu Properties dialog box (refer to Figure 15-1), click the Customize button in the Notification Area section. The Notification Area Icons window appears (see **Figure 15-4**). The icons that appear here are currently in the notification area or were recently.

Choose behaviors for each icon.

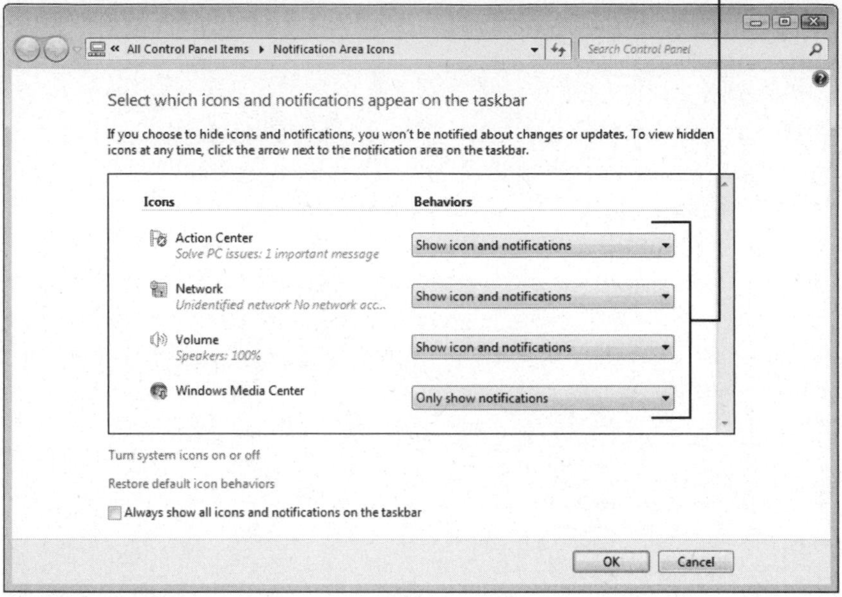

Figure 15-4

5. Icons take up space on the taskbar and can be distracting. On the other hand, you may need to know what an icon is trying to tell you. For each icon, you can choose a behavior for that icon from the Behaviors drop-down lists:

- **Show Icon and Notification:** With this choice, both the icon and associated pop-up messages appear. Select this if the icon itself displays useful information by changing under different conditions, such as the speaker icon with or without a red slash to indicate the mute condition. Some icons change and some don't.

- **Hide Icon and Notifications:** With this choice, the icon doesn't appear directly in the notification area. You won't receive messages from this icon, either. Select this option if an icon just seems to take up space or its messages distract you. (Ignore messages at your own peril. Some are irksome; some are vital.)

- **Only Show Notifications:** This choice hides the icon but lets messages pop up. This is a good choice if the icon itself never changes.

6. If you use the second or third behavior options, you can display the hidden icons by clicking the triangle to the left of the notification area. All of the hidden icons appear in one little window (refer to Figure 15-3). As with the other icons, you can hover, click, double-click, or right-click to access different functions related to each icon. Click outside the pop-up to hide it again.

Pin Icons to the Taskbar

1. Two kinds of icons appear in the main part of the taskbar. If a window is open, its icon is there. Other icons are *pinned* to the taskbar so that they're always there and can be used to open a window or start a program. In Figure 15-1, shown earlier, the first three icons in the taskbar are pinned and can be used to start IE, Windows Explorer, and Media Player, respectively. The fourth icon is for the active window, Taskbar and Start Menu Properties.

2. For these steps, you practice by pinning an icon for Solitaire to the taskbar. Choose Start⇨Solitaire. (Click OK if Solitaire displays a hardware message.) Right-click the Solitaire icon in the taskbar. Choose Pin This Program to Taskbar from the drop-down list shown in **Figure 15-5**.

Right-click the icon on the taskbar.

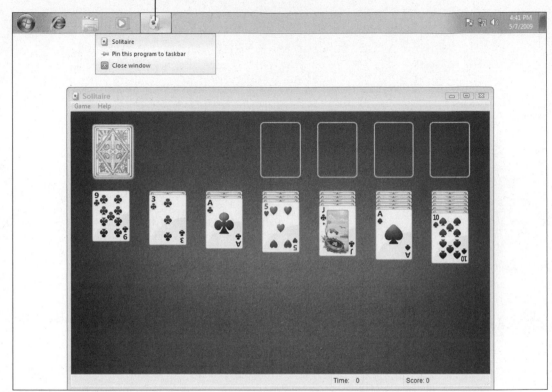

Figure 15-5

3. Close Solitaire. The icon is still on the taskbar because you pinned it there. If you want fast access to Solitaire, this is hard to beat. Consider pinning any program you use often.

4. Right-click Solitaire in the taskbar. Click Unpin This Program from Taskbar. The icon disappears unless Solitaire is running, in which case, the icon stays there until you close the program. Consider unpinning icons in the taskbar that you never use.

Use Taskbar Jump Lists

1. *Jump Lists* are shortcuts to documents or functions associated with a program. Display a Jump List in the taskbar by clicking an icon and dragging down (or up, if your taskbar is at the bottom). Click and drag down from the Media Player icon on the taskbar. **Figure** 15-6 shows the Media Player Jump List. (Keep in mind that yours will show some different options based on what you've played recently in Windows Media Player.)

Click and drag from a taskbar icon to see its Jump List.

Figure 15-6

2. The Media Player Jump List displays frequently played tracks or playlists, as well as tasks, such as Resume Previous List (where *List* refers to *playlist*). This Jump List provides an easy way to play these tracks without having to start Media Player first, before choosing what to play. Click an option to play music.

3. On the taskbar, click and drag down or up from the Windows Explorer icon (the yellow folder). **Figure 15-7** shows the Windows Explorer Jump List. (Yours will be different based on what you've explored recently.) Folders you have frequently accessed appear on the Jump List. When you hover your mouse pointer over one of the items, such as Pictures, a pushpin appears to the right. Click on the pushpin to *pin* that selection to the Jump List. That pinned selection appears in the Pinned section at the top of the Jump List. Pinned items are always accessible in the Jump List. Click on the pin to *unpin* this from the Jump List. The item still appears, but it may be replaced by other items as you use Windows Explorer.

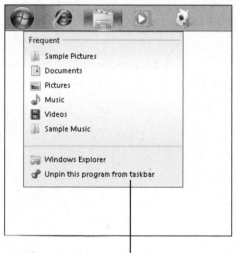

The Windows Explorer Jump List

Figure 15-7

4. Click and drag down (or up) from any other icons in the taskbar. The options available may be different for other icons. Use Jump Lists to quickly jump to a file or option. Pin the most useful files.

 Let me stress the combined value of Jump Lists with the taskbar at the top of the screen. You can click and drag down and select a pinned item with much less movement of the mouse than if the taskbar is at the bottom, where you click and drag up the full length of the Jump List to reach pinned items. The difference is more significant than may be apparent now.

 On the Start menu, programs with Jump Lists, such as Paint and WordPad, display a triangle (arrow) to the right of the menu item. The Jump List for such menu items appears when you hover your mouse pointer over the program name. You don't need to click and drag to display Start menu Jump Lists.

Customize Your Start Menu

1. Throughout this book, you use the Start menu to start programs, such as Solitaire or WordPad, and to access files, folders, and libraries, such as Documents or Pictures. As you've seen, the Start menu's Search box is often the most direct way to run a program. (Pinned taskbar icons are even more direct.) Still, you can customize the Start menu to make it more useful. Right-click the Start button and choose Properties. The Start Menu tab of the Taskbar and Start Menu Properties dialog box appears (see **Figure 15-8**).

2. Click the drop-down list next to Power Button Action. This determines the behavior of the Power button that appears at the bottom of the Start menu. Choose the option you'll use most often: Sleep, Hibernate, or Shut Down. Both Sleep and Hibernate return you to the programs and documents you had open when you chose that option. Shut Down closes programs and documents. For a laptop, choose Hibernate to save the most power while still being able to quickly return to the programs you were running. For a desktop, you may prefer the quicker resumption from Sleep.

Start Menu tab

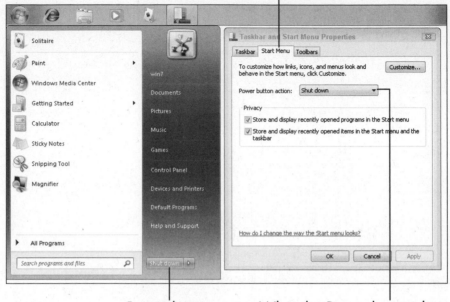

Power button   What the Power button does

Figure 15-8

3. Under Privacy, the two check boxes enable you to easily rerun programs and reopen documents through the Start menu. In an environment where other people see the Start menu, some users prefer that this information not appear and would deselect both of these check boxes. I recommend you leave the options selected.

4. Click the Customize button on the Start Menu tab. The Customize Start Menu dialog box appears (see **Figure 15-9**). There are many ways to customize the Start menu. In general, use the check boxes to determine which features appear on the Start menu. Deselect features you never use to reduce clutter.

Display Computer as a link.

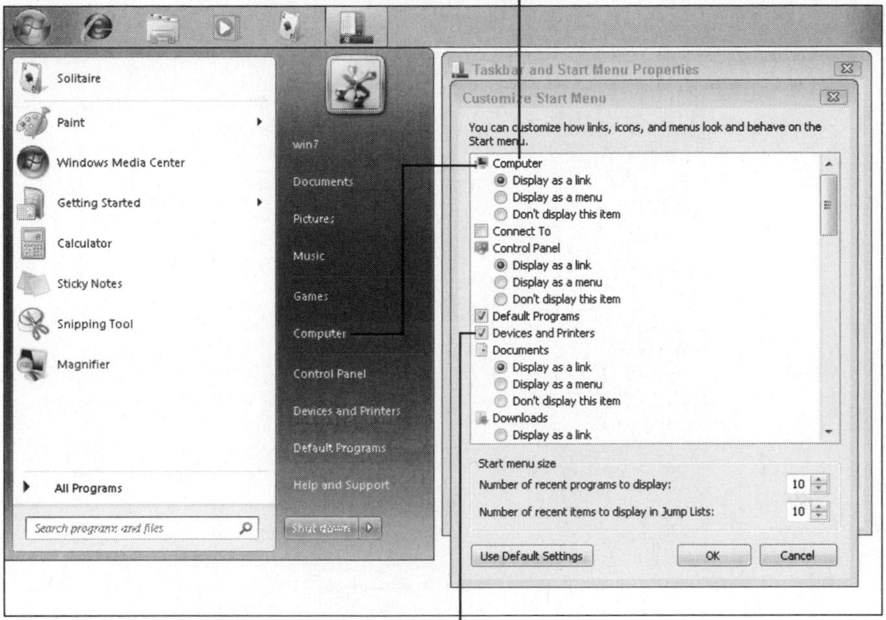

Checked items appear in the Start menu.

Figure 15-9

Many of the options in the Customize Start Menu dialog box give you a choice of three settings:

- **Display as a Link:** This setting makes the item a link you click to open a separate window. Initially, all the items on the right side of the Start menu (in the black area) have this effect (see Figure 15-9), including Computer.

- **Display as a Menu:** This setting causes a menu to pop out when you hover your mouse pointer over or click this item. **Figure 15-10** shows Computer with Display as a Menu selected. The drives appear to the right of Computer for easy access.

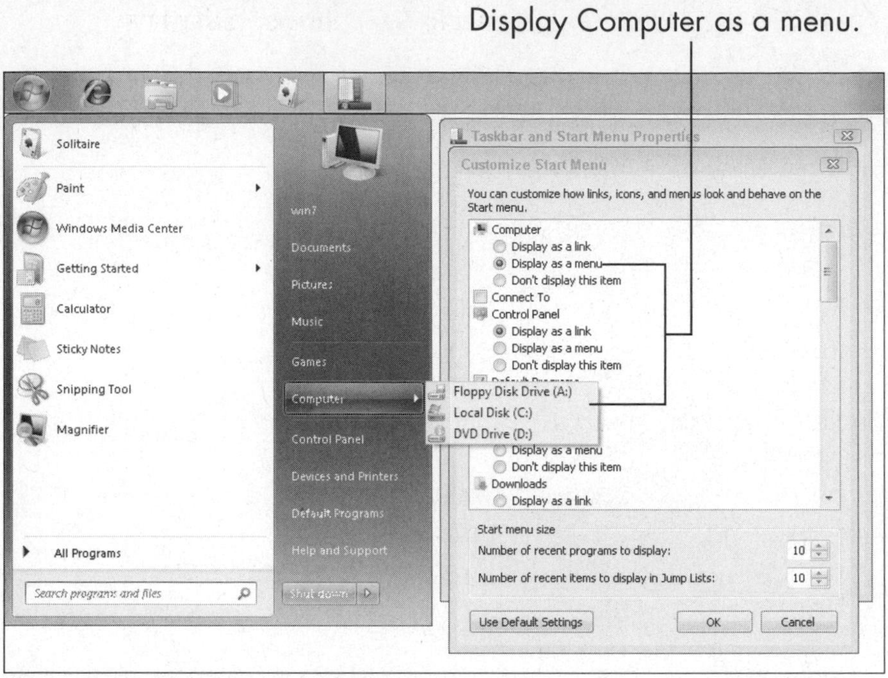

Display Computer as a menu.

Figure 15-10

- **Don't Display This Item:** Of course, this setting removes the item from the Start menu. Reduce Start menu clutter: Don't display items you don't ever use. Windows Explorer is pinned to the taskbar and pressing +E opens Computer, so you may prefer to use the Don't Display This Item option for Computer. (However, I like having more than one way to get to everything important.)

Here are a few changes for you to consider:

- If you'll be traveling with a laptop, select the **Connect To** check box to provide a way to connect to wireless networks. See Chapter 8 for information on connecting to a wireless Internet connection.

- Deselect the **Default Programs** check box — you won't use it.

- Under the **Downloads** check box, choose Display as a Link.

- If you don't play games, choose Don't Display This Item under the **Games** check box.

- If you use a network, select the **Network** check box.

- Select the **Recent Items** check box. This provides another way to reopen documents.

In the Start Menu Size, you find these options:

- **Number of Recent Programs to Display:** This option determines how many programs appear in the Start menu. The default value of 10 is probably fine.

- **Number of Recent Items to Display in Jump Lists:** This option determines how many documents or other items appear in Start menu Jump Lists (coming up). The default value of 10 is probably fine.

Figure 15-11 shows seven recent programs on the left, with room for three more before older items drop off to make room for newer ones. On the right, the Jump List for Getting Started displays nine items with room for one more before older items drop off to make room for newer ones. No items are deleted or lost; these two options just determine how many items you can see at one time.

5. When you're done making changes, click OK to close the Customize Start Menu dialog box. (Refer to Figure 15-9.) Then click OK to close the Taskbar and Start Menu Properties dialog box.

Recently used programs

Jump List items

Figure 15-11

Pin Icons to the Start Menu

1. The programs that appear on the Start menu are recently used or recommended by Windows 7. As you use more programs, this initial list on the Start menu changes to show only your most recently used programs. Pin the programs to the Start menu that you want always available, as other items come and go. Right-click any item on the Start menu, including those listed under All Programs. Choose Pin to Start Menu. **Figure 15-12** shows Solitaire pinned to the Start menu. Note that a line separates pinned programs (above) from those Windows 7 lists (below).

A pinned program

Figure 15-12

 I'm not *really* obsessed with Solitaire — it's just a convenient example.

2. To remove a program you pinned to the Start menu, right-click that program and choose Unpin from Start Menu.

Making Windows 7 Easier to Use

You can change Windows 7 in many ways that may make using your computer easier and more comfortable. In this chapter, you choose adjustments that may make all the difference to you.

If you strain and squint to make things out onscreen, change your screen to make everything larger. Increase the size of the screen font and adjust the sharpness of text.

Go from double-clicking to single-clicking to open programs and documents.

Add a new method for selecting files: check boxes. With check boxes, you don't need any keystrokes as you make selections and those selections are very obviously marked.

Windows 7 provides a magnifier for zooming into an area of the screen. An onscreen keyboard can substitute for a mechanical keyboard. And Windows 7 can read screen content to you.

Make Your Screen Easier to See

1. Two factors work together in determining the appearance
of a computer screen:

- **The display** — the TV-like device sometimes called
a monitor or an LCD — has a width and height
you can't change. Displays are measured diagonally.
Sizes range from 17 to 25 inches for desktops and
8 to 17 inches on laptops.

- **Screen resolution** determines how much content
fits on the screen.

To change your screen resolution, right-click the desktop.
Choose Screen Resolution. The Screen Resolution dialog
box appears, as shown in **Figure 16-1**.

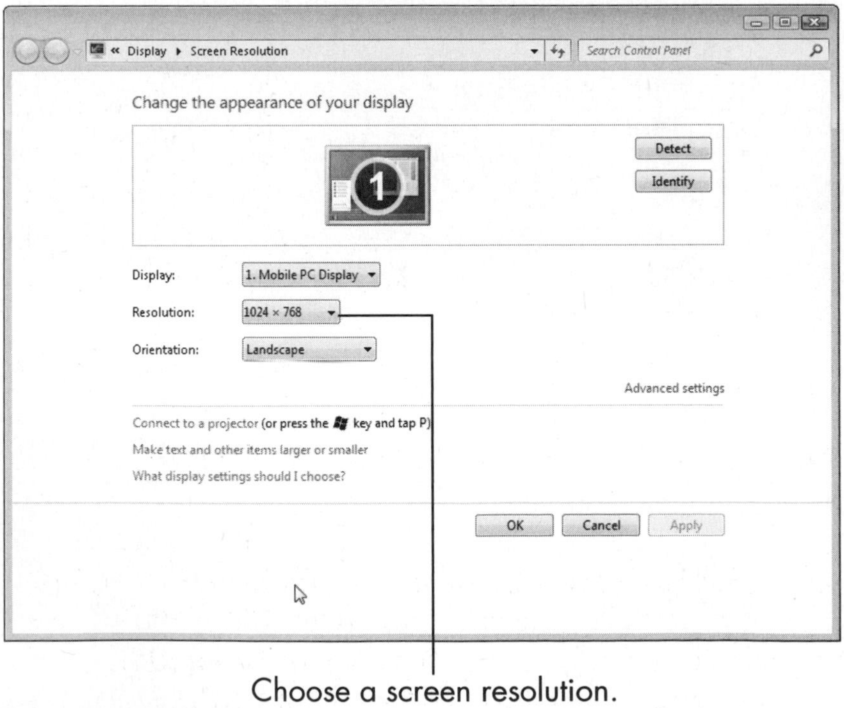

Choose a screen resolution.

Figure 16-1

If your desktop display is too small, consider buying a new one to replace it. See Chapter 7 for information on adding a second display before you give the old one away.

2. Click the Resolution drop-down list. Available resolutions appear with width and height measured in *pixels* (dots). The slider marks the current resolution. In **Figure 16-2**, the current resolution is 1024 x 768, a very common resolution ideal for displays around 16 inches.

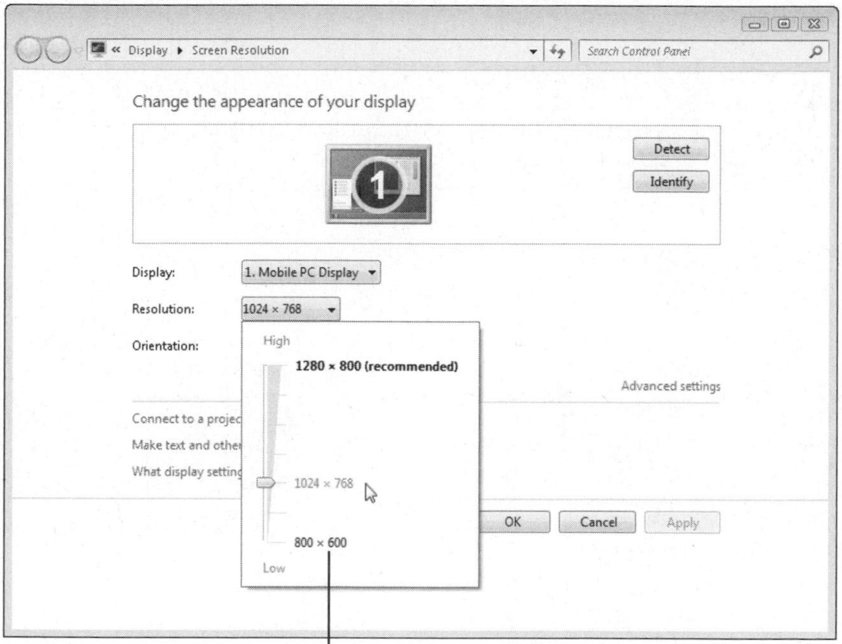

Choose a lower resolution to make the items onscreen larger.
Figure 16-2

3. The choices available to you in the dialog box may be different from those in the figure. If you have 800 x 600 as an option, select that. Otherwise, click the next resolution lower than the current resolution (down the menu). Click the Apply button to see this resolution.

4. A dialog box appears to ask Do You Want to Keep These Display Settings? If you want to try this resolution for a while, click the Keep Changes button. If you don't want this resolution, click the Revert button to return to the previous resolution. This dialog box has a 15-second timer. If you don't respond, it reverts automatically. That's a safety measure. If you choose a resolution that prevents you from seeing the dialog box — that's possible — don't panic; just count to 15 and let Windows 7 fix the problem. For the purposes of these steps, click the Keep Changes button if you can read the dialog box comfortably.

5. Here's the catch about screen resolution: Lower resolution makes everything onscreen bigger but shows less. Higher resolution shows more onscreen but smaller, which may be harder to read. You may need to use a particular resolution for a while to judge the effect. Look at how your desktop, taskbar, and Start menu change with the resolution. Start IE and browse a familiar Web site. Play a game you've played before.

6. In the Screen Resolution dialog box, choose 1280 x 1024 or the next resolution higher than the current one (up the menu). Click Apply. If you can read the dialog box, click the Keep Changes button. Check out this resolution by looking at familiar screens.

7. In the Screen Resolution dialog box, return to your original screen resolution.

8. Feel free to try other resolutions to find the one that works best for you. You may need to return to this section after you use a resolution for a while.

 If you use a high screen resolution, you may want to increase screen font size. See the following task, "Change Screen Font Size," for steps to increase font size.

Change Screen Font Size

1. You can increase the size of text on the screen by 25 or 50 percent. Right-click the desktop and choose Screen Resolution. The Screen Resolution dialog box appears (refer to Figure 16-1). Click the Make Text and Other Items Larger or Smaller link. The Display window appears (see **Figure 16-3**).

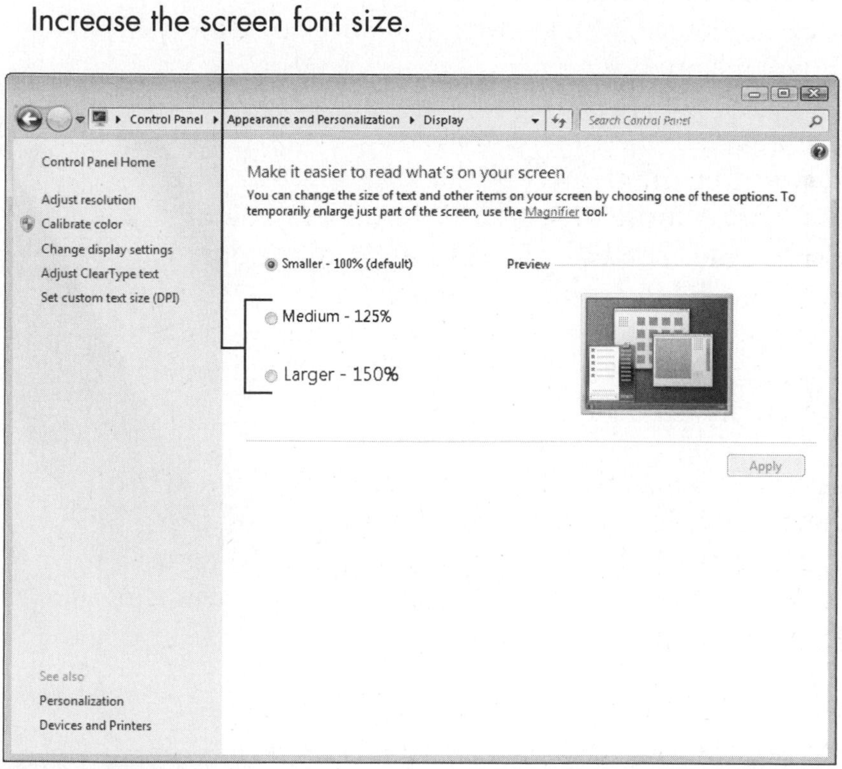

Increase the screen font size.

Figure 16-3

2. Increase the screen font size by choosing Medium (125%) or Larger (150%) and clicking Apply. Be aware that you may see consequences from choosing this increase, including

- A warning that some items may not fit on your screen with the current screen resolution

- Some dialog boxes that are too large for a screen resolution of 1024 x 768 or lower

3. If you encounter a problem seeing an entire dialog box, you may be able to move it to see the missing areas, or you may have to reset the screen font size to 100 percent. Click Apply.

4. To complete the change, click the Log Off Now button, as shown in **Figure 16-4**.

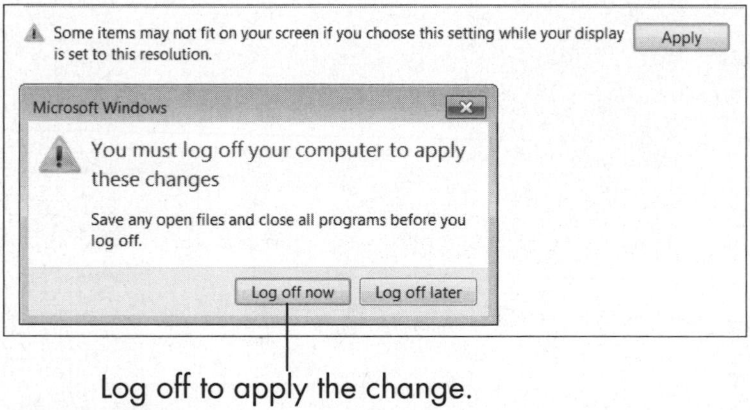

⚠ Some items may not fit on your screen if you choose this setting while your display   [Apply]
is set to this resolution.

Microsoft Windows ✕

⚠ You must log off your computer to apply these changes

Save any open files and close all programs before you log off.

[Log off now] [Log off later]

Log off to apply the change.

Figure 16-4

5. Log in by choosing your user icon and, if necessary, entering your password. **Figure 16-5** shows the Start menu with each option selected.

 As you increase screen resolution, consider increasing screen font size to keep the text legible.

 Some programs may have their own options for adjusting text size onscreen. In IE and some other programs, press Ctrl+= (the Ctrl key and the equal sign key, which also has a plus sign on it) to increase text size. Or press Ctrl+- (the Ctrl key and the minus key) to decrease text size. Press Ctrl+0 (the zero key above the letters) to return to 100 percent. If your mouse has a wheel, hold down the Ctrl key and roll the wheel away from you to increase or towards you to decrease text size.

Medium font size   Larger font size

Figure 16-5

Turn On ClearType Text

1. ClearType improves legibility of text on an LCD display. On the Start menu, type **clear** and click Adjust ClearType Text. (There is also a link from the Display window where you adjust screen font size.) **Figure 16-6** shows the first screen of the ClearType Text Tuner, a series of dialog boxes that help you fine-tune text sharpness.

Select to use ClearType.

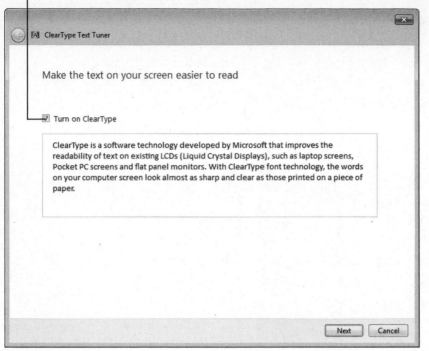

Figure 16-6

2. Select the Turn On ClearType check box if it isn't already selected. You may notice an immediate improvement in text legibility in the box. Click Next.

3. In each of the next four dialog boxes, click the box containing the sharpest text. This is like a visit to the eye doctor — better or worse? One or two? Don't fret; just go with what looks sharpest. Click Next on each screen.

4. The last screen indicates you've finished tuning the text on your monitor (screen). Click Finish.

 As you use your computer, if you notice text isn't as sharp as you want, repeat these steps.

Stop Double-Clicking for Good

1. For icons on the desktop or in Windows Explorer, you click once to select the icon, and you double-click to open that item. You can reduce the double-click to a single-click — which may not seem like much of a change — but consider the following:

- You already single-click items on the Start menu and taskbar, as well as most buttons and menu items.

- Even links on Web pages involve a single-click to open or browse that link.

- Double-clicking to open an icon, such as the Recycle Bin on the desktop, seems an odd exception.

2. You can make icons behave more consistently with the rest of Windows 7. Open the Start menu and type **folder** in the Search text box. In the list of search results, click Folder Options. On the General tab (see **Figure 16-7**), under Click Items as Follows, select the option called Single-Click to Open an Item (Point to Select). Click OK.

3. Hover your mouse pointer over the Recycle Bin icon (or any other icon) on the desktop to select it. Click the icon to open it. You won't double-click much anymore (once you break that habit).

4. This change requires an adjustment if you've used Windows before. You may open things you only intended to select. You'll get used to this and love it if you give it some time.

Choose Single-click.

Folder Options

General | View | Search

Browse folders

○ Open each folder in the same window
○ Open each folder in its own window

Click items as follows

○ Single-click to open an item (point to select)
   ○ Underline icon titles consistent with my browser
   ◉ Underline icon titles only when I point at them
◉ Double-click to open an item (single-click to select)

Navigation pane

☐ Show all folders
☐ Automatically expand to current folder

Restore Defaults

How do I change folder options?

OK | Cancel | Apply

Figure 16-7

Check to Select

1. In Windows Explorer, if you want to select more than
one file at a time, you can use the Ctrl key to select additional files. For an alternative method, have Windows 7
add a check box to each file. Use the check box to select
each file. On the Start menu, type **folder** in the Search
box and then, in the list of search results, click Folder
Options. On the View tab (see **Figure 16-8**), under
Advanced Settings, scroll down to the Use Check Boxes
to Select Items check box and select it. Click OK.

2. Choose Start⇨Pictures. Open the Sample Pictures folder. As you move the mouse pointer over each picture, a small check box appears in the upper-left corner of the icon (see **Figure 16-9**) or left of the filename in Details view. Click in that check box to select that photo. Repeat to select additional photos. If a photo is selected, click in the check box to deselect that photo. Close the window after you've seen how these check boxes work.

Select Use Check Boxes to Select Items.

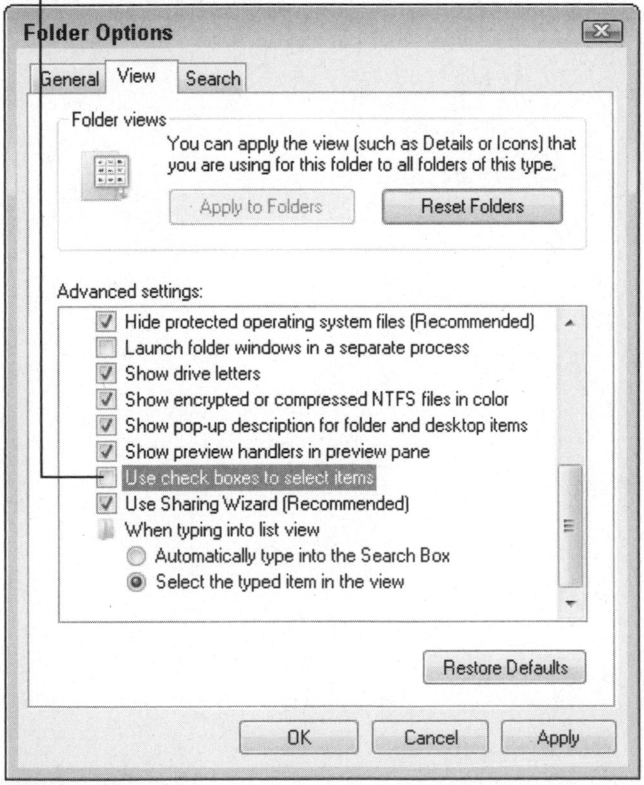

Figure 16-8

This change works especially well with the change in the earlier task "Stop Double-Clicking for Good." With both changes, click anywhere on the icon to open it or click on the check box to select it.

Selecting files is just a step before copy, move, rename, delete, and more. See Chapter 4 for information on working with files.

Hover over an item to see the check box.

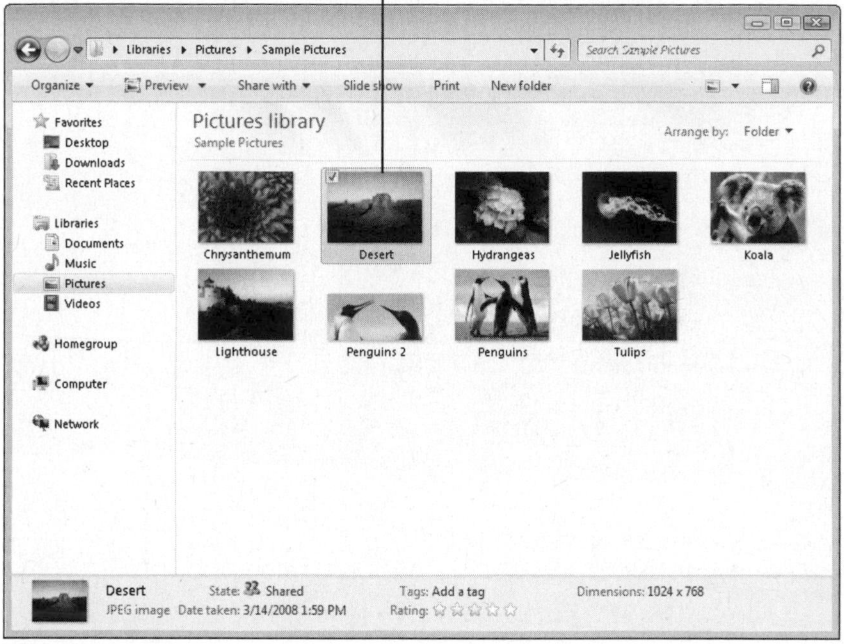

Figure 16-9

Get Recommendations for Specific Needs

1. In the Start search box, type **access**. In the search results list that appears, click Ease of Access Center. Maximize the window by clicking the middle of the three buttons in the upper-right corner of the window, just left of the Close button (the X). The Ease of Access Center, shown in **Figure 16-10**, provides even more ways to adjust the usability of Windows 7.

 Pressing +U also displays the Ease of Access Center.

2. Click the link to Get Recommendation to Make Your Computer Easier to Use. In a series of five screens, select all statements that apply to you. Click Next on each screen.

Click to take a survey and get recommended settings.

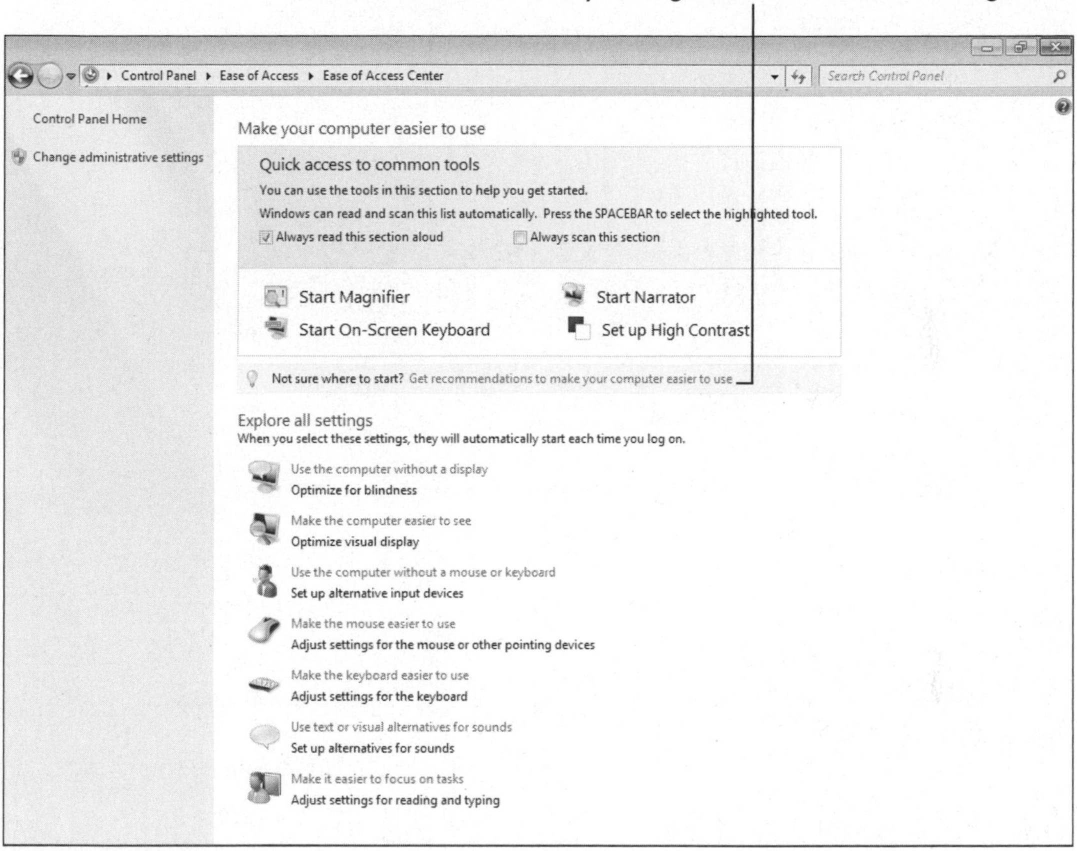

Control Panel ▸ Ease of Access ▸ Ease of Access Center

Search Control Panel

Control Panel Home

Change administrative settings

Make your computer easier to use

Quick access to common tools

You can use the tools in this section to help you get started.

Windows can read and scan this list automatically. Press the SPACEBAR to select the highlighted tool.

☑ Always read this section aloud   ☐ Always scan this section

Start Magnifier   Start Narrator

Start On-Screen Keyboard   Set up High Contrast

Not sure where to start? Get recommendations to make your computer easier to use

Explore all settings
When you select these settings, they will automatically start each time you log on.

Use the computer without a display
Optimize for blindness

Make the computer easier to see
Optimize visual display

Use the computer without a mouse or keyboard
Set up alternative input devices

Make the mouse easier to use
Adjust settings for the mouse or other pointing devices

Make the keyboard easier to use
Adjust settings for the keyboard

Use text or visual alternatives for sounds
Set up alternatives for sounds

Make it easier to focus on tasks
Adjust settings for reading and typing

Figure 16-10

3. On the fifth screen, click Done. The Recommended Settings appear based on your responses, as shown in **Figure 16-11**. Turn on features you wish to use, such as Narrator. Adjust settings on this screen or follow links to set up appropriate functions.

 Although this survey and the resulting recommendations are a good place to start, the following sections provide information on separate functions the Recommended Settings combines into one page.

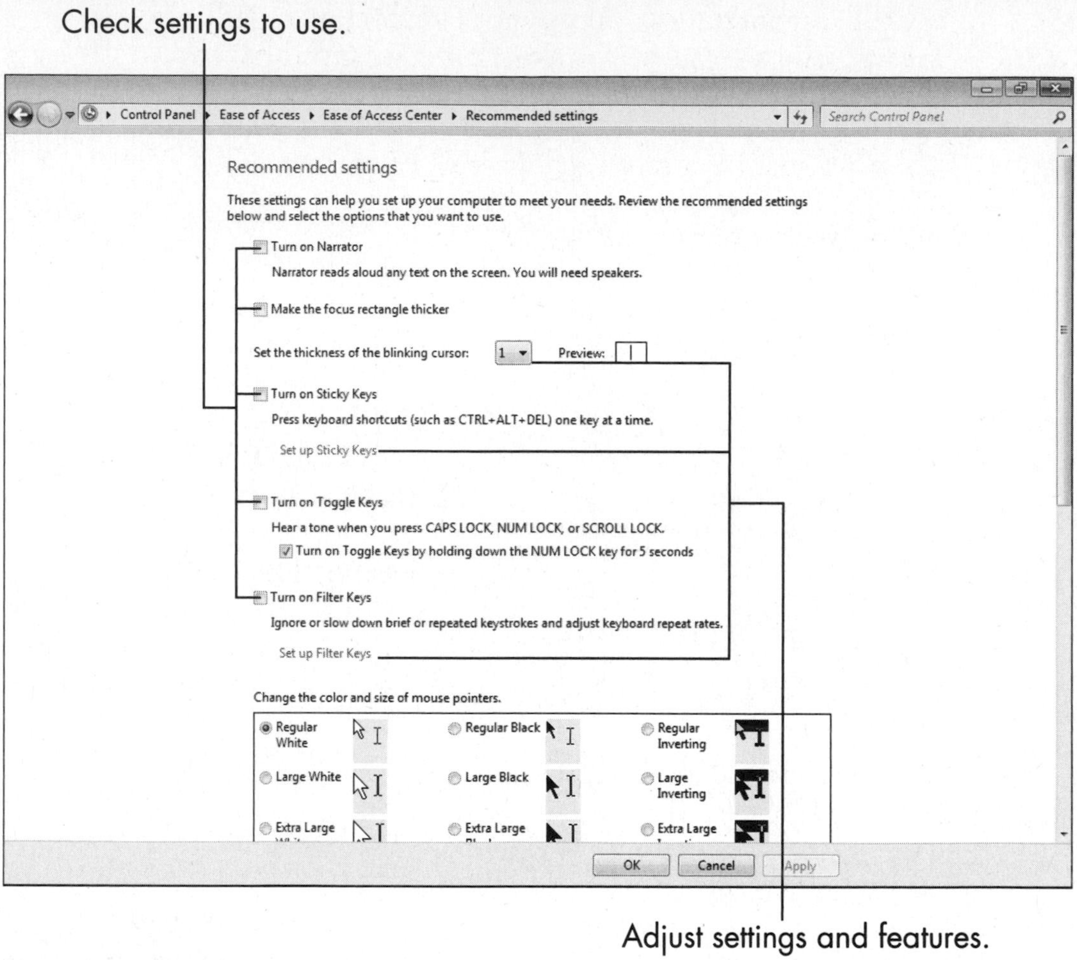

Check settings to use.

Recommended settings

These settings can help you set up your computer to meet your needs. Review the recommended settings below and select the options that you want to use.

☐ Turn on Narrator

Narrator reads aloud any text on the screen. You will need speakers.

☐ Make the focus rectangle thicker

Set the thickness of the blinking cursor: 1 ▼   Preview:

☐ Turn on Sticky Keys

Press keyboard shortcuts (such as CTRL+ALT+DEL) one key at a time.

Set up Sticky Keys

☐ Turn on Toggle Keys

Hear a tone when you press CAPS LOCK, NUM LOCK, or SCROLL LOCK.

☑ Turn on Toggle Keys by holding down the NUM LOCK key for 5 seconds

☐ Turn on Filter Keys

Ignore or slow down brief or repeated keystrokes and adjust keyboard repeat rates.

Set up Filter Keys

Change the color and size of mouse pointers.

◉ Regular White   ○ Regular Black   ○ Regular Inverting

○ Large White   ○ Large Black   ○ Large Inverting

○ Extra Large White   ○ Extra Large Black   ○ Extra Large Inverting

OK   Cancel   Apply

Adjust settings and features.

Figure 16-11

Start Magnifier

1. The Magnifier places (or, in techy terms, *docks*) a panel across the top of your screen. As you move the mouse, the area around the mouse appears magnified in this panel. In the Ease of Access Center, click the Start Magnifier button (refer to Figure 16-10).

2. Click the magnifying glass to display the Magnifier toolbar (see **Figure 16-12**). With these tools, you can increase (click the Plus button) or decrease (click the Minus button) magnification. Click the Views drop-down list to switch the magnification panel from docked to full screen. Click the gear icon for Magnifier Options; for instance, you can

- Adjust the percentage change of zoom.

- Turn color inversion on or off.

- Change the tracking from following the mouse (default) to following keyboard focus or the text insertion point.

- Click the link to Control Whether Magnifier Starts When I Log On.

Click OK to keep changes to these options or Cancel to discard changes.

Click to control magnification.

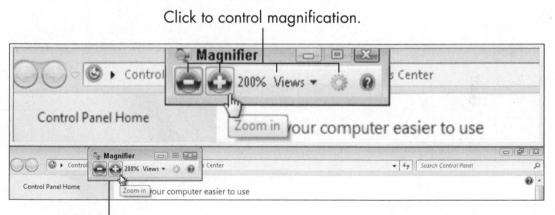

Magnifier toolbar

Figure 16-12

3. To turn off the Magnifier, click the X in the Magnifier toolbar.

Use the On-Screen Keyboard

1. Using the On-Screen Keyboard, you can type with the mouse or other pointing device, such as a joystick, pen, or mouth-stick. In the Ease of Access Center, click Start On-Screen Keyboard.

2. Using your mouse or other pointing device and the On-Screen Keyboard, click the Windows logo key, (it's between Ctrl and Alt). The Start menu appears. Click the letters **k-e-y** (see **Figure 16-13**). As you select letters with the On-Screen Keyboard, words matching what you've typed appear across the top of the keyboard. You can click the correct word (*keyboard,* for example). The word *keyboard* is inserted into the Start search box, and matching items appear.

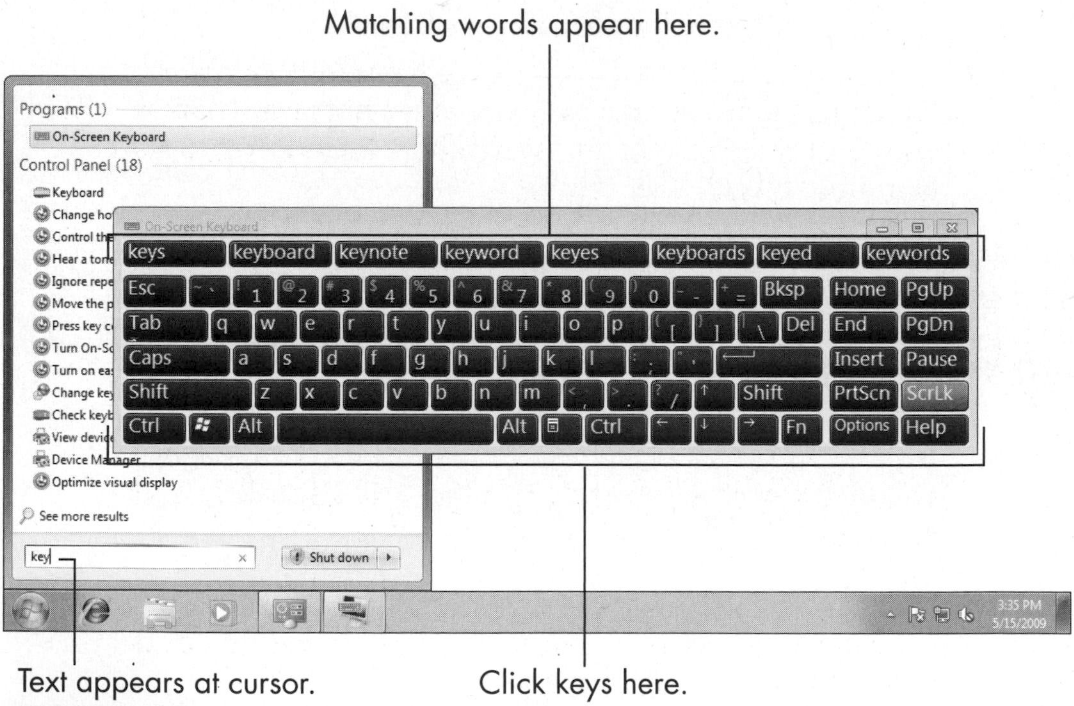

Matching words appear here.

Text appears at cursor.   Click keys here.

Figure 16-13

3. You can drag the On-Screen Keyboard by the title bar to reposition it. Minimize by clicking the first of the three buttons in the upper-right corner of the keyboard if you need it later.

4. On the On-Screen Keyboard, click the Options button. You can turn off the audible click that accompanies clicking the keys. You can turn on the display of the numeric keypad. Consider the option to Hover Over Keys, which enables you to select a key by hovering over it instead of clicking it, if clicking the keys isn't practical.

 Windows 7 has another On-Screen Keyboard called the Tablet PC Input Panel. Search for tablet on the Start menu. You may prefer either of these virtual keyboards.

Let Narrator Read to You

1. Narrator is a *screen reader*, which is software that reads screen text aloud. Press the   key. Type **narrator** (**narr** is enough) in the Start menu search box. Press Enter to start Narrator.

2. The Narrator Settings dialog box opens (see **Figure 16-14**). This window stays on top of other windows, unless you minimize it. Narrator reads aloud the contents of any window you click in. Initially, Narrator reads its own window's content. If you click in IE, Narrator begins reading the contents of the Web page you are browsing. You may want to adjust speaker volume or volume control in the taskbar.

3. Narrator reads the content based on *focus*, which is the currently selected item. Onscreen, the item with focus is highlighted by a box of dots.

4. Press Tab to move the focus in the window from one item to the next. Each time you press Tab, you move the focus to the next item, and Narrator reads the text of that item and its tooltip, if any. Pressing Shift+Tab moves the focus to the previous item.

Figure 16-14

5. Press the Tab key to move the focus to the Quick Help button. Narrator reads just the button text and tooltip. Press Enter to listen to Quick Help, which announces these keystrokes, among others:

- Press the Ctrl key to stop Narrator from reading the current content.

- Press Ctrl+Shift+Enter to make Narrator read information about the current item. Use this to repeat text Narrator reads.

- Press Ctrl+Shift+spacebar to make Narrator read the entire active window, top to bottom.

6. Press the   key. The Narrator reads the Start menu search box. Type **help** to select Help and Support under Programs. Press Enter.

 On the Start menu, if you need to move between selections, press the down- or up-arrow keys.

7. In Windows Help and Support, type **narrator** and press Enter. Press Tab to move among search results. Listen for Hear Text Read Aloud with Narrator. Press Enter. This

Help page includes a list of keyboard shortcuts. Press Ctrl+Shift+spacebar to hear the whole page.

8. Switch back to Narrator using Alt+Tab. (Hold down Alt and tap Tab repeatedly until Narrator is selected.) In the Narrator window, press Tab until Exit is selected and then press Enter. Press Enter again to select Yes. Narrator closes.

Explore All Access Settings

Although there are many other options you may appreciate in the Ease of Access Center (+U), I want to highlight a few (refer to Figure 16-11). Some of these options appear in more than one place, including the recommendations discussed in the task "Get Recommendations for a Specific Need."

➡ **Click the Use the Computer without a Display link.** You can then change how long pop-up notifications display from the default 5.0 seconds to up to 5 minutes. These pop-ups don't stick around long enough, it seems to me. If you use Narrator, select the Turn On Narrator check box to turn it on automatically when Windows 7 starts and select the Turn On Audio Descriptions check box. Click OK to return to the Ease of Access Center.

➡ **Click the Make the Computer Easier to See link** and then select the Make the Focus Rectangle Thicker check box. This option puts a thicker box around selections in dialog boxes. Change the Set the Thickness of the Blinking Cursor setting from the default of 1 to 3 or more (note the Preview). If you use the Magnifier, select the Turn On Magnifier check box to turn it on automatically when Windows 7 starts. Click OK to return to the Ease of Access Center.

➡ **Click the Make the Mouse Easier to Use link** and then select the Activate a Window by Hovering Over It with the Mouse check box. This option makes it unnecessary to click in a window to make it active — hovering your mouse pointer makes it active. If you have trouble with windows rearranging automatically as you drag them, select the Prevent Windows from Being Automatically Arranged When Moved to the Edge of the Screen check box. See Chapter 14 for information on modifying the mouse pointer.

➡ **Click the Make the Keyboard Easier to Use link** and then choose these options:

   • Select the Underline Keyboard Shortcut and Access Keys check box to add an underline to menu items below the letter you use with the Ctrl key, such as Ctrl+S for Save.

   • If you have trouble pressing combinations of keystrokes, such as Ctrl+S, select the Turn on Sticky Keys check box to turn combinations into sequences: press Ctrl and release, press S and release.

   • If you sometimes accidentally press Caps Lock, Num Lock, or Scroll Lock, select the Turn On Toggle Keys check box to hear a tone when you press one of these keys.

➡ **Click the Use Text or Visual Alternatives for Sounds link** and then select the Turn On Visual Notifications for Sounds check box if you have trouble hearing the Windows 7 alert and error sounds. See Chapter 14 for information on changing the sounds in Windows 7.

Part VI

Staying Safe and Keeping Windows 7 Healthy

The 5th Wave   By Rich Tennant

"Well, the first level of Windows 7 security seems good – I can't get the shrink-wrapping off."

Updating Windows 7

*T*hings change. As millions of people put
Windows 7 to the test every single hour,
Microsoft discovers glitches with how
Windows 7 works. Especially important are
any weaknesses in security that turn up only
when software is under fire in the real world.
Windows Update is the process for installing
patches (updates) to plug these holes in
Windows 7.

If you have an always-on Internet connection,
such as DSL or cable, Windows Update automatically downloads and installs the most
important updates as they become available
(usually, once a month). Security patches are
among the most important, so they're among
those updates downloaded automatically.

Less important, optional updates include
updates to device *drivers*, the programs that
make Windows 7 work with specific hardware,
such as your display and printer. Windows
Update keeps track of optional updates but
leaves the decision of whether to install — and
the installation — up to you. For this reason,
you need to run Windows Update and check
out the optional updates, at least occasionally,
perhaps once every month or two.

In this chapter, I show you how to work with the ever-changing world of Windows. You can start by activating Windows 7, a one-time process for validating your computer. And for the ever-changing part, you see how to work with Windows Update. Finally, you explore the option of upgrading from your current edition of Windows 7 to another in order to acquire additional features, such as more backup options.

 If you have a laptop but no Internet connection, take your computer to someplace with a free public wireless connection, such as a coffee shop or library. See Chapter 8 for information on connecting to the Internet before trying to activate or upgrade Windows 7 or trying to use Windows Update.

Activate Windows Now

1. You have to activate Windows 7 within 30 days of your first use. During activation, your computer contacts Microsoft over the Internet to confirm you have a legitimate copy of Windows 7. (If you aren't currently connected to the Internet, you need to connect before you can activate Windows 7.) To activate Windows 7, click Start and type **activate** in the Search Programs and Files text box. Click Activate Windows in the resulting list of matching programs.

 You can also activate Windows 7 by clicking on the pop-up notification that appears daily until you activate.

2. Click the words Activate Windows Online Now (as shown in **Figure 17-1**). After about a minute, you may see a message indicating activation was successful, and you'll know that you're done.

3. If you see the dialog box labeled Type Your Product Key, you need to enter the 25-character product key that appears on the Windows 7 Installation disc or on a sticker attached to your computer. Type the 25 characters (dashes are added automatically) in the text box. Click Next. If you get an error message, double-check the product key you entered against the copy on the computer or disc.

Click to activate Windows.

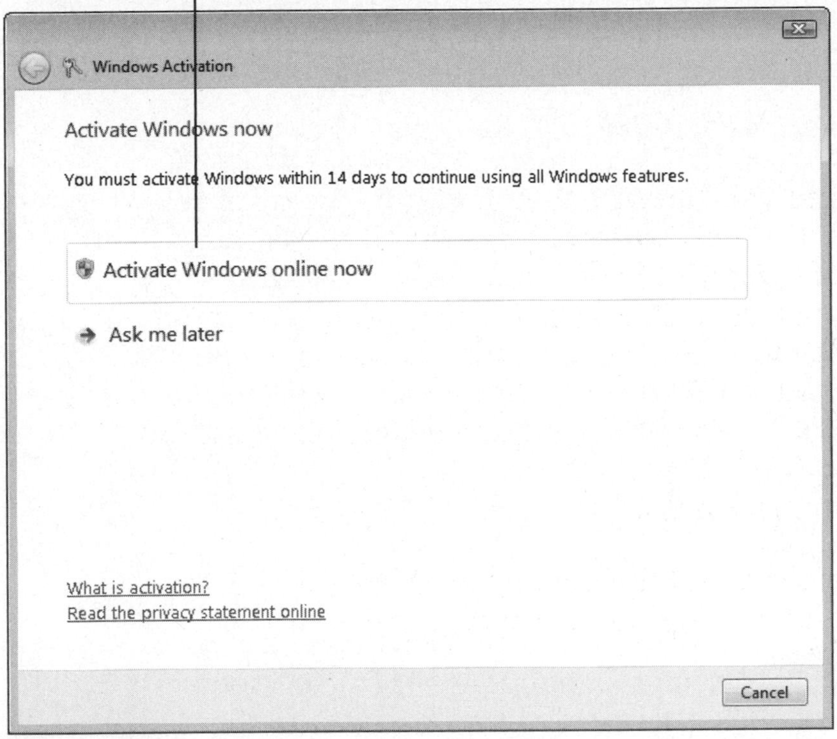

Figure 17-1

Perform a Windows Update

1. To run Windows Update, click Start and type **update** in the Search Programs and Files text box. Click Windows Update in the resulting list of matching programs. **Figure 17-2** shows the Windows Update screen that appears next.

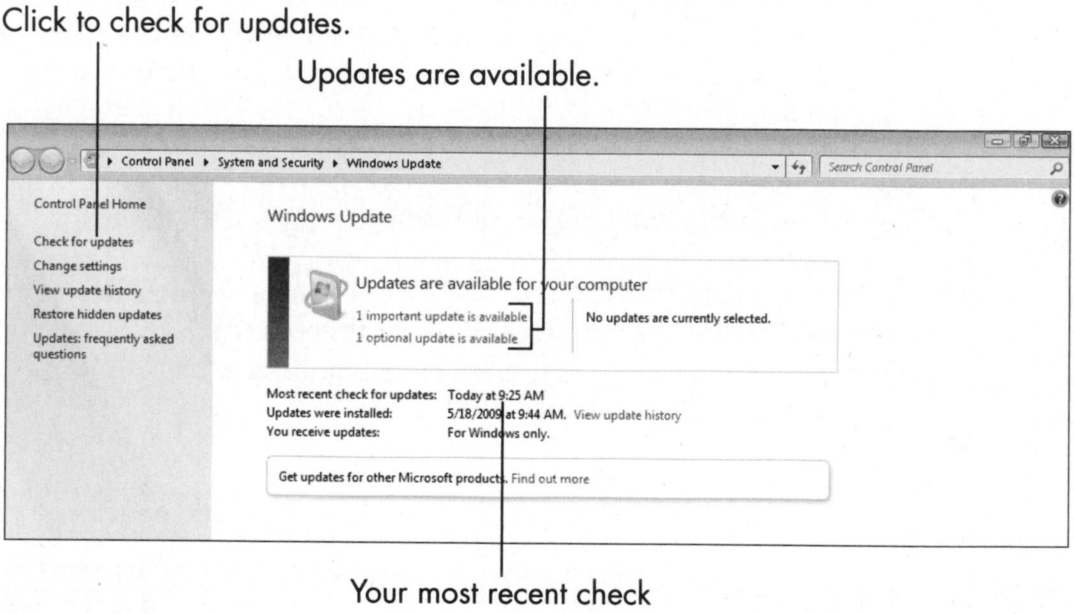

Click to check for updates.

Updates are available.

Your most recent check

Figure 17-2

2. Windows Update indicates the following:

- **Important Updates Available:** Microsoft recommends you install important updates as soon as possible. (Critical updates are automatically installed.) Important updates include noncritical security updates.

- **Optional Updates Available:** Optional updates are just that — optional — and include device drivers. However, you should consider making these updates carefully. If a device is working well, an update may not improve the situation.

- **Most Recent Check for Updates:** The date and time when Windows 7 checked for updates, which should be the current day or very recent. If the most recent check is a week old or older, click the Check for Updates link in the Navigation pane on the left.

- **Updates Were Installed:** The date and time when Windows 7 was last updated. If you want to know what update was performed, click View Update History.

- **You Receive Updates:** Initially, Windows Update is for Windows 7 only. See "Get Updates for Other Microsoft Products," later in this chapter.

3. Click the link for Important Update (if there is one). **Figure 17-3** shows one example of the resulting screen.

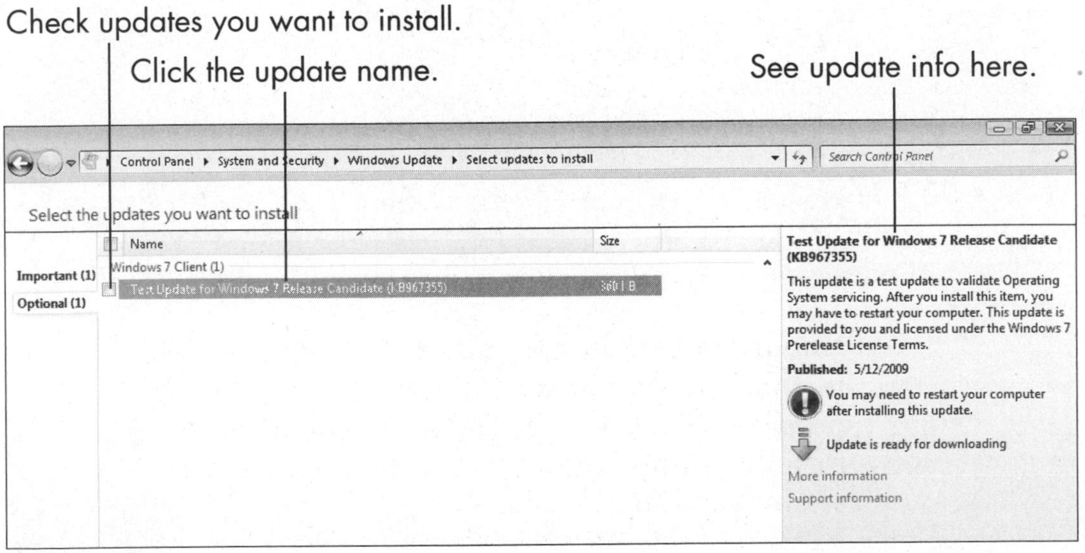

Check updates you want to install.

Click the update name.

See update info here.

Name	Size	**Test Update for Windows 7 Release Candidate (KB967355)**
Windows 7 Client (1)		This update is a test update to validate Operating System servicing. After you install this item, you may have to restart your computer. This update is provided to you and licensed under the Windows 7 Prerelease License Terms.
Test Update for Windows 7 Release Candidate (1-B967355)	360	B	**Published:** 5/12/2009

Important (1)

Optional (1)

Select the updates you want to install

You may need to restart your computer after installing this update.

Update is ready for downloading

More information

Support information

Figure 17-3

4. Click the link for Optional Updates (if there is one) on the Select Updates to Install screen or from the initial Windows Update screen.

5. To learn more about an update, click the name of the update. The area to the right then shows you some information for the selected update. Click the More Information link if you want to know even more.

 Notice whether the update description includes a warning (marked by an exclamation point in a circle) that you may need to restart your computer after installing this update. You won't have to restart immediately, in most cases. You can shut down at the end of the day and start normally the next day, instead, although both shutdown and start-up may take a few minutes longer than usual.

 Even with a description, you can't always determine how important an update is for your computer. Sometimes you have to guess. In general, I suggest installing important updates and not installing the updates labeled *optional*, especially if you don't know the updates will benefit your computer. You can opt to install an update later.

6. To select an update for installation, click the check box next to its name. Click OK to continue or Cancel if you don't want to perform an update. When I selected both updates available and clicked OK, I saw the screen shown in **Figure 17-4**.

7. To complete the update, click Install Updates. After you start the update, you shouldn't cancel or stop the update or close this window. You can minimize the window, if you want to do other things.

When the download and installation of the update are completed, the Windows Update screen reports The Updates Were Successfully Installed. If a restart isn't required, click OK to close Windows Update. If Windows Update seems to think it's best to restart your computer (and you agree), click the Restart Now button.

Remember that you should close other open programs and save open documents before you click the Restart Now button. If you want to wait to restart, just close the Windows Update window.

Click here to install selected updates.

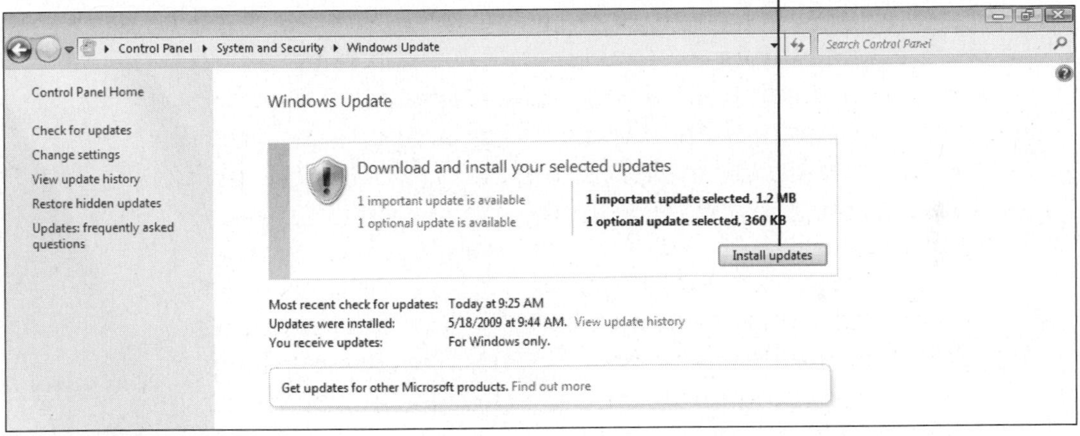

Figure 17-4

8. Take note of the messages that the update process has for you.

- During restart or shut down, you may see a message that updates are being installed. If you're shutting down, don't turn off your computer until this process finishes.

- When the computer starts, you may see messages about installing and configuring updates.

- Windows Update may display a notification in the taskbar concerning recent updates.

9. If you wish to confirm that the update was completed, start Windows Update (as you did in Step 1) and check for yourself. You should see a message similar to the one in **Figure 17-5**.

Click here to change update time.

Your computer is up to date!

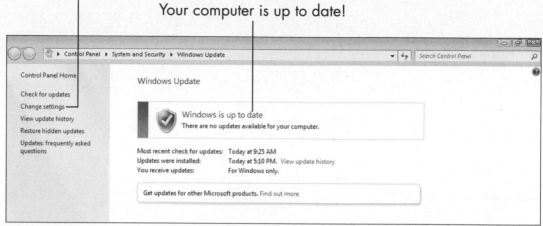

Figure 17-5

Change the Time When Windows Update Runs

1. For some reason, Microsoft schedules Windows Update to run at 3 AM every day. If necessary, Windows 7 will turn on your computer automatically so that Windows Update can run. If your computer is in the guest room, avoid waking guests by clicking Change Settings in the Navigation pane on the left of the Windows Update window.

2. You see the Choose How Windows Can Install Updates window, as shown in **Figure 17-6**. Click the down arrow next to Install New Updates At and select a time from the drop-down list. Change the time to one when the computer is likely to be on, such as 12 PM.

3. Click OK to save your change.

 The only way to guarantee the computer won't turn on in the middle of the night is to plug your computer into a power strip and turn that off after you shut down. For laptops, remove the battery if you intend to prevent Windows 7 from starting on its own.

Change the time for updates here.

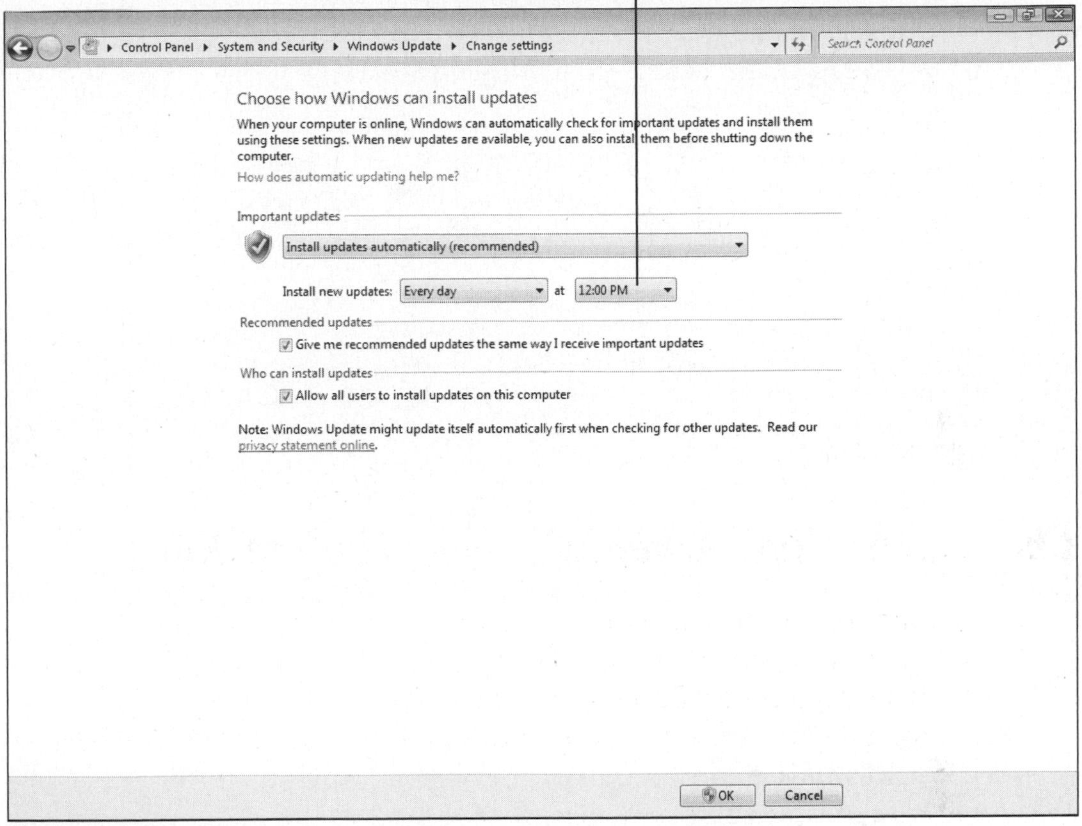

Figure 17-6

Get Updates for Other Microsoft Products

1. Windows Update automatically installs important updates for Windows 7. If you use other Microsoft software — in particular, Microsoft Office for word processing (Word) or spreadsheets (Excel) — you can have Windows Update check for additional updates, as well. In Windows Update, click the Find Out More link, if the screen displays that option next to Get Updates for Other Microsoft Products (refer to Figure 17-2). If you don't have this option, the choice to check for additional updates may already be selected (see Step 5).

2. Internet Explorer launches and automatically browses the Microsoft Update site shown in **Figure 17-7**. Select the check box to agree to the Terms of Use. (What choice do you have, really?) Then click Install.

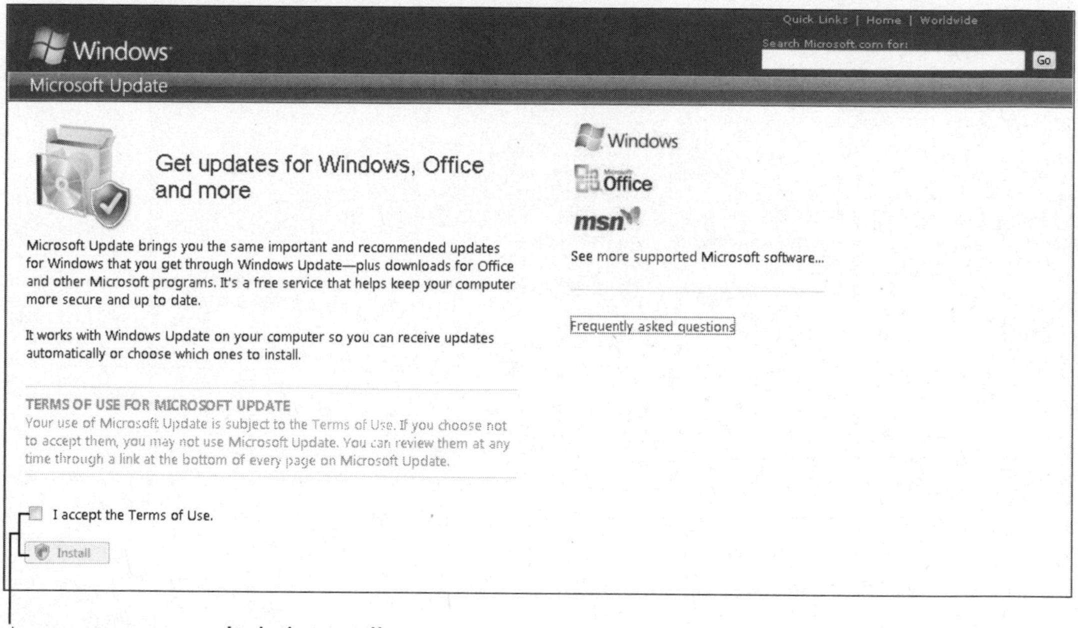

Accept terms and click Install.

Figure 17-7

3. User Account Control may display a dialog box to confirm running Windows Update. Click Yes.

4. The next Web page indicates Microsoft Update was successfully installed. Click the X in the upper-right corner to close the browser window.

5. Windows Update automatically starts and searches for updates. If Windows Update doesn't start, see "Perform a Windows Update," earlier in this chapter, to start it. The You Receive Updates option now states `For Windows and Other Products from Microsoft Update`, as shown in **Figure 17-8**.

Your chosen updates are here.

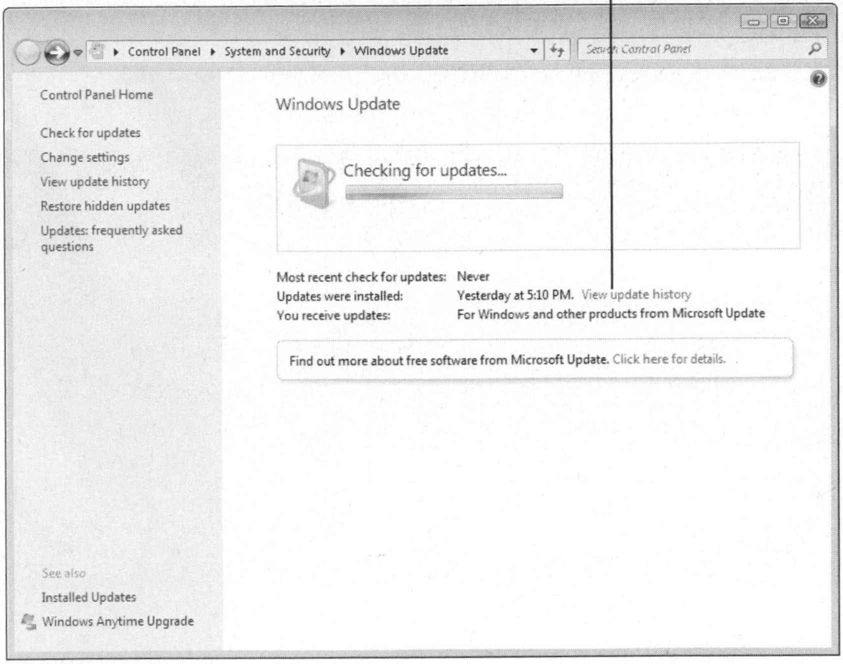

Figure 17-8

6. If updates are found and you want to install them, continue with the steps (starting with Step 4) in the "Perform a Windows Update" section, earlier in this chapter.

Discontinue Additional Updates

1. You may change your mind and decide you don't want updates for Microsoft products or notification of new software. No problem! Run Windows Update by clicking Start and typing **update** in the Search Programs and Files text box. Then click Windows Update in the resulting list of matching programs.

2. Click Change Settings in the left pane of the Windows Update window that appears. In the resulting dialog box, you should see the options you want to discontinue in the Microsoft Update and Software Notifications sections, as shown in **Figure** 17-9. (These options don't appear in the Choose How Windows Can Install Updates dialog box unless you've completed the steps in the preceding section.)

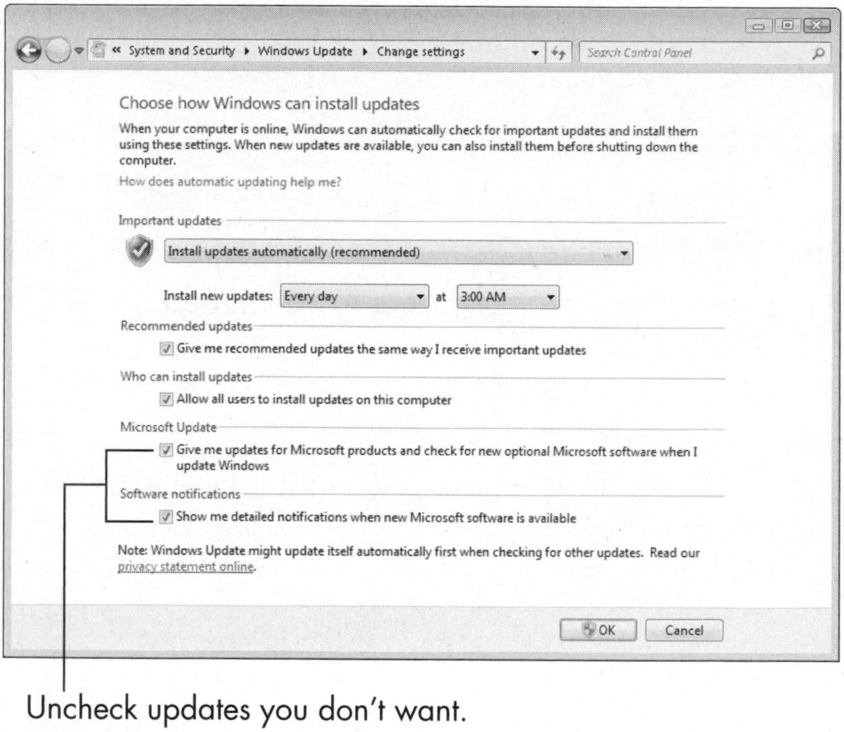

Uncheck updates you don't want.

Figure 17-9

3. Each update option has a separate check box. Deselect the check box next to the options you want to discontinue. Then Click OK.

Upgrade Windows Anytime

1. Windows 7 has several editions with different features. See URL for details comparing editions. For a fee, you can upgrade to another edition. If you decide to upgrade to a version with more features or want to know more about your options, click Start, type **anytime** in the Search Programs and Files text box, and click Windows Anytime Upgrade in the resulting list of matching programs.

2. The Windows Anytime Upgrade screen displays your current edition in the upper-right corner. **Figure 17-10** shows that I'm running Windows 7 Home Premium. If you have Windows 7 Ultimate, you're done (since there's nothing to upgrade to from Ultimate).

 If you have Windows 7 Starter, you may want the multimedia options in Home Premium. The Ultimate edition is less compelling.

3. Click the link labeled Go Online to See If Your Computer Is Ready to Upgrade to Another Edition of Windows 7. Click Download the Windows 7 Upgrade Advisor. On the next screen, click Download.

4. In the File Download Security Warning dialog box, click Save. In the Save As dialog box, click Save. After download completes, click Run. If the dialog box doesn't stay open after downloading, choose Start⇨Computer and click Downloads on the left. Double-click the Upgrade Advisor installer. Click Next and OK as needed.

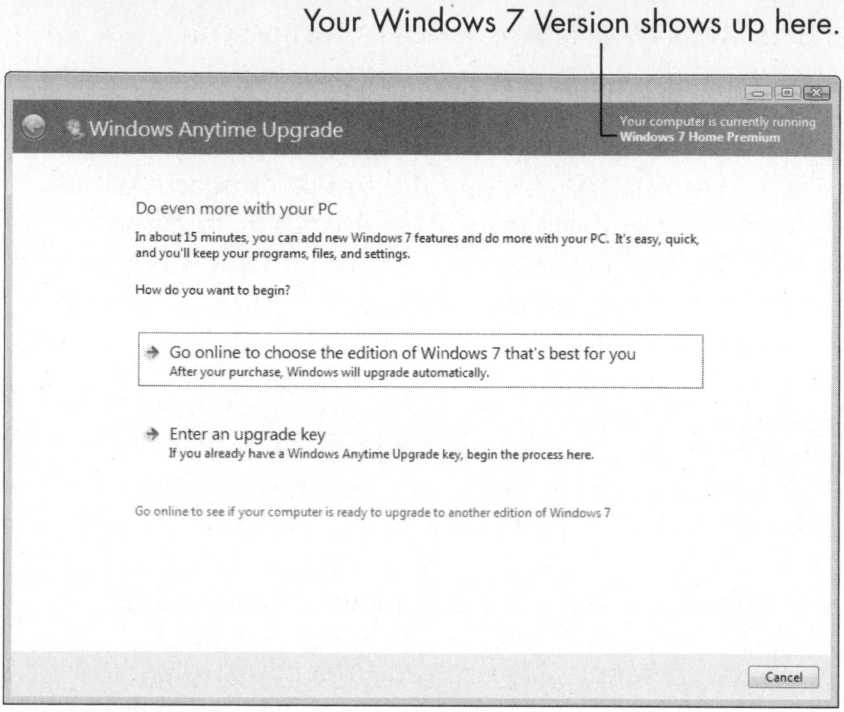

Your Windows 7 Version shows up here.

Figure 17-10

5. After the installer finishes, click Start. Click Windows 7 Upgrade Advisor on the Start menu. If the User Account Control dialog box prompts you for confirmation, click Yes.

6. On the first Advisor screen, click Start Check. The process takes a few minutes to run. Read the resulting Report screen. If you want to refer to the report later, click Save Report. Click Close.

7. Click Go Online to Choose the Edition of Windows 7 That's Best for You. Click Compare the Editions of Windows 7. Find your current edition in the columns of the chart. Look at editions to the right of your current edition. Do you see any features you want? If you don't see a feature you want, then you don't need to continue; close the window. If you see a feature you want, consider the following tip before proceeding to the next step.

If your edition of Windows 7 lacks a feature you want or need, you may be able to find other programs with the missing feature. There are many good — even free — programs available for download from the Web. Take the time to research a program before you download and install it, to avoid unreliable or dangerous software. Two good sources for software reviews are www.downloadsquad.com and www.howtogeek.com.

8. Click the button to upgrade from your current edition to the edition you intend to buy. Confirm your selection. On the payment screen, fill in the required information. Click Checkout.

9. After a few minutes, Windows 7 completes downloading the missing features and upgrading the edition. Click Restart Now. When Windows 7 restarts, the Congratulations screen indicates your new edition.

Protecting Your Computer

Windows 7 uses the Action Center to keep you informed of security and maintenance issues that need attention, such as antivirus protection and file backup. The Action Center alerts you to issues you should investigate by displaying a flag with an *X* over a red circle in the notification area of the taskbar.

The Action Center divides issues into Security and Maintenance sections. As far as maintenance goes, Windows 7 automatically performs certain functions to protect your computer. But in the last section of this chapter, I do show you how to check your hard drive for file system errors. Your hard drive's well-being is essential for your computer's overall well-being.

Then you have security issues. For most new computers running Windows 7, the pressing security issue is protection against viruses. *Viruses* are programs designed to work undetected against your interests, and they can employ a variety of tactics. A virus may

➠ **Search your system** for information that's useful for identity theft, such as your Social Security number (which should not be anywhere on your computer), credit card numbers, or bank and investment account numbers.

➠ **Install** *spyware,* such as a *keystroke logger,* a program that records every keystroke you type, as a way to snag passwords as you enter them into a program or on a Web site.

➠ **Spread to other systems** through e-mail, over a network connection, or by way of flash drives.

Given the severity of risk viruses pose to your security, you'll be surprised that Windows 7 doesn't include antivirus software, although the company that sold your computer may have added some. In this chapter, you find out how to download, install, and run this vital software.

Check the Action Center

1. If you see the Action Center icon (the image of a flag) in the taskbar's notification area, hover your mouse pointer over that icon for a summary tooltip. When the icon also has an *X* over the flag image, you know that the Action Center has a message for you. Click the icon to see a list of the Action Center messages. In **Figure 18-1**, the Action Center notification pop-up indicates one important message (finding an antivirus program) and a second, presumably less-important issue (setting up a backup).

Summary of messages

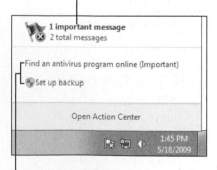

Specific messages

Figure 18-1

2. You can click a specific message within the pop-up notification to see related details, and you can also click Open Action Center for access to all messages. **Figure 18-2** shows the result when you choose to open the Action Center.

If you don't see the Action Center icon in the taskbar, click Start and type **action** in the Search Programs and Files text box; then click Action Center from the resulting list.

Security and Maintenance section headers

Control Panel ▸ System and Security ▸ Action Center

Search Control Panel

Control Panel Home

Change Action Center settings

Change User Account Control settings

View archived messages

View performance information

Review recent messages and resolve problems

Action Center has detected one or more issues for you to review.

Security

Virus protection (Important)

Windows did not find antivirus software on this computer.

Turn off messages about virus protection

Find a program online

Maintenance

Set up backup

Your files are not being backed up.

Turn off messages about Windows Backup

Set up backup

If you don't see your problem listed, try one of these:

Troubleshooting
Find and fix problems

Recovery
Restore your computer to an earlier time

See also

Backup and Restore

Windows Update

Windows Program Compatibility Troubleshooter

Figure 18-2

 Most Action Center issues have an option to Turn Off Messages about the particular issue. Don't turn off a message until you determine that it's truly irrelevant to you. On the other hand, the X — indicating a problem to resolve — appears over the Action Center icon until you address it or turn off the messages (for an issue you can safely ignore).

3. Click anywhere on the Security heading to expand that section of the Action Center, as shown in **Figure 18-3**. Most of the items in this area are marked On or OK. Here's a brief description of each item under Security:

- *Network Firewall:* The firewall scans Internet traffic and blocks activity from programs that don't have explicit permission to use Internet access. When you install a program that uses the Internet, you may be asked to approve the connection the first time. The safest practice is to reject online connections that you don't initiate or recognize.

- *Windows Update:* See Chapter 17 for information on Windows Update.

- *Virus Protection:* Having virus protection for your computer is essential. See the task "Install Antivirus Software," later in this chapter, for instructions on making it so.

- *Spyware and Unwanted Software Protection:* If this service is on, you have basic protection from malicious software.

- *Internet Security Settings:* These settings pertain to your browser. The default settings may be adequate. To learn more, see the following tip.

 I recommend *Using the Internet Safely For Seniors For Dummies* (Wiley Publishing, Inc.), by Nancy Muir and Linda Criddle, as a guide for helping you deal with online security confidently.

- *User Account Control (UAC):* This function notifies you of programs that try to make changes to your system and requires that you confirm any such changes. In particular, UAC lets you know when a program tries to run or install software that may be malicious.

- *Network Access Protection (NAP):* If this service is off, that isn't a problem, unless this computer connects to a business network that requires NAP to protect the business network from machines that aren't properly protected.

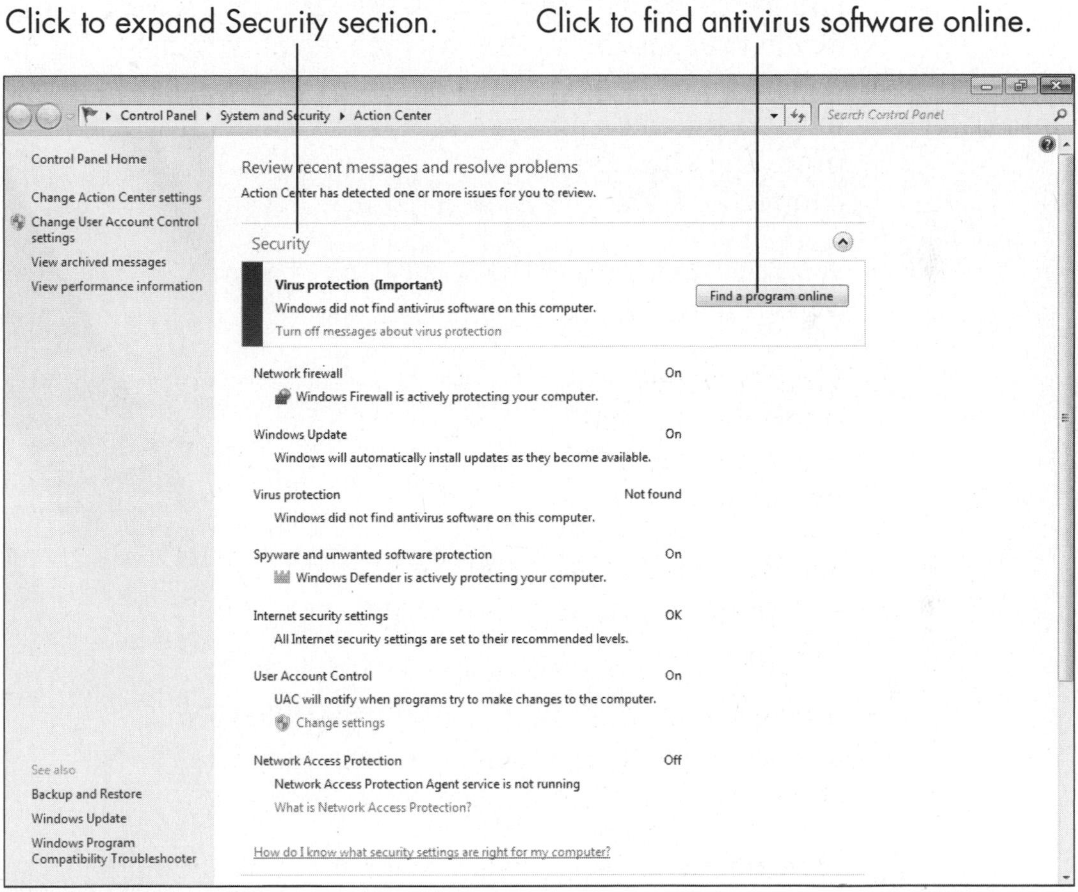

Click to expand Security section.　　　Click to find antivirus software online.

Figure 18-3

4. Click the Security heading to collapse that section. Then click the Maintenance heading to see what that section includes. Among other options, setting up backups is an item that Windows 7 likes to remind you of. (See Chapter 19 for information on backing up your data.) You can click the Maintenance heading to collapse that section.

Check the Action Center weekly or monthly to see whether any new messages have appeared. This is Windows 7's primary means of alerting you to potential problems.

Install Antivirus Software

1. In the Action Center, if Windows didn't find antivirus software on your computer, it prompts you to get cracking and get some. You'll need an Internet connection and Internet Explorer (IE) for this task. See Chapter 8 for information about connecting to the Internet and Chapter 9 for information on using IE.

2. In the Action Center, click the button to Find a Program Online (refer to Figure 18-3) under the Security heading. A Web page of Microsoft security software providers appears in your browser. Each company listed provides antivirus software. Some of these programs are free; some operate as an annual subscription. You may click on the company logo of any of these companies.

 For these steps, I lead you through the process of downloading and installing free avast! antivirus software, an antivirus product that I recommend and have used for years.

3. In the IE address bar, type **avast** and press Ctrl+Enter, which automatically adds www. and .com to the address. The Web page shown in **Figure 18-4** appears. On the avast! home page, click the Free Software tab and then click the Download button under Home Edition. (If these options don't appear on the home page, click the Download navigation button at the top, then Programs, then Home Edition. Click the Download button.) A second download page may appear, in which case, click the Download Now button. *Note:* Watch out for ads on these pages that also say download — those other products are not what you're after.

Click to download.   Click for free software.

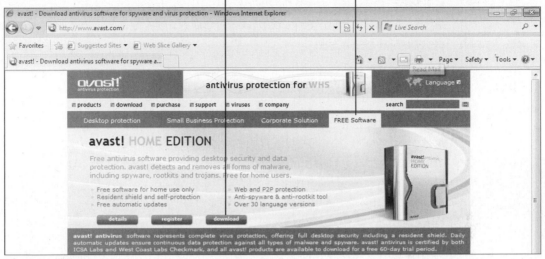

Figure 18-4

4. The IE Information Bar appears below the tab to indicate IE has blocked the download, as shown in **Figure 18-5**. (Don't worry; this is the normal, precautionary reaction that you want to happen with IE.) Click the Information Bar and then click Download File. The File Download Security Warning appears. Click Save.

Click to continue the download.

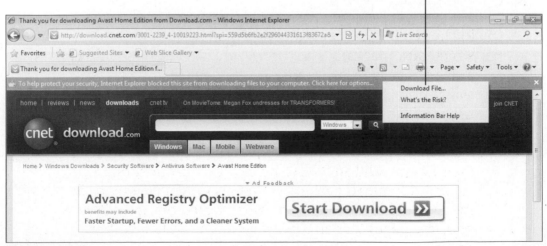

Figure 18-5

5. The Save As dialog box appears. Without changing anything, click the Save button.

6. After a few seconds, the Download Complete dialog box appears. Click the Run button. (If this dialog box doesn't appear, click the Start button and click Downloads or type **down** in the Start menu's search box and click Downloads. Double-click avast_home_setup.) The User Account Control dialog box appears to confirm your intent to run the setup. Click Yes.

7. In the first avast! Antivirus Setup dialog box (shown in **Figure 18-6**), choose your language and click Next. avast! downloads additional files and shows you another dialog box. If you're running any other programs, such as WordPad or Solitaire, close those programs to reduce interference with the setup. Click Next.

Choose your language here.

Figure 18-6

8. The avast! setup continues with a series of dialog boxes.
Your part is simple — see the following table.

This Dialog Box Appears	You Do This
Read Me	Click Next.
License Agreement	Click I Agree, then Next.
Destination	Click Next.
Configuration	Click Next.
Installation Information	Click Next.
The Installation Progress	Nothing.
A pop-up asking if you want to schedule a boot-time antivirus scan	Click Yes.
Setup Finished	Click Restart and Finish.

9. Windows 7 exits and restarts. Before Windows 7 loads
again — because you clicked Yes to schedule a boot-time
antivirus scan — avast! scans your system for viruses.
Don't be concerned as filenames flash on the screen
during this process. This could take up to half an hour.

 If your antivirus software finds a virus, it may ask you
what to do. The best option is to delete a virus when
it is found. However, some viruses infect documents.
In such a case, you can choose the Quarantine option
if you don't have a backup copy of the infected
document. Quarantine moves the infected document
to a safe area. You'll need to search the Web and
download a program that can extract the virus from
the document. It is better to have a backup of your
documents — see Chapter 19 to create a backup
before trouble comes.

Register Your Antivirus Software

1. After you install antivirus software, the company providing the software usually offers you the opportunity to register your software. Registering gives you access to updates. Antivirus software changes almost daily in the fight against virus developments.

2. If you followed the steps in the preceding section and installed avast!, you can proceed with these steps to register it. When avast! finishes the initial scan, Windows 7 starts again. The Welcome to avast! Home Edition dialog box appears, as shown in **Figure 18-7**. This dialog box informs you that you have 60 days to obtain a free registration key. avast! requires a new, free registration key every 14 months. To obtain the key immediately, click the link labeled avast! Home Registration Page. Otherwise, click OK to close the dialog box.

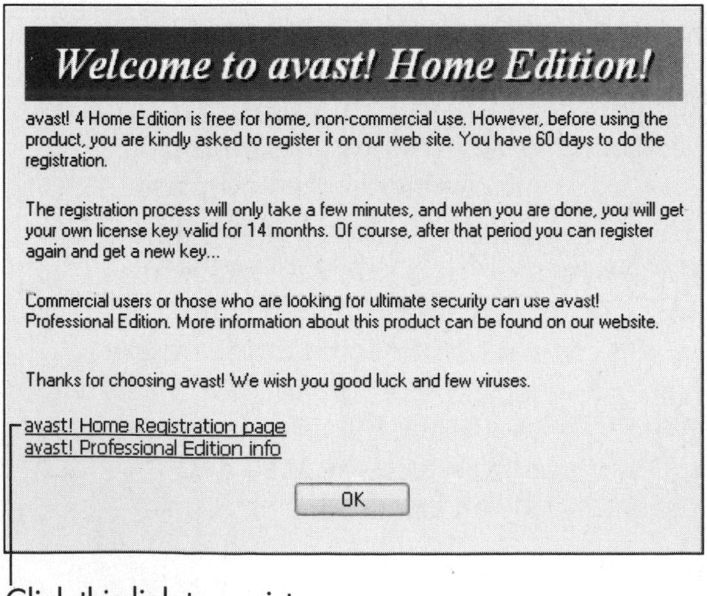

Welcome to avast! Home Edition!

avast! 4 Home Edition is free for home, non-commercial use. However, before using the product, you are kindly asked to register it on our web site. You have 60 days to do the registration.

The registration process will only take a few minutes, and when you are done, you will get your own license key valid for 14 months. Of course, after that period you can register again and get a new key...

Commercial users or those who are looking for ultimate security can use avast! Professional Edition. More information about this product can be found on our website.

Thanks for choosing avast! We wish you good luck and few viruses.

avast! Home Registration page
avast! Professional Edition info

OK

Click this link to register.

Figure 18-7

3. On the avast! Registration page, click the I'm a New User link. The next page prompts you for some information. Enter your e-mail address twice, your name, and your country. Click the check box to confirm you'll use the program at home. Enter the Control Letters that appear onscreen. Click Register. A confirmation message appears onscreen, saying that an e-mail message has been sent to your address. This message contains your license key.

4. Open your e-mail program and look in your inbox for a message from avast! with your license key. Refer to Chapter 10 for information on using e-mail.

5. To enter your license key, click the left arrow in the notification area on the taskbar. Right-click over the avast! icon. (It's a white *a* on a blue circle.) Click About avast! and click the License Key button in the About avast! dialog box.

6. If the User Account Control dialog box appears, click Yes. Then, in the Registration dialog box, enter your registration key. The easiest and most accurate way to enter the registration key is to select the key in the e-mail you received, press Ctrl+C to copy, click in the Registration text box (shown in **Figure 18-8**), and press Ctrl+V to paste. If you can't copy the key, enter the key as it appears in the e-mail. Click OK. avast! thanks you; click OK again.

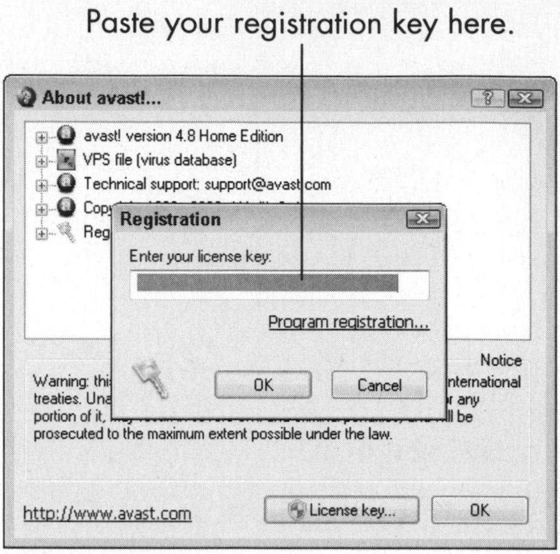

Paste your registration key here.

Figure 18-8

7. Return to the Action Center (see the task "Check the Action Center" for steps). If there are no current issues, the Security section is collapsed; you can assume all is well.

8. If Virus Protection (under Security) is highlighted, avast! may need permission to update. Click the Update Now button. The Action Center may ask "Do You Want to Run This Program?" as in **Figure 18-9**. Click the Don't Show Me This Again check box and click Yes, I Trust the Publisher and Want to Run This Program. avast! downloads and installs updates. From this point on, avast! automatically installs updates and protects your computer from virus threats.

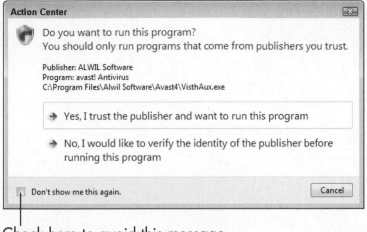

Check here to avoid this message.

Figure 18-9

Scan a Folder or Disk for Viruses

1. Although avast! — or any other antivirus program — automatically scans for viruses, you may want to manually scan certain disks or folders, including the following:

- **Flash drive:** Always scan a USB flash drive that has been used with another computer, because flash drives can carry viruses from one computer to another.

- **Downloads folder:** Files in the Downloads folder have come from the Internet via the browser or e-mail. Scan this folder before opening downloaded files or moving files to other folders.

- **Network folder:** Although every computer on your network should be equally protected, you never know what someone else is doing with his or her computer, so scan a network folder before opening or copying files from that folder.

2. To scan a disk for viruses, choose Start⇨Computer (+E). Right-click over the disk or flash drive. Choose Scan. (The avast! icon appears next to this option.) To scan a folder, right-click over the folder and choose Scan *Folder Name* from the shortcut menu, as shown in **Figure 18-10**.

Right-click folder or disk.

Click Scan.

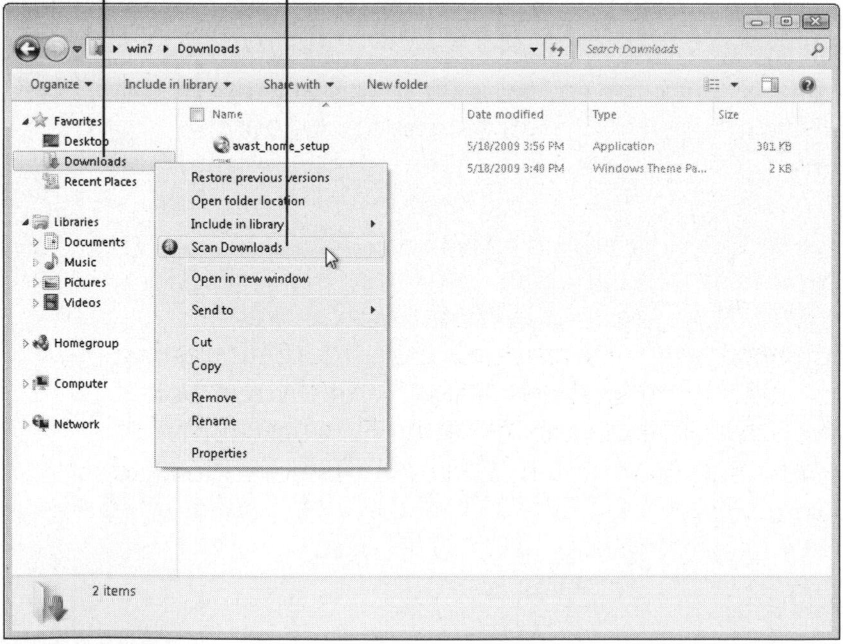

Figure 18-10

3. As the scan begins, the avast! Quick Scanner dialog box appears. A folder or disk with few files takes just seconds to scan. A large number of files may take several minutes to scan. The dialog box disappears automatically, unless a virus is found. If a virus is found and avast! asks what to do, choose to delete or quarantine the virus. In most cases, delete the virus. If you got this infected file from a friend, warn her to update her antivirus software and run a scan.

Schedule a Disk Check

1. Hard disks store information in magnetically charged bits. Over time, hard disks can lose their ability to record information in random areas. Windows 7 can scan your hard disk for potential problems. If problems are found, Windows 7 tries to move data out of the affected area and marks that area to be avoided for data storage in the future. To run the error-checking function, choose Start⇨Computer (or press +E). Right-click over the Local Disk (C:) and choose Properties. The General tab of the Properties dialog box appears, as shown in **Figure 18-11**.

 If you want to give your hard disk a more interesting name than Local Disk, type a name in the text box above Local Disk on the General tab. Click Apply. The new name appears in Windows Explorer, instead of Local Disk.

Give your hard drive a name here.

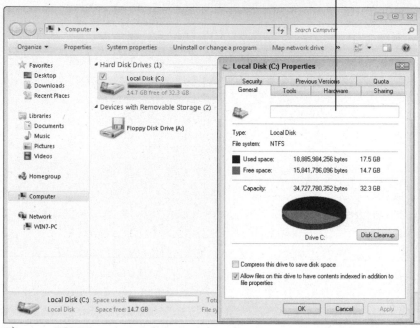

Figure 18-11

2. Click the Tools tab; then click the Check Now button in the Error-Checking panel. **Figure 18-12** shows the resulting Check Disk Local Disk (C:) dialog box.

3. The Automatically Fix File System Errors check box should already be selected. Select the check box called Scan for and Attempt Recover of Bad Sectors. (The *bad sectors* are those weakened or corrupted areas of the disk's surface.) Click the Start button.

4. Windows 7 reports that it can't check the disk while it's in use (see **Figure 18-13**). Click the Schedule Disk Check button.

Choose options for your disk check.

Click Start.

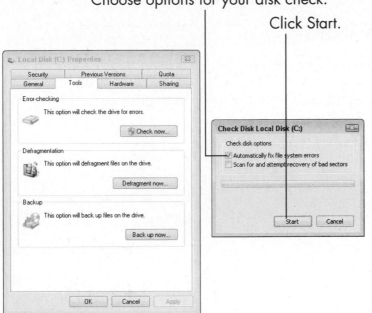

Figure 18-12

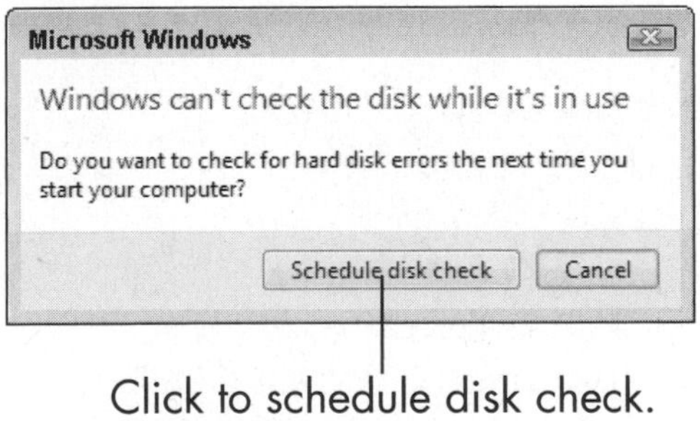

Click to schedule disk check.

Figure 18-13

5. The next time you start your computer, the error-checking function will start before Windows 7 loads. You may see a message giving you 9 seconds to press any key to bypass the check. Let the check run without interruption. A simple text screen of white text on a black background will indicate progress. The scan could take up to an hour or so. After the scan is complete, Windows 7 loads normally. You won't receive any reports, but you can assume the error-checking function has done its job. Run this test every couple of months or anytime your computer acts weird.

Keeping Your Data Safe

Chapter 19

*1*f your computer is stolen, lost, or destroyed, you can replace it — at a price. But, the *documents and photos* you create — your data — are irreplaceable. Consider how miserable you might be if you lost a favorite photo or precious document forever.

As you work with your computer, any number of things can go wrong. Everyone loses something on the computer eventually. This is no reason to fear, but it is good reason to create *backups*, which are duplicates of your data that you keep in separate storage. You can back up just your most precious files, all of your files, or even the entire computer if you have the space for a very large backup.

In this chapter, you find out how to use Windows 7's tools to back up selected data or everything on your computer. I also show you how to *restore* files (put them back on the computer) and urge you to practice with at least one file so that you're ready for the real drill. You can also follow the steps in this chapter to create an emergency disc for starting the computer and repairing problems with Windows 7.

If you just have a few precious photos or documents, you can copy those files to a flash drive. See Chapter 4 for those simple steps.

Back Up Your Documents and Photos

1. Open the Start menu and type **backup** in the Search Programs and Files text box. Choose Backup and Restore from the list of matching results. The Backup and Restore window opens, as shown in **Figure 19-1**.

Click to set up backup.

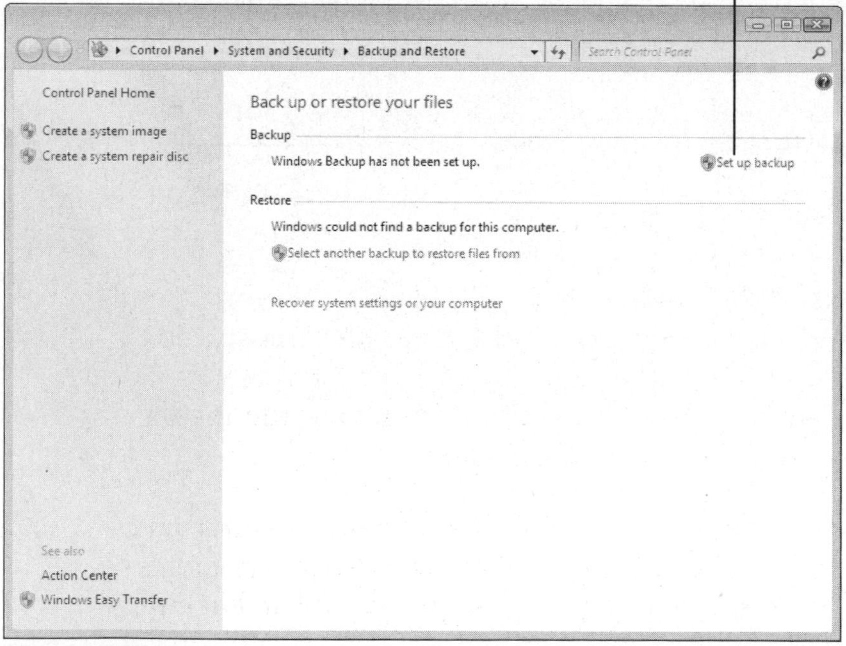
Control Panel ▸ System and Security ▸ Backup and Restore
Search Control Panel
Control Panel Home
Create a system image
Create a system repair disc
Back up or restore your files
Backup
Windows Backup has not been set up.
Set up backup
Restore
Windows could not find a backup for this computer.
Select another backup to restore files from
Recover system settings or your computer
See also
Action Center
Windows Easy Transfer

Figure 19-1

2. Click the Set Up Backup link. A dialog box shows up and displays the message `Starting Windows Backup`. Wait for this process to finish. The next dialog box allows you to select where you want to save your backup. If the

Save Backup On list box is empty, you don't have a device to back up to. Suitable *backup media*, as shown in **Figure 19-2**, includes:

- **Recordable DVD or CD:** This is the option of last resort, assuming you have no other options. Discs are less convenient to handle, carry, and store than other options.

- **Memory card:** This option uses the same kind of memory card as digital cameras. If you have a spare card and a card slot or reader, this may suffice.

- **Flash drive:** This option may be better than the previous options for ease of use and capacity.

- **External hard drive:** This is the best option. An external hard drive allows you to back up much more than any other option, creating a more complete backup.

If necessary, attach or insert the backup media you intend to use and click the Refresh button. If [Recommended] appears next to one of the choices, that's the one you should use. If none is recommended, choose the media with the most free space. Click Next.

 Removable media (such as discs, memory cards, and flash drives) are marked as unsuitable for a *system image*. A system image is the most complete backup, which can be used to restore your entire disk, including all changes to Windows 7 and all installed programs, as well as your data. You may be able to back up your own files — all your documents, photos, music, and so on — to media that doesn't have sufficient room for an entire system image.

Choose the recommended media option.

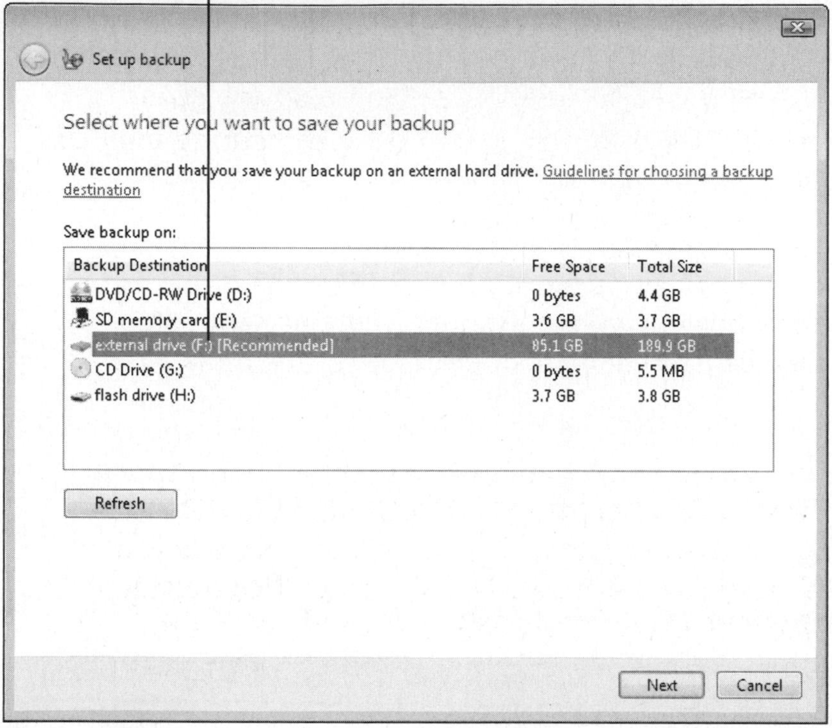

Figure 19-2

You can move backward through the Set Up Backup dialog boxes by clicking the Back button (an arrow on a blue circle) in the upper-left corner. Use it if you need to review or change an earlier step.

3. The What Do You Want to Back Up? dialog box appears. Only one of the two following options may be available, depending on the backup media you chose earlier:

- **Let Windows Choose:** Windows 7 backs up all data files that are in standard libraries and folders for all users. If the backup media has sufficient space, a system image is created. Choose this option if you have an external hard drive attached.

- **Let Me Choose:** You select the folders to back up on the next screen. Only data files are backed up; files belonging to programs or Windows 7 are not backed up. This option requires less free space on the backup media and less time to perform the backup. However, you risk missing something in the backup.

Click an option button and then click Next.

4. If you selected Let Windows Choose in the previous step, skip to the next step.

If you selected Let Me Choose in the previous step, the What Do You Want to Back Up? dialog box enables you to select folders to back up, as shown in **Figure 19-3**. The data files for your username should remain selected. You need to select other folders only if you store files outside the standard Windows 7 user folders. See Chapter 4 for information on using these standard folders. Click Next.

5. In the next dialog box, review your backup settings. Click the Change Schedule link, and the How Often Do You Want to Back Up? dialog box appears, as shown in **Figure 19-4**. If you don't want the backup to run automatically, deselect the Run Backup On a Schedule check box. If you do want an automatic backup, how often do you want to do it? Schedule a backup when the computer is likely to be on but not in heavy use; if you use removable media, such as a flash drive, you need to leave it in place when the backup is scheduled or be present to insert the media when it's needed.

- **How Often:** A daily backup provides the greatest insurance against data loss. A weekly backup may suffice, although you put six days of document changes at risk if something goes wrong before the next backup. A monthly backup may not be frequent enough to keep your data safe.

Select folders to include in the backup.

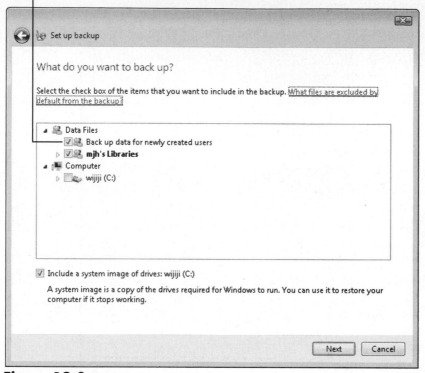

Figure 19-3

- **What Day:** If you select Weekly in the previous option, choose a day of the week. If you select Monthly, choose a day of the month.

- **What Time:** What time of day is the computer on but not in heavy use? For me, that's lunch- or dinnertime.

Click OK to close the dialog box.

6. In the Review Your Backup Setting dialog box (see **Figure 19-5**), click the Save Settings and Run Backup button to begin the backup.

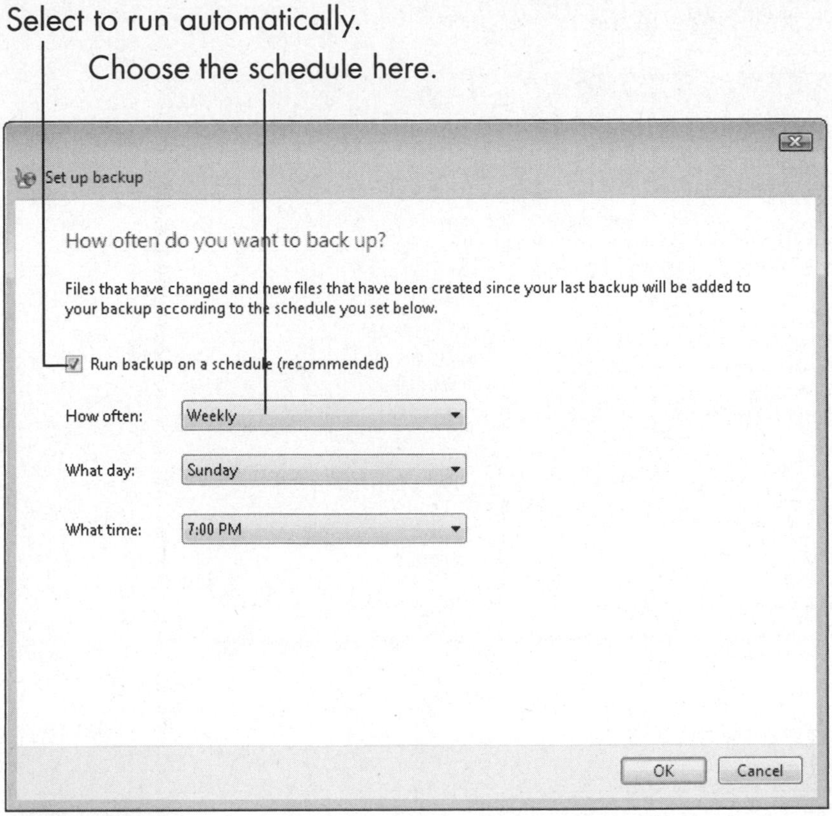

Select to run automatically.

Choose the schedule here.

Set up backup

How often do you want to back up?

Files that have changed and new files that have been created since your last backup will be added to your backup according to the schedule you set below.

☑ Run backup on a schedule (recommended)

How often: Weekly ▼

What day: Sunday ▼

What time: 7:00 PM ▼

OK   Cancel

Figure 19-4

7. The original Backup and Restore window appears with an indication that the backup is in progress. Click the View Details button if you want the nitty-gritty; click Close on the View Details screen to return to this dialog box.

 Although you can use the computer during backup, the process may be faster if you don't run other programs at the same time. Also, don't shut down or turn off the computer until the backup is complete. Leave your computer on overnight, if necessary.

8. When the backup is complete, the Backup and Restore window displays the time of the next backup and the last (previous) backup, which just completed (see **Figure 19-6**). At any time after setting up backup, you can do the following from this window:

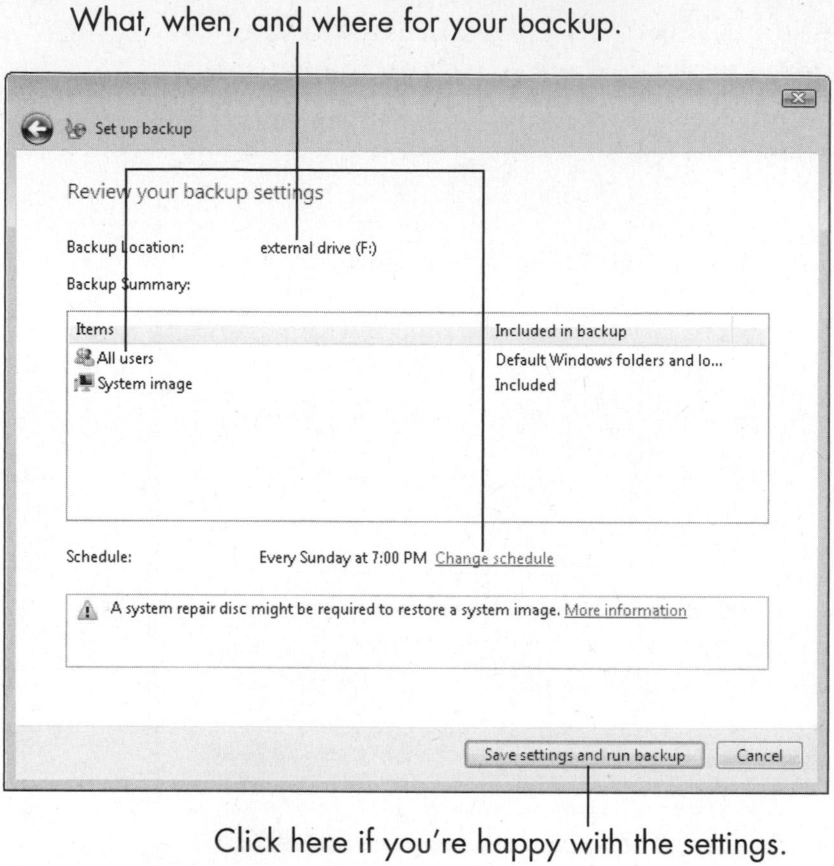

What, when, and where for your backup.

Click here if you're happy with the settings.

Figure 19-5

- **Change Settings:** Clicking this link takes you through all of the preceding steps in this list so you can adjust when, where, and what you're backing up.

- **Manage Space:** Click this link only if your backup media is 80 percent full. You can delete older backups to make room for newer backups.

- **Back Up Now:** Click this button to run an unscheduled backup.

If you don't want a scheduled backup to run, click the Turn Off Schedule link on the left side of the screen. You can still run a backup manually whenever you like or click the Turn On Schedule link.

Manage your backups from this window.

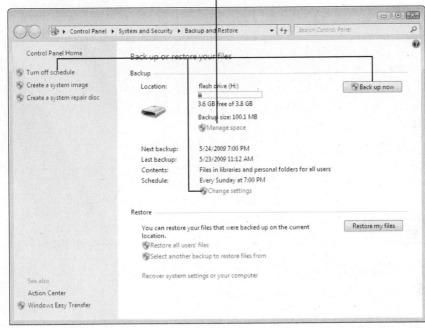

Figure 19-6

Restore Files from Backup

1. If you're lucky, you'll never need your backup. However, if you lose a file (or more), you can restore the missing files from your backup. Consider restoring a file for practice, just so you have some experience before you really need to restore a file (under the pressure of loss). Open the Start menu and type **backup** in the Search text box. Choose Backup and Restore from the resulting list. The Backup and Restore window opens (refer to Figure 19-6). Click the Restore My Files button.

2. In the Restore Files dialog box (see **Figure** 19-7), use any of three ways to locate files or folders you intend to restore:

- **Search:** Click this button if you know the filename but not the location of the original. In the search dialog box, type part of the name of the file you intend to restore. Click the found file to select it to restore. Click Select All if you intend to restore all the found files. Click OK.

- **Browse for Files:** Click this button to open a dialog box of folders. Click the backup name and then open the folder that contained the original file. Click the found file to select it to restore. Click Add Files.

- **Browse for Folders:** Click this button to open a dialog box of folders. Click a folder to restore all the files in that folder. Click Add Folder.

The files you select with the preceding methods appear in the dialog box. Repeat these steps if you need to select additional files or folders to restore.

 If you can't find a backup of the file you want to restore and you made more than one backup, in the first Restore Files dialog box, click the Choose a Different Date link. Choose All from the Show Backups From drop-down list. Pick a backup that is likely to have the file you intend to restore. You may have to repeat this process for more than one backup.

3. After you've selected one or more files or folders in the preceding step, click Next in the original Restore Files dialog box (shown in Figure 19-7).

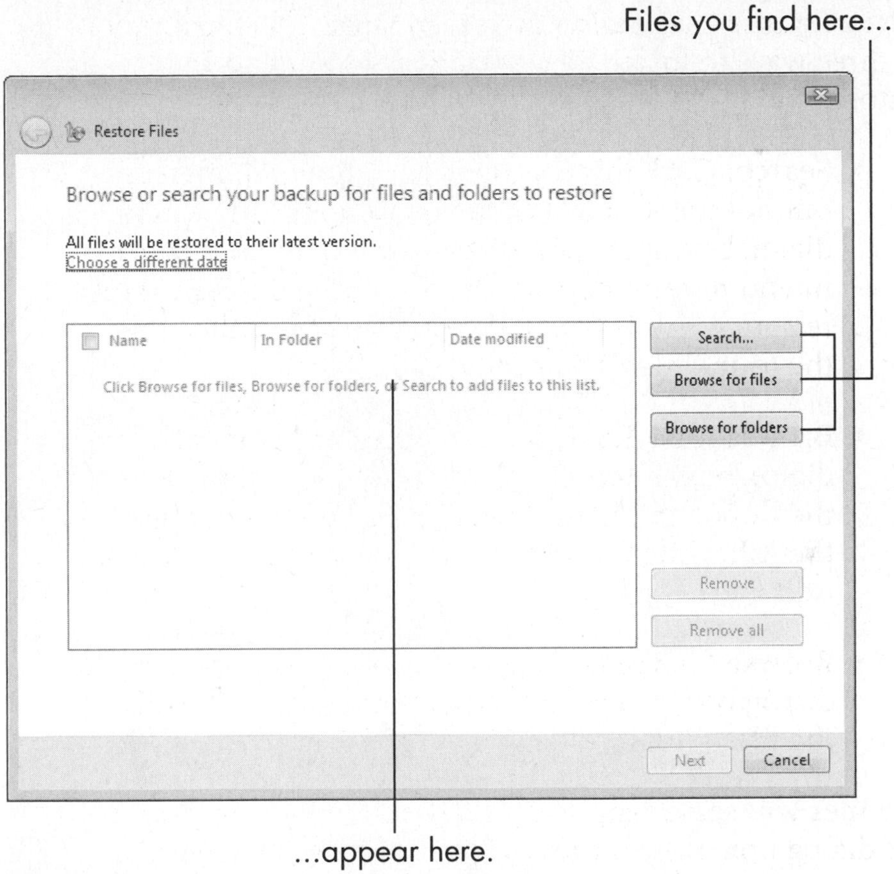

Files you find here...

...appear here.

Figure 19-7

4. The next dialog box (see **Figure 19-8**) asks for the location to which you want these files restored:

- **In the Original Location:** Puts the file back where it was originally. This is the more likely choice.

- **In the Following Location:** Allows you to specify a different location from the original. Use this if you want the restored file in a different location from the original. If you choose this option, you have to specify the new location and indicate whether you want subfolders to be restored with the restored files.

Choose this option, in most cases.

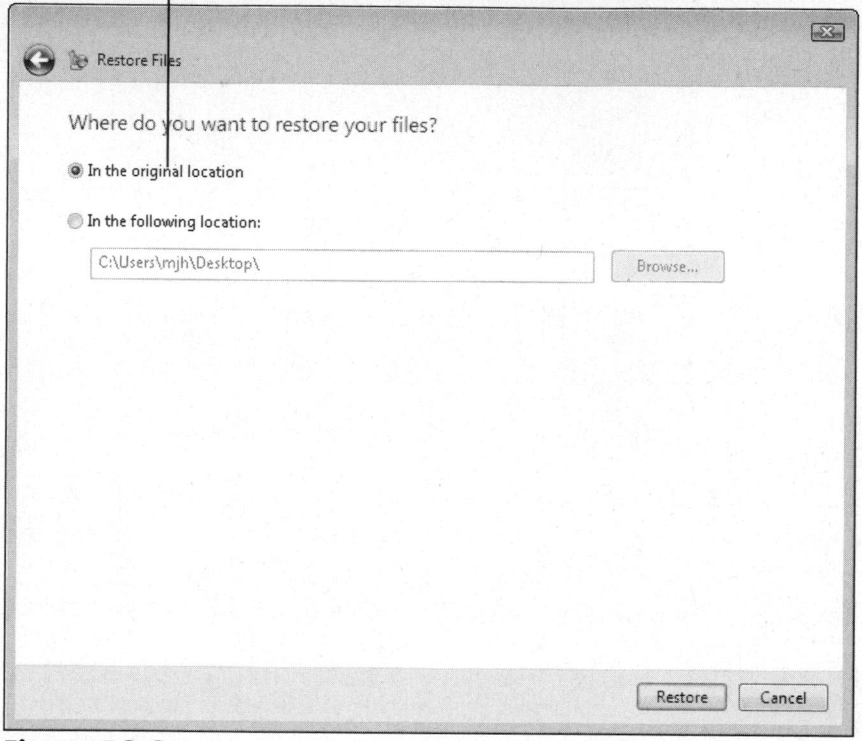

Figure 19-8

5. If you restore a file to a location that already contains a file of the same name, such as restoring a backup when the original is still in the folder, you see the dialog box shown in **Figure 19-9**. Consider these choices:

- **Copy and Replace:** The file in the original location will be replaced by the file restored from backup. Choose this option if the current file is wrong and the backup is a better file.

- **Don't Copy:** The backed-up version isn't restored. Nothing changes.

- **Copy, But Keep Both Files:** The original file and the restored file will both be in the original location. The restored file will include (2) in the filename.

- **Do This for All Conflicts:** Select this check box if you're restoring multiple files and intend one of the preceding choices to apply to every file with a duplicate filename.

Choose what to do with duplicate files.

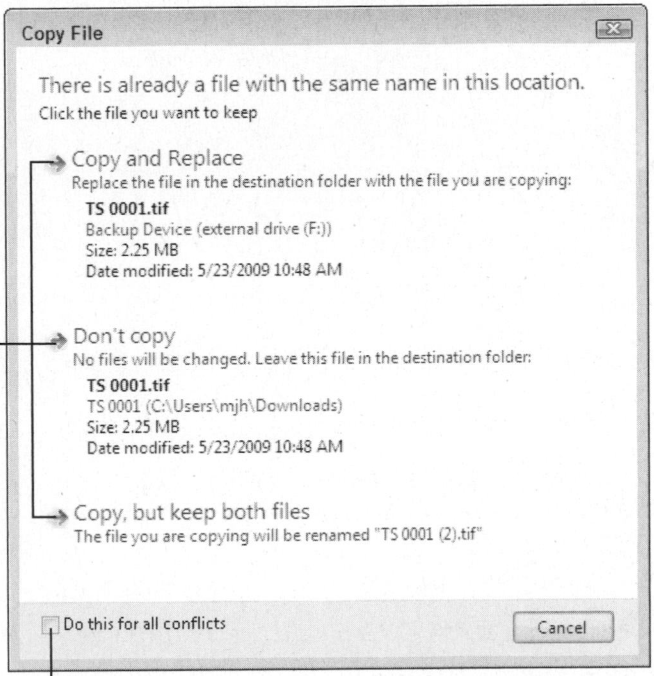

Select to apply your choice to all duplicates.

Figure 19-9

6. The final dialog box appears. Your files have been restored. You can click the View Restored Files link, which opens the folder you restored these files to. Click Finish to close the dialog box.

Create a System Repair Disc

1. If your computer came with a Windows 7 DVD, you can use that DVD to start the computer and effect some repairs, including restoring a system image created in

Backup and Restore. Restoring a system image resets everything to the conditions at the time the image was created, and of course, having a recently created system image is best. See the earlier task "Back Up Your Documents and Photos" for instructions on the type of backup media and choices to make. If you don't have a Windows 7 DVD, you need to create a Repair Disc for this purpose. Open the Start menu and type **backup**. Choose Backup and Restore. The Backup and Restore window opens, as shown in **Figure 19-10**.

Click here to create your own repair disc.

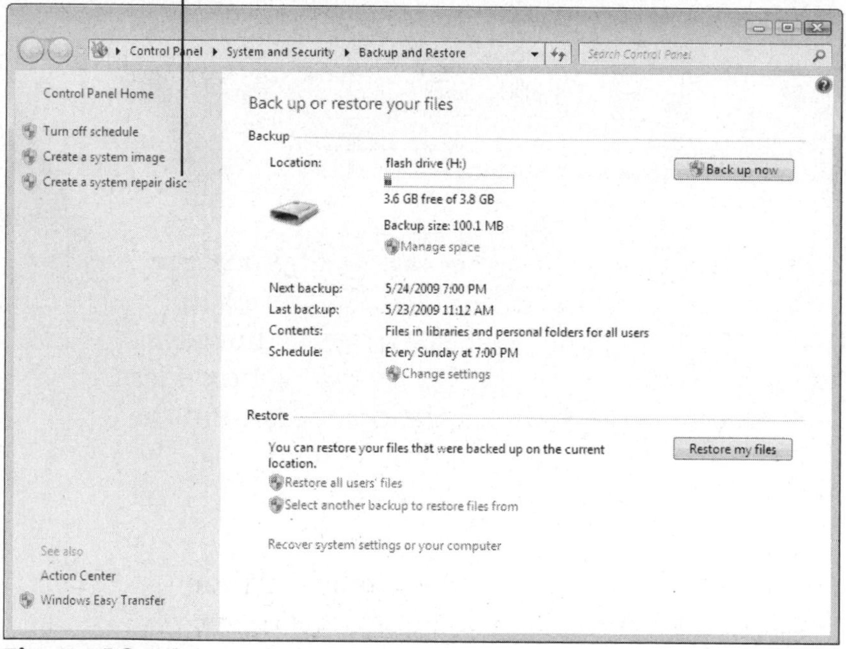

Figure 19-10

2. Click the Create a System Repair Disc link. The dialog box shown in **Figure 19-11** appears.

3. Insert a blank DVD into your DVD drive. (Look for a button to open the DVD tray on the front of a desktop or around the edge of a laptop. Some computers have a DVD slot into which you insert the DVD.) Click the Create Disc button.

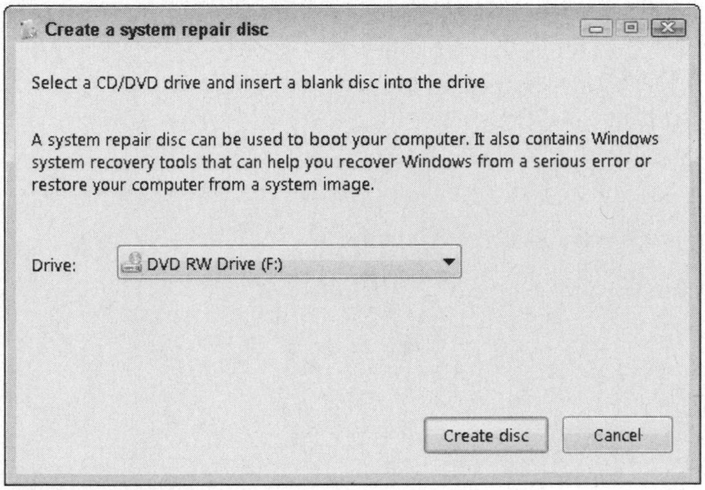

Create a system repair disc

Select a CD/DVD drive and insert a blank disc into the drive

A system repair disc can be used to boot your computer. It also contains Windows system recovery tools that can help you recover Windows from a serious error or restore your computer from a system image.

Drive: DVD RW Drive (F:)   ▼

Create disc   Cancel

Figure 19-11

4. Windows 7 prepares the System Repair Disc. When the process is done, an informational dialog box pops up, indicating you should label the disc. Close the message dialog box. Click OK to close the Create dialog box. Eject the disc by pressing the button on the computer. Put the disc in a safe place, where you can find it in an emergency.

When the disc is done, Windows 7 may start the AutoPlay dialog box. Close AutoPlay, if it opens.

Many computers come with a Restore Disc from the computer manufacturer. That disc restores your computer to the exact condition it was in when you received it (using a restore hard disk partition you may notice in Windows Explorer). A Restore Disc isn't the same as a Windows 7 Repair Disc. You may want both.

Use the System Repair Disc

1. If Windows 7 won't start or starts with significant problems, you may need to use the System Repair Disc to fix problems. (See the preceding section for instructions to create a System Repair Disc.) Insert the System Repair Disc in the DVD drive and restart the computer. If necessary, turn off the power, count to ten, and turn the power back on.

2. For just a few seconds, the screen displays Press any key to boot from CD or DVD. Press any key. If you aren't quick enough, you'll have to start the computer again.

3. The screen displays white text on a black background: Windows is loading files. The first System Recover Options dialog box appears. Change the keyboard input method if US isn't correct. Click Next.

4. The next dialog box indicates System Recover is searching for Windows installations. Click Next.

5. The next screen offers these choices:

- **Use Recovery Tools That Can Help Fix Problems Starting Windows.** Choose this option.

- **Restore Your Computer Using a System Image That You Created Earlier.** Choose the other option unless you're certain this is the one you want. (You have a second chance to take this option after choosing the other.)

6. Click Next.

7. Choose a Recovery Tool:

- **Startup Repair:** Automatically fix problems that are preventing Windows from starting. Choose this option if Windows 7 won't start. This option isn't likely to do any harm.

- **System Restore:** Restore Windows to an earlier time. Choose this option if Windows 7 starts but you think something significant about how it runs has changed. This might happen after you install a new program or update a program. You'll pick from a list the most recent restore point based on date and time. Because this option rolls back Windows 7 settings, you may lose recent changes you made to Windows 7 or other programs, but not your data.

- **System Image Recovery:** Recover your computer using a system image you created earlier. Choose this option if the first two don't fix a problem and you have a relatively recent system image. Attach the backup media you used to create the system image. (See the earlier task "Back Up Your Documents and Photos.") Because this option rolls back the entire computer to the date and time the image was created, you'll lose data created or changed since the image was created, unless you have that data on a separate device, such as a flash drive.

- **Windows Memory Diagnostic:** Check your computer for memory hardware errors. Choose this harmless diagnostic if your computer mysteriously hangs, freezes, or crashes. See Chapter 18 for information on scheduling a disk check as a separate measure.

- **Command Prompt:** Open a command prompt window. Use this if you're familiar with typing commands at a prompt.

Use the first three options in the order listed, restarting after each one.

8. After using any of these tools, click Restart. Click Shut Down if you've had enough for now.

 Index

Business/Accounting & Bookkeeping

Bookkeeping For Dummies
978-0-7645-9848-7

eBay Business
All-in-One For Dummies,
2nd Edition
978-0-470-38536-4

Job Interviews
For Dummies,
3rd Edition
978-0-470-17748-8

Resumes For Dummies,
5th Edition
978-0-470-08037-5

Stock Investing
For Dummies,
3rd Edition
978-0-470-40114-9

Successful Time
Management
For Dummies
978-0-470-29034-7

Computer Hardware

BlackBerry For Dummies,
3rd Edition
978-0-470-45762-7

Computers For Seniors
For Dummies
978-0-470-24055-7

iPhone For Dummies,
2nd Edition
978-0-470-42342-4

Laptops For Dummies,
3rd Edition
978-0-470-27759-1

Macs For Dummies,
10th Edition
978-0-470-27817-8

Cooking & Entertaining

Cooking Basics
For Dummies,
3rd Edition
978-0-7645-7206-7

Wine For Dummies,
4th Edition
978-0-470-04579-4

Diet & Nutrition

Dieting For Dummies,
2nd Edition
978-0-7645-4149-0

Nutrition For Dummies,
4th Edition
978-0-471-79868-2

Weight Training
For Dummies,
3rd Edition
978-0-471-76845-6

Digital Photography

Digital Photography
For Dummies,
6th Edition
978-0-470-25074-7

Photoshop Elements 7
For Dummies
978-0-470-39700-8

Gardening

Gardening Basics
For Dummies
978-0-470-03749-2

Organic Gardening
For Dummies,
2nd Edition
978-0-470-43067-5

Green/Sustainable

Green Building
& Remodeling
For Dummies
978-0-4710-17559-0

Green Cleaning
For Dummies
978-0-470-39106-8

Green IT For Dummies
978-0-470-38688-0

Health

Diabetes For Dummies,
3rd Edition
978-0-470-27086-8

Food Allergies
For Dummies
978-0-470-09584-3

Living Gluten-Free
For Dummies
978-0-471-77383-2

Hobbies/General

Chess For Dummies,
2nd Edition
978-0-7645-8404-6

Drawing For Dummies
978-0-7645-5476-6

Knitting For Dummies,
2nd Edition
978-0-470-28747-7

Organizing For Dummies
978-0-7645-5300-4

SuDoku For Dummies
978-0-470-01892-7

Home Improvement

Energy Efficient Homes
For Dummies
978-0-470-37602-7

Home Theater
For Dummies,
3rd Edition
978-0-470-41189-6

Living the Country Lifestyle
All-in-One For Dummies
978-0-470-43061-3

Solar Power Your Home
For Dummies
978-0-470-17569-9

Internet

Blogging For Dummies,
2nd Edition
978-0-470-23017-6

eBay For Dummies,
6th Edition
978-0-470-49741-8

Facebook For Dummies
978-0-470-26273-3

Google Blogger
For Dummies
978-0-470-40742-4

Web Marketing
For Dummies,
2nd Edition
978-0-470-37181-7

WordPress For Dummies,
2nd Edition
978-0-470-40296-2

Language & Foreign Language

French For Dummies
978-0-7645-5193-2

Italian Phrases
For Dummies
978-0-7645-7203-6

Spanish For Dummies
978-0-7645-5194-9

Spanish For Dummies,
Audio Set
978-0-470-09585-0

Macintosh

Mac OS X Snow Leopard
For Dummies
978-0-470-43543-4

Math & Science

Algebra I For Dummies
978-0-7645-5325-7

Biology For Dummies
978-0-7645-5326-4

Calculus For Dummies
978-0-7645-2498-1

Chemistry For Dummies
978-0-7645-5430-8

Microsoft Office

Excel 2007 For Dummies
978-0-470-03737-9

Office 2007 All-in-One
Desk Reference
For Dummies
978-0-471-78279-7

Music

Guitar For Dummies,
2nd Edition
978-0-7645-9904-0

iPod & iTunes
For Dummies,
6th Edition
978-0-470-39062-7

Piano Exercises
For Dummies
978-0-470-38765-8

Parenting & Education

Parenting For Dummies,
2nd Edition
978-0-7645-5418-6

Type 1 Diabetes
For Dummies
978-0-470-17811-9

Pets

Cats For Dummies,
2nd Edition
978-0-7645-5275-5

Dog Training For Dummies,
2nd Edition
978-0-7645-8418-3

Puppies For Dummies,
2nd Edition
978-0-470-03717-1

Religion & Inspiration

The Bible For Dummies
978-0-7645-5296-0

Catholicism For Dummies
978-0-7645-5391-2

Women in the Bible
For Dummies
978-0-7645-8475-6

Self-Help & Relationship

Anger Management
For Dummies
978-0-470-03715-7

Overcoming Anxiety
For Dummies
978-0-7645-5447-6

Sports

Baseball For Dummies,
3rd Edition
978-0-7645-7537-2

Basketball For Dummies,
2nd Edition
978-0-7645-5248-9

Golf For Dummies,
3rd Edition
978-0-471-76871-5

Web Development

Web Design All-in-One
For Dummies
978-0-470-41796-6

Windows Vista

Windows Vista
For Dummies
978-0-471-75421-3

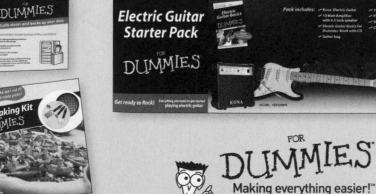